Augustine R. Whiteway

Hints to Solicitors

Being a treatise on the law relating to their duties as officers of the High Court of Justice. With notes on the recent changes affecting the profession, and a vade mecum to the law of costs

Augustine R. Whiteway

Hints to Solicitors
Being a treatise on the law relating to their duties as officers of the High Court of Justice. With notes on the recent changes affecting the profession, and a vade mecum to the law of costs

ISBN/EAN: 9783337113810

Printed in Europe, USA, Canada, Australia, Japan

Cover: Foto ©Suzi / pixelio.de

More available books at **www.hansebooks.com**

HINTS TO SOLICITORS,

BEING A

TREATISE ON THE LAW

RELATING TO

THEIR DUTIES AS OFFICERS OF THE HIGH COURT OF JUSTICE.

With Notes on the Recent Changes Affecting the Profession,

AND A

VADE MECUM TO THE LAW OF COSTS.

BY

A. R. WHITEWAY, M.A.,

OF

TRINITY COLLEGE, CAMBRIDGE, OF THE EQUITY BAR AND MIDLAND CIRCUIT,
AUTHOR OF "HINTS ON PRACTICE."

LONDON:
STEVENS AND SONS, 119, CHANCERY LANE,
Law Publishers and Booksellers.
1883.

PREFACE.

Claims to originality in a Law Book are not only generally unfounded but also undesirable. Indeed for the rendering of the subject to be at all complete the writer must have been "a gatherer and disposer of other men's stuff." Statements made by him to have authority should be the reproductions of those made by great judges as noted by careful reporters; and their very words must be often used for greater accuracy. To be exact is essential, and to know what may be safely omitted in a reference to a judgment is no mean knowledge (*a*).

If this is true of law books generally, how much more is it so of a book written for solicitors about the practical details of their own profession. More critical readers could hardly be found, nor men more able to say at once whether such a book is wanted; and if so, whether the one before them meets the want in any degeee. And yet their very knowledge of the difficulties with which they have to contend should make them well-disposed towards any earnest attempt to deal with these subjects; for they

(*a*) See the instance given in the note to p. 130, Warren's Law Studies, ed. 1.

would not fall into the error of expecting from a book professing only to give hints, an exhaustive treatise on so large a matter.

It goes without saying that it is not a simple one, and that its proper understanding is of deep importance to the body of men best able to judge of it; and yet the latest book upon the subject (*b*) does not profess to touch upon, but, indeed, expressly excludes party and party costs; while the passing of the Judicature Acts and various enactments especially relating to the profession makes the only other still in use (*c*) now out of date for practical purposes.

Although I have taken pains to consult all recent works which deal with the subject matters of this book, it appears to me that there is still a useful field for a handy treatise dealing with the solicitor's duties, work and difficulties, and to which he can readily turn for a hint on a point which possibly materially affects himself, where he might not desire to seek the assistance of counsel, and which otherwise could only be obtained by a prolonged search among recent enactments, voluminous rules and a variety of recent cases; many of which last can only be found either in the weekly notes or in the columns of the law papers.

These remarks are particularly applicable to decisions in chambers and the practice with regard to costs.

The solicitor's duties are constantly increasing, and his responsibility is in no way diminished by recent legisla-

(*b*) Mr. Cordery's able work on the Law Relating to Solicitors, 1878.

(*c*) Pulling's Law Relating to Attornies, 1862.

tion, whilst his disabilities are multiplied. The next step may be to deprive him of much of the assistance of counsel upon which he has been accustomed to rely in the rough and ready work at chambers (*d*); while the lengthy and complicated rules which during the last few years have appeared with such frequency, demand incessant attention from the country as well as from the London solicitor.

A copious index with cross references, a full list of cases cited, and extensive marginal notes will, it is hoped, make this book easy of reference, without which ease its object would fail.

The writer will be thankful for and will acknowledge any practical suggestions for a future edition, should such be required.

A. R. W.

9, OLD SQUARE, LINCOLN'S INN, W.C.
April, 1883.

(*d*) See *In re Chapman*, 10 Q. B. D. 54.

TABLE OF CONTENTS.

	PAGE
Table of Cases	xi

CHAPTER I.

Articled Clerks 1

CHAPTER II.

As Officers of the Court 12

CHAPTER III.

Retainer 22

CHAPTER IV.

Privilege 36

CHAPTER V.

General view of Lien 44

CHAPTER VI.

Lien II 56

CHAPTER VII.

Change of Solicitors 62

CHAPTER VIII.

Disabilities 68

CHAPTER IX.

PAGE
Agreements and Undertakings . . . 71

CHAPTER X.

Town Agents 84

CHAPTER XI.

As Trustees 90

CHAPTER XII.

As Advocates 94

CHAPTER XIII.

As Draftsmen 97

CHAPTER XIV.

Negligence 104

CHAPTER XV.

Unqualified Practitioners 113

CHAPTER XVI.

General Costs 118

CHAPTER XVII.

Taxation of Costs 138

CHAPTER XVIII.

Taxation between Solicitor and Client . . 145

CHAPTER XIX.

Where Taxing Master's opinion final . 152

CHAPTER XX.

Costs payable by a Client 161

CHAPTER XXI.

PAGE
Taxation after Twelve Months 173

CHAPTER XXII.

Party and Party Costs 177

CHAPTER XXIII.

Costs out of a Fund 187

CHAPTER XXIV.

Statutory Charges 194

CHAPTER XXV.

Priorities of Costs and Charges . . . 203

Conclusion 208

APPENDIX.

Solicitors Remuneration Act, 1881 215
The rules under it 221
Remarks upon the Act 232
Solicitors Act, 1870 239
Solicitors Act, 1843, ss. 37—41 247
An item disallowed on taxation 254
List of cases on negligence 256

Index 265

TABLE OF CASES.

A. and B. solicitors, In re, 16
Abercrombie v. Jordan, 34, 116
— v. Jordan, In re Hunt, 114
Adams, Ex parte, 2
Alcock, Ex parte, 142
Allen Davies v. Chatwood, In re, 27
— v. Jarvis, 176
Andrew v. Hawley, 104
Articled Clerk, Ex parte, 9
Ashworth v. Outram, 136, 179
Atkinson, In re, 169
Attorney and Solicitors Act, 1870, In re, 99
Attorney-General v. Stewart, 147
— v. Kerr, 147
Austin v. Jackson, 197

Baile v. Baile, 49, 200
Bailey v. Birchall, 200
Baines v. Wormsley, 158
Baker v. Loader, 192
— v. Oakes, 122
Bambrigge, In re, 144
Banyard, Ex parte, 4, 5
Barker v. Hemming, 133, 205
— v. St. Quentin, 26
Barnes v. Addey, 90
Barrett v. Hammond, 16
Barring, In re, 166
Batley v. Kynock, 179
Beaufort (Duke of) v. Earl of Ashburnham, 181
Belamy v. Ffrench, 66
Bell v. Aitkin, 159, 167
Benson, In re, 4
Berrie v. Howitt, 199
Bevan and Whitting, In re, 65
Beynon v. Godden, 133
Birchall v. Pugin, 206
Bird v. Harris, 22
Birt, In re, Birt v. Birt, 34
Blair, Ex parte, In re Mackie, 176
Blake, In re, 13
— v. Appleyard, 128
Bloyce, In re, 155
Blunt v. Heslop, 140
Blyth and Fanshaw, In re, 184, 186
Bodenham, Ex parte, In re Jephson, 82
Bonser v. Bradshaw, 197, 200, 201
Bookham v. Potter, Ex parte Rogers, 95
Bozon v. Bolland, 61, 65
Bracey, In re, 169
— v. Carter, 111
Branford v. Branford, 43
Bray v. Hine, 88
Bremner v. Bremner and Brett, 59
British Mutual Investment Co. v. Cobbold, 107
British Mutual Investment Co. v. Peed, 41
Broadhouse, Ex parte, 95
Bromsall, Ex parte, 3, 14
Brooks v. Beckett, 143

Broughton v. Broughton, 91
Brown, In re, 152, 170
— a solicitor, In re, 79
— v. North, 135
— v. Sewell, 132, 153, 154
— v. Tolley, 112
— v. Trotman, 197
Brownsall, Ex parte, 14
Brunswick, Duke of, In re, 116
Bryant v. Herbert, 125
Bulkley v. Wilford, 73
Bullock v. Corry, 39
Burchall, In re, 169
Burdick v. Garrick, 90, 118, 119
Burrell, In re, 150
— v. Jones, 80
Burge v. Burton, 89, 91
Burton v. Earl of Darnley, 39
Butler v. Knight, 26

CALVERT v. Scinde Railway Co., 159 182
— Ex parte, In re Messenger, 60
Carew, In re, 78
Carter v. Green, 146
Cartwright, In re, 175
Catlin, In re, 67, 169
Catlow v. Catlow, 196, 202
Chamberlayne, Ex parte, 92
Champernown v. Scott, 46
Chapman, In re, 151, 156
— v. Chapman, 110
— v. Midland Railway Co., 130
Charlton v. Charlton, 144
Chatfield v. Sedgwick, 128, 129
Chennell, In re, Jones v. Chennell, 145, 149
Child v. Kelly, 86
Churchyard v. Watkins, 106
Churton v. Frewen, 180
City of Brussels, 11
City of Manchester, 136
Clack v. Carton, 91
Clark v. Malpas, 159, 181
Clarke, In re, Ex parte Newland, 49
Cobb v. Becke, 87
Cockburn v. Edwards, 145
Cole v. Frith, 127
— v. Grove, 84
Collett v. Foster, 112
Collins v. Welsh, 129
Connop v. Chattie, 26
Cooper v. Pritchard, 112
Corticine Floor Co. v. Jull, 130, 185
Cowper v. Green, 60
Cox v. Coleridge, 94
Cracknell v. Janson, 158
Cradock v. Piper, 91
Crawcour v. Salter, 42
Cross v. Kennington, 148
Cumberland, Ex parte, 9

DARVILLE, Ex parte, 4
Davies v. Marshall, 181
— v. Lowndes, 58
Davis' Trusts, In re, 11
Daw v. Eley, 20
Dawkins v. Rokeby, 19
Dawson v. Shepherd, 133
Dax v. Ward, 111
Day v. Batty, 185
De Bray v. Griffin, 202
De Roufigny v. Peale, 108
Dendy, In re, 142
Dickens, Ex parte, 166
Ditton, In re, Ex parte Woods, 143, 159, 165
Dodd v. Evans, 182
Doe dem. Davies v. Eyton, 29
Donaldson v. Holdane, 109
Downam v. Williams, 81
Drake, In re, 78
Du Boison v. Maxwell, 58
Dufaur v. Blakeway, 144

EADIE v. Addison, 40
Earle v. Hopwood, 99
Earl de la Warr v. Melis, 179
Eastside v. Outram, 37
Edd v. Winson, 136
Edwards, Ex parte, 52, 87, 88
Eley v. The Positive Government Life Assurance Co., 24

Elmslie & Co., In re, Ex parte Tower Subway Co., 175, 176
Emanuel, In re, 151, 164
Emden v. Carte, 50, 190, 194
Engleheart v. Moore, 140
Evans v. Bear, 16
Everett v. Loudham, 21

FAITHFUL, In re, 47, 65
—— v. Ewen, 51, 207, 208
Fane v. Fane, 129
Farewell v. Coker, 88
Farmer v. May, 124
Farrington, In re, 158
Fergusson v. Davison, 126
Fernandez, In re, 76
Ferrell, In re, 152
Fiddey, In re, 201
Field v. Great Northern Railway Co., 123
Findon v. Parker, 99
Firth, Ex parte, In re Cowburn, 137
Fish v. Kelly, 109
Fleming v. Manchester, Sheffield and Lincolnshire Railway Co., 125
Flux, Argles and Rawlins, In re, 169
Foster v. Edwards, 123, 136
— v. Elsley, 35
— In re, Ex parte Dickens, 85, 159, 166
— v. Great Western Railway Co., 122
— v. Monmouthshire Canal Co., 113
Foxon v. Gascoigne, 198
Fray v. Vowles, 26, 105, 106
Fritz v. Hobson, 131
Frost v. London, Brighton and South Coast Railway Co., 178
Furlong v. Howman, 60

GALATTI v. Wakefield, 126
Garnett v. Bradley, 121, 123, 124
General Share Trusts Co. v. Chapman, 59
Gibbs v. Daniel, 71
Gibson v. Jeyes, 70
Gilbert v. Cooper, 82
Giles v. Hamer, 192, 197
Gillimore v. Gill, 191
Godefroy v. Dalton, 104, 108, 110
— v. Jay, 106
Gomley v. Wood, 91
Goodland v. Ayscough, 131
Grant v. Banque Franco Egyptienne, 133
—— v. Holland, Ross v. Grant, 67, 133
Gray v. Kirby, 86
Greenough v. Gaskill, 36
Gregg, In re, 141
Gresley v. Moulsey, 68, 69
Greville, In re, 7
Griffin, Ex parte, In re Adams, 205
Grills v. Dillon, 135
Grundy, Kershaw & Co., In re, 54, 79, 131

HALL & Barker, In re, 175
— v. Bennett, 25
— v. Tepper, 195
Hambridge v. De la Crouée, 25
Hamer v. Giles, 61, 192, 197, 206
Hamet v. Panet, 10
Hammond v. Barclay, 57
Hanley v. Casson, 86
Harbin v. Darby, 92
Harding, In re, 173
Hargreaves v. Scott, 153
Harlock v. Ashberry, 135
Harnett v. Vise, 119, 122
Harper, Ex parte, In re Pooley, 33, 36, 156, 189
— v. Williams, 80
Harpham v. Shacklock, 112
Harrington v. Binns, 107
Harris v. Aaron, 136
— v. Petherwick, 122
— v. Quine, 49
— v. Tremenheere, 73
Harrison, In re, 173
— v. Lentner, 132
— v. Wearing, 154
Hartland v. Murrell, 179

Hawkins v. Harwood, 104, 107
Haynes v. Cooper, 50
Heath v. Crealock, 39
Heather, In re, 142, 169
Heinrich, The, 204
— v. Sutton, 28, 32, 196, 201
Henderson v. Dodds, 148
Herbert, Ex parte, 5
Heritage, In re, Ex parte Docker, 170, 175
Hill, In re, 3, 10, 13, 14
— v. Finney, 110
— v. Fletcher, 82
Hills v. Reeves, 112
Hirst v. Procter, 103
Hobson v. Shearman, 195
Hoby v. Built, 108, 111
Holmes' Estate, In re, 72
Holroyd & Smith, In re, 142
Holt, In re, 17
Hope, In re, 114
— v. Liddell, 41
Hornby v. Cardwell, 134
Horton, In re, 35, 85, 117
Houseman v. Houseman, 192
Howell v. Young, 107
Hubbard v. Phillips, 109
Hunt v. Austin, 52
Husband v. Bolland, 65

Ingwell v. Hooper, 90
Ireson v. Pearman, 99, 105
Iveson v. Conington, 81
Izard, Ex parte, In re Moir, 134

Jacand v. French, 109
Jacob v. Majnay, 32
James v. James, 147
Jarman, Ex parte, 49, 169, 171
Jeffreys v. Evans, 143
Jenkins v. Biddulph, 108
Jennings v. Johnson, 74, 183
Johnston v. Alston, 25
Johnstone v. Cox, 193
Jonas, In re, 137
Jones, Ex parte, 87
— In re, 113, 138
Jones v. Frost, 202
— v. James, 139, 170
— v. Read, 74
Joyce, Ex parte, 7, 9
Judd v. Green, 136

Keane, In re, Lumley v. Desborough, 201
Kevan v. Crawford, 146
King, In re, 3, 15, 115
— v. Savery, 70
Kirkwood v. Webster, 153, 178
Kynaston v. Macknider, 121

La Grange v. MacAndrew, 135
Laidler v. Elliot, 108
Law Society v. Shaw, 85
— v. Waterlow, 85
Lawrence v. Fletcher, 53, 88, 89
Leadbitter, In re, 171
Leader, The, 207
Lee, a Solicitor, In re, Ex parte Nevill, 163
— v. Sankey, 90
Lewes v. Morgan, 69
Lewis, In re, Ex parte Munro, 75, 75
— v. Pennington, 41
Lightfoot v. Keane, 60
Little v. Kingswood Collieries' Co., 34
Local Board of Health of Leamington, Ex parte, 96
London, Brighton and South Coast Railway Co., In re, 47, 65
Lord v. Warmleighton, 64
Loughborough, In re, 139
Lowe v. Holme, 126
Lucas v. Peacock, 61, 196
Ludlow v. Kingdom, 158
Lydall v. Martinson, 134
Lyle v. Ellwood, 11

Mackay v. Ford, 96
Mackley v. Chillingworth, 180
Macgregor v. Keily, 141
M'Corcuodale v. Bell, 39, 42

Malins v. Greenway, 86
Mandus v. Lancashire and Yorkshire Railway Co., 136
Mann v. Harbord, 179
Manning v. Wilkin, 104
Marseilles Extension Railway and Land Co., In re, Ex parte Evans, 176
Mason and Taylor, In re, 208
— v. Brentini, 127
— v. Catsley, 41
Mayor of Swansea v. Quirk, 36, 38
Mercus Co., Ex parte, 121
Mercer v. Graves, 204
— v. King, 110
Messenger, In re, Ex parte Calvert, 60
Meynott v. Meynott, 179
Midland Railway Co. v. Brown, 153
Mildmay v. Quicke, 131
Miller v. Atlee, 58
Minet v. Morgan, 40
Mitchell v. Homfray, 71
Moore v. Froud, 92
Mordue v. Palmer, 146
Morgan v. Minett, 71, 72, 73, 209
— v. Etford, 133
Morley, In re, 159
Morrison, Ex parte, 54, 191, 194
Morton v. Palmer, 137
Moses, Ex parte, 6
Moss, In re, 44, 63, 210
Murray, In re, 49
Myers v. Defries and others, 122, 123

Neville, Ex parte, 164
New British Mutual Investment Co. v. Peed, 41
Newbiggin-by-the-Sea Gas Co. v. Armstrong, 30, 32
Newington Local Board v. Eldridge, 46
Newman, In re, 171
Newton v. Boodle, 152
Nias v. Northern and Eastern Railway Co., 40
Nolan v. Copeman, 179
Norfolk (Duke of) v. Arbuthnot, 130
Norman, In re, 172
North Western Railway Co. v. Sharp, 108
Northampton Coal, Iron and Wagon Co. v. Midland Wagon Co., 135
Nurse v. Durnford, 30, 32, 150
Nye v. Macdonald, 11

O'Brien v. Lewis, 71
Oliver, In re, 138
Ottley v. Gilby, 111, 118
Owen v. London and North Western Railway Co., 160
— v. Ord, 22

Paddon v. Winch, 39, 41
Payne v. Layton, 54
Palmer v. Jones, 150
Pappa de Rossa, 157
Parker, In re, 138
— v. Rolls, 100, 105
Parkinson v. Atkinson, 181
Parsons v. Tinling, 123, 124
Patch v. Ward, 42
Payne v. Layton, 54
Pearce v. Beattie, 92
Peatfield v. Barlow, 88, 89
Penley v. Anstruther, 141
Penn v. Jack, 151
— v. Bibby, 151
— v. Fernie, 151
Peppercorn, In re, 7
Philippine, The, 204
Phillipps v. Phillipps, 132
Piller v. Roberts, 134
Pinkerton v. Easton, 198
Pisani v. Attorney-General of Gibraltar, 70
Plant v. Pearman, 110
Polini v. Gray, 135
Pollard, In re, 20
Pontifex v. Midland Railway Co., 125
Poole, In re, 14

Poole v. Pass, 149
Pooley v. Driver, 130
Potter v. Chambers, 127
— v. Jackson, 193
— v. Rankin, 159
Potts v. Sparrow, 99, 110
Prance, In re, 141
Pringle v. Gloag, 53, 120, 157, 205
Pritchard v. Roberts, 197, 200, 201
Pugwell v. Hooper, 38

Ramsbotham v. Senior, 39
Ransom, In re, 169
Raymond v. Lakeman, 75
— v. Tapson, 48
Read v. Bailey, 134
Reades v. Bloom, 113
Reece v. Rigby, 110
Rees v. Williams, 78
Reeve v. Palmer, 108
Regina v. Avery, 38
— v. Biggins, 94
— v. Justices of Cumberland, 25
— v. Lichfield Town Council, 25
— v. Upper Boddington, 38
Rex v. Sankey, 46
Reynell v. Sprye, 38, 41
Rhodes v. Bate, 71
Richards v. Suffield, 34
Richardson, In re, Richardson v. Richardson, 148, 150, 192
Robarts v. Buée, 204
Robbins v. Fennell, 86
— v. Heath, 86
Robins v. Goldingham, 52, 63
Robinson, In re, 174
Rodick v. Gandell, 54
Rogers v. Jones, 185
— Ex parte, 95
Rolfe v. Maclaren, 128
Ross v. Laughton, 64
Rush, In re, 15
Russell, Ex parte, In re Butterworth, 188

Saffron Waldon Second Benefit Building Society v. Rayner, 23
Sandeman, In re, 185
Savage, In re, 18
Sayer, In re, 4, 5
— Ex parte, 4
Scarth v. Rutland, 75
Schjott v. Schjott, 19, 29
Scholefield v. Lockwood, 199
Seaman v. Netherclift, 19
Sewell, Ex parte, 5
Sharp v. Lush, 150, 185
Sheffield v. Eden, 59
Sheffield Waterworks Act, 1864, In re, 160
Sherry, In re, 6
Shippey v. Gray, 207
Shitler v. Shitler, 147
Shrewsbury (Earl of) v. Trappes, 182
Siddons v. Lawrence, 122
Simmonds v. Great Eastern Railway Co., 63
Simmons v. Storer, 154
Sinclair v. Great Eastern Railway Co., 160, 178
Singer Manufacturing Co. v. Loog, 179
Slack v. The Midland Railway Co., 131
Smith v. Buller, 152, 177
— v. Dale, 27
— v. Daniell, 42, 154
— v. Dimes, 139
— v. Keal, 112
— v. Pococke, 106
Snell, In re, 24, 60, 157, 162, 166
Solicitor, In re, 15, 17
South Essex Estuary and Reclamation Co., In re, 54
Southwark and Vauxhall Water Co. v. Quick, 41
Sparrow v. Hill, 132, 153
Spencer, In re, Spencer v. Hart, 143
Spenser v. Topham, 70
Stannard v. Ullithorne, 100, 105
Steel v. Scott, 66
Steele v. Hutchins, 150
Stephens v. Lord Newborough, 153, 161, 166

Stephenson v. Higginson, 115
Stevens v. Avery, 88
Stevenson v. Rowland, 105
Stewart, In re, 14
Stirke, In re, 173
Stooke v. Taylor, 126
Street v. Hope, 16
Streeter, Ex parte, In re Morris, 96, 212
Sullivan v. Purson, Ex parte Morrison, 54
Swinbanks, Ex parte, In re Shanks, 162
Swinfen v. Chelmsford, 104

Tabram v. Horn, 23
Tardew v. Howell, Shitler v. Shitler, 147
Taylor, In re, 170, 171, 172
— v. Batten, 42
— v. Gorman, 101
— v. Harlstone, 35
Terrell, In re, 185
Thomas v. Jones, 148
— v. Harris, 105
Thompson, In re, 78
Tibbitts, In re, 144
Tillett v. Stracey, 153, 155
Tilney v. Stansfield, 18
Toleman v. England, In re, Ex parte Bramble, 54
Tower Subway Co., Ex parte, 175, 176
Trenchard, Ex parte, 3
Turnbull v. Janson, 181
Turner, In re, 3, 15
— v. Collins, 146, 149
— v. Deane, 47
— v. Hancock, 34
— v. Heyland, 122
Turton v. Barber, 39
Tyne Alkali Co. v. Lawson, 121
Twynam v. Porter, 191

Underwood, Ex parte, 63
Union Cement and Brick Co., In re, Ex parte Pulbrook, 54

Upperton, In re, 144
Upton v. Brown, 15

Vicary v. Great Northern Railway Co., 123
Vines v. London, Brighton and South Coast Railway Co., 178

Wainwright, Ex parte, In re Wainwright, 189, 193
Wake v. Harrop, 80
Wakefield v. Newton, 47, 159
Walford v. Walford, 118
Walker v. Smith, 71
Ward, In re, 87, 138
— v. Eyre, 89
— v. Kepple, 88
— v. Lawson, 74
— v. Wild, 125
Warner v. Mosses, 153, 178
— v. Murdock, 120
Watson v. Murrell, 80
— v. Rodwell, 69, 174
— v. Row, 26
Waugh v. Waddell, 139, 143
Webb v. Mansell, 131
Webster v. Le Hunt, 66
— Ex parte, In re Morris, 134
Weeks v. Goode, 61
Wells v. Mitcham Gas Light Co., 154, 155
West of England Banking Co. v. Batchelor, 53, 56
Wheatcroft, In re, 59
Whitcombe, In re, 78
Whitehead v. Lord, 66
Whiteman v. Hawkins, 107
Whitney v. Smith, 91, 93
Widgery v. Tepper, 195
Wilkinson v. Barber, 146
Williams, In re, 63
— v. Preston, 25, 33
— v. Swansea Canal Navigation Co., 176
Williamson, Ex parte, 3
Willmott v. Barber, 120
Wilmshurst, Hollock & Co. v. Barrow Ship Building Co., 127

Wilson *v.* Emmett, 63
Witt *v.* Corcoran, 136
Wood *v.* Wacey, 54
Woodfin *v.* Seray,
Working Men's Mutual Society, In re, 181
Wormsley, In re, Baines *v.* Wormsley, 158
Worth, In re, 151
Wyche, In re, 174

YGLESIAS *v.* Royal Exchange Assurance Corporation, 159
Yorkshire Wagon Co. *v.* Newport and Abercome Coal Co., 133
Young *v.* English, 48

HINTS TO SOLICITORS.

CHAPTER I.

ARTICLED CLERKS.

THE provisions relating to the service and admission of articled clerks do not present many difficulties, and being generally known to the profession, it is not intended to recapitulate them here; indeed, mention will be made only of a few things to be noticed with regard to them that applications to the Courts have lately brought to light.

Duration of clerkship.

The duration of a clerkship is five years, except in the case of those who have passed certain specified preliminary examinations at the universities, when four suffice; and in the case of such as have taken a degree there, and persons who have served for ten years as clerks to solicitors, three years is the period of probation.

Coupling of periods of service.

With reference to this period, 6 & 7 Vict. c. 73, s. 13 enacts that, when a clerk shall have been discharged before its expiration through (among other causes) mutual consent, if the clerk enters into another contract of service, the Court may allow the periods of service to be coupled. The Solicitors' Act, 1877 (40 & 41 Vict. c. 25, s. 15), which gives to

Solicitors Act, 1877, as to

irregular service.

the Master of the Rolls further discretionary power as to the period of service, was no doubt intended to meet hard cases, as, for instance, Ex parte *Adams*, 4 Ch. D. 39. The words of the section are: "Where any person articled to a solicitor has not served as a clerk under such articles strictly within the provisions of the Solicitors Act, 1843, and the Solicitors Act, 1860, and any Act amending the same, but subsequently to the execution of his articles bonâ fide serves (either continuously or not) one or more solicitors as an articled clerk for periods together equal in duration to the full term for which he was originally articled, and has obtained such certificate as he is required by this Act to obtain; it shall be lawful for the Master of the Rolls, in his discretion, if he is satisfied that such irregular service was occasioned by accident, mistake, or some other sufficient cause, and that such service, though irregular, was substantially equivalent to a regular service, to admit such person to be a solicitor in the same manner as if such service had been a regular service, within the meaning of the said Acts and any Act amending the same."

Ex parte *Adams*.

In the case above quoted the clerk was articled to his father for five years, from September, 1870, and he served till October, 1873, when his father by an indenture assigned his services to another solicitor for fifteen months, after which he returned to his father and served under the original articles till September, 1875. The Court held that the fifteen months could not be reckoned as part of the five years service, as such service had been under an assignment, and the conditions of 6 & 7 Vict. c. 73, ss. 6 and 12, had not been fulfilled. The clerk continued to serve with his father for another fifteen months after September, 1875, though without fresh articles; but the Court held that he had not duly served under the contract within the meaning of sec. 3, which prohibits the admission of a clerk unless "he shall have been bound by contract in writing to serve as clerk for and during the term of five years to a practising solicitor in England or Wales, and shall have duly served under such contract for and during the term of five years." It held that he must, therefore, complete his five years service under fresh articles for fifteen months; but that, under the circumstances, he might be allowed to go in for his examination at once. This is a good instance of the class of case in which the Master of the Rolls, under sec. 15 of the Act of 1877, is now empowered to give relief.

Cancellation of articles by mutual consent.

Ex parte *Williamson*, 4 Ch. D. 581, shows that "mutual consent" will be construed liberally for the clerk; see also Ex parte *Trenchard*, L. R. 9 Q. B. 406, where the Court was divided as to whether the facts in that case amounted to a virtual cancellation by mutual consent. The latter case is also a precedent for three several periods of service under three different sets of articles having been allowed to make up the full term.

Stamping articles.

Articles of clerkship require a stamp of £80, which should be impressed before execution. They can, however, be stamped up to six months after execution, upon payment of a fine of £10, and even after six months by leave of the Treasury and payment of a heavier fine. The clerk's master must enrol them (together with an affidavit by himself of his due admission, and of the proper execution of such articles) within six months from their date with the Clerk of the Petty Bag, who marks them

Enrolment of articles and affidavit of their execution in Petty Bag Office.

with the date of such enrolment before returning them to him. This takes place upon the master's application within a few weeks time.

Further enrolment by Registrar of Solicitors.

Within three months of such enrolment the articles are produced to and further enrolled by the Registrar of Solicitors. If all this is not done at the proper time, the clerk's service dates simply from the time at which it is done, except by order of the Court. Application for such order is made by motion under 23 & 24 Vict. c. 127, s. 7, of which notice must be given to the Registrar.

Non-enrolment within prescribed period.

Although the articles have not been enrolled within the prescribed period of six months, the Court has often granted leave to enrol nunc pro tunc, where the omission has arisen from circumstances for which a tangible excuse is offered. A strong affidavit explaining how the mistake arose must be made, and that there was no neglect on the part of the applicant; but it must contain no such statement as that it arose from inadvertence: In re *Benson*, 10 Beav. 435. The omission must have been the result of some accident or unforseen circumstance; not the having been disappointed in receiving money to pay for the stamp: Ex parte *Darville*, L. R. 6 C. P. 244; Ex parte *Banyard*, L. R. 10 C. P. 638.

Omission to enrol must have been the result of accident.

But if the failure has arisen from the non-payment of a debt due to the clerk, which he had a reasonable expectation to obtain in time, the excuse will be held sufficient: In re *Sayer*, L. R. 10 C. P. 570; in which case the form of the order is given as being—

In re *Sayer*; form of order.

"That the service of the applicant be computed from the date of the execution of the articles; that he present himself for the examination to be held next term; that notice of the application be given to the

Incorporated Law Society, and the affidavit used in support of the application laid before them; that the rule be not drawn up until after four days have elapsed from the service of the notice upon the Society; and that an affidavit of the service of the notice and affidavit upon the Society be produced to the master on drawing up the rule."

The real question is, whether labour has been honestly thrown away; per Blackburn, J., in Ex parte *Sayer*, 33 L. T. N. S. 560; quoted and approved by Lord Coleridge, C.J., in Ex parte *Banyard*, L. R. 10 C. P. 643. The latter case also clearly shows that because the Treasury have allowed articles to be stamped on payment of a fine (without which they could not be enrolled), it does not follow that the Court will, therefore, order enrolment. The two things are distinct, though the former is a necessary preliminary to the latter: Ex parte *Sewell*, 11 W. R. 673. But it would appear from Ex parte *Herbert*, 31 L. J. Q. B. 33, that it will be assumed that the Treasury has arrived at a right conclusion, and that unless objections are raised to the enrolment which were not brought under the notice of the Treasury, service will be ordered to count from the date of the articles.

Ex parte *Banyard*.

Where articles have been lost, a verified copy can be, by leave, enrolled.

Where articles have been lost.

The service under articles must be continuous, with the exception of a reasonable amount of absence for holidays, or short intervals of absence owing to sickness. Where a clerk was absent for several months on a sea trip, though for ill health, Blackburn, J., said that he could have been acquiring no experience at all during that period, and would not allow it to count, though the clerk had before the application

Service must be continuous.

Absence for several months.

successfully passed the required examination: Ex parte *Moses*, L. R. 9 Q. B. 3; see also *Ford* v. *Drew*, 5 C. P. D. 59.

Service by ten years men.

In the case of ten years men, the ten years service need not, however, be so rigorously continuous, and may commence at an early age, say fifteen. The applicant ought not to have been a mere errand boy for any part of the time, but must have been a regular general clerk: In re *Sherry*, L. R. 3 Q. B. 164.

Engagement during articles in other occupation.

Perhaps the greatest difficulty under the enactments with reference to articled clerks is that which the provision contained in 23 & 24 Vict. c. 127, s. 10, has given rise to, namely, that a clerk may not engage in any employment whatsoever, other than the employment of a clerk to his master or his partner in the business of a solicitor. This section has been re-enacted by the Solicitors Act, 1874, s. 4, except in cases where the clerk has, before entering into any employment, obtained—

Solicitors Act, 1874, employment under articles, s. 4.

(1.) The consent of his master thereto;

(2.) The consent of one of the judges permitting the same. Fourteen days' notice of this application to a judge is to be given to the Registrar, stating—

(*a.*) The names and addresses of the applicant and his master;

(*b.*) The nature of the employment;

(*c.*) Its probable duration.

The judge may make such order upon terms; and if he does so, the clerk, before admission, must show that he has fulfilled the terms imposed.

Since the passing of the latter Act, giving leave to apply as above, no case appears to have been reported in the Law Reports which explains what is meant by the words "any employment whatsoever other than the employment of a clerk to his master or his partner in the business, practice, or employment of a solicitor." In 1873, however, Lord Coleridge, C.J., In re *Greville*, L. R. 9 C. P. 15, clearly showed that the older enactment must be construed literally.

In re *Greville*.

There a clerk held during the term of his articles the office of vestry clerk; but it was shown that the duties of the office had not interfered with the due performance by him of his duties under articles, or with his legal studies; for the work of the vestry clerkship was done in the evening, with one or two trifling exceptions, not amounting in the aggregate to more than three and a half days, and he had never been absent without the consent of his principal. Lord Coleridge there said that the clerk had held an office and been engaged in an employment other than that of an articled clerk; and that to hold otherwise would be to trifle with the words of the statute, and to afford a most striking illustration of the well known saying that hard cases make bad law. His lordship then proceeded to say that the application of the decision in In re *Peppercorn*, L. R. 1 C. P. 473, was not to be extended. There the clerk became steward of a manor, in which he and his family were beneficially interested, and the stewardship devolved upon him as part of the family property, and through a family arrangement, in order to protect the property. That decision, in fact, rested on its own peculiar circumstances, and certainly since the Act of 1874 it would hardly be safe to rely upon it.

Articled clerk steward of a manor. In re *Peppercorn*.

The kind of difficulty which now arises is rather analogous to than the same as that In re *Greville*. The case of Ex parte *Joyce*, 4 Ch. D. 596, is an illustration. There an articled clerk with a fixed salary agreed with his master to take all the profits of the

Ex parte *Joyce*.

business, and to account to him for them at the expiration of his articles; and should they go into partnership upon his admission, that the master should have the amount of such profits as his share of the capital. The business, most of which was introduced by the clerk, was managed by him upon these terms, and he received and paid all moneys, and his name was outside the office door. It was held by the Master of the Rolls that, as the clerk had no interest in the business during the articles, except his salary and the contingency of retaining the clients whom he introduced during his articles, if he afterwards became admitted, that the business was his master's in truth as well as in theory; and that the clerk was really the clerk and not the proprietor of the business.

Service, definition of.

Service was in that case defined as being the attendance of the clerk during office hours at his master's office, and the performance of the ordinary duties of a clerk.

Agreements between master and clerk.

This case is further valuable as showing the nature of an agreement between a clerk under articles and his master that will be allowed to be made. Jessel, M.R., said that he was not aware of any law which prohibits an articled clerk, who has a connection of his own fairly acquired, from saying to a solicitor, "I will become your articled clerk upon these terms; you shall pay me a salary, and you shall have for your own benefit the profits of all the business which I shall introduce to you until I myself become admitted, and you shall agree that when I become admitted, you will not transact any business for those clients whom I so introduced to you, but that you will leave to me the entire business which I so introduced;" and that the following variation is also admissible.

Instead of the master retaining these profits for himself, if the clerk and his master agree to go into partnership at the end of the period of articles, when the clerk becomes admitted, then these profits to form the clerk's share of the capital of the partnership, and the partnership to be entered into upon terms to be agreed upon. The real point in this class of cases is, whether the clerk intended to comply with the law, or whether he hoped to evade it.

Test.

Where there has been cause for suspicion, and the examiners were justified in doubting the bona fides of such an arrangement as the foregoing, the clerk may not get his costs upon an application such as that in the case of Ex parte *Joyce*, as he usually does when successful.

Costs of clerk on application to Court.

Before a clerk can be admitted as a solicitor, he must be of full age; and if there is any provision in his articles that he is not to practice in competition with his master, even though he may not be bound by this if he was under age when such articles were entered into, should he remain under them when over age, he certainly will be taken to have adopted such provision.

Clerk must be of full age to be admitted.

Service after coming of age.

It is now necessary for a clerk when he desires to be admitted to give a notice of his desire six weeks before the first day of the month in which he proposes to be admitted. This is given at the Petty Bag Office, and is signed by the clerk. It must state where he and his master live, and also where he has lived during the twelve months last past. A strict compliance with the regulations in force with reference to admission is required, and the Court will not generally relieve when such is not observed: Ex parte *An Articled Clerk*, L. R. 7 Q. B. 587; Ex parte *John Cumberland*, L. R. 10 Q. B. 138.

Notice of desire to be admitted.

Affidavit of due service.

Before actual admission, an affidavit has to be sworn by the clerk that he has duly served his master, and that he has not engaged in any other employment without leave of the Court, and that he has given the notices above referred to.

Judge may refuse to admit.

If this affidavit is false, he can be struck off the rolls if he has been admitted; and if facts discreditable to the applicant are brought to the notice of the judge upon his application for admission, he may refuse to admit him: Cockburn, C.J., In re *Hill*, L. R. 3 Q. B. 546.

Upon being admitted, he can practice in all the divisions of the Court, and also in all the Ecclesiastical Courts (40 & 41 Vict. c. 25, s. 17), and the inferior courts.

As advocates.

In the chapter upon solicitors as advocates, something has been said about the practice of police magistrates in London to hear articled clerks; but it may be taken generally that an articled clerk has no locus standi to be heard as an advocate for a client in any Court by reason of his position as a solicitor designate.

Notaries.

To practise as a notary in London, service for seven years is necessary under articles with a notary in actual practice; but to practise ten miles from London, five years service with a solicitor is sufficient, if specially appointed by the faculty which defines the district within which he is to practise: 3 & 4 W. IV. c. 70. The limits of his jurisdiction are important, and an act done by him in his notarial capacity outside them would appear to be ineffectual: *Hamet* v. *Panet*, L. R. 2 Ap. Ca. 121.

As nothing more than a few words will be said about notaries in this book, they may well follow here.

To practise within three miles of London, it is necessary to be a member of the Scriveners' Company.

Stamp duty.

The stamp duty is the same as in the case of solicitors, but if the certificate is not taken out for one year, re-admission is necessary: 37 Geo. III. c. 90, s. 31; which enactment, according to Mr. Pulling, ed. 3, p. 489, note z, is still in force as to notaries.

Duties.

Their duties are chiefly in connection with protesting bills of exchange and ships' protests, and evidencing the validity of documents to be sent abroad, although the same weight of evidence is not given by a Court governed by the law of France to the certificate of an English notary public as to the certificate of a French one: *Nye* v. *Macdonald*, L. R. 3 P. C. 331.

Unqualified persons.

Notaries' work, especially in the matter of ships' protests in out-ports, is sometimes partly done by persons who are not notaries, as, for instance, the British chaplain, before whom protests are frequently sworn. If, however, a person not being a notary prepares briefs and affidavits, his charges will not be allowed on taxation: *The City of Brussels*, L. R. 4 A. & E. 294.

Evidence before.

Affidavits in an action sworn abroad, at a distance from the residence of a consul, may be sworn before a notary on the written consent of the other side: *Lyle* v. *Ellwood*, L. R. 15 Eq. 67.

A notary's signature to the affidavit must be verified by affidavit, unless the fund to which it relates is very small: In re *Davis' Trusts*, L. R. 8 Eq. 98.

CHAPTER II.

SOLICITORS AS OFFICERS OF THE COURT.

Jud. Act, 1873, s. 87. THE 87th section of the Judicature Act, 1873, makes all solicitors officers of the Supreme Court, and authorises that Court, and the High Court of Justice, and the Court of Appeal, respectively, and any division or judge thereof, to exercise the same jurisdiction in respect of such solicitors as any one of the Superior Courts might have done before.

Jud. Act, 1881, s. 24. Moreover, the Master of the Rolls, with the concurrence of the Lord Chancellor and the Lord Chief Justice of England, or, in case of difference, of one of them, has now had vested in him since the passing of the Supreme Court of Judicature Act, 1881, s. 24, the powers which he before had jointly with the Lord Chief Justice of the Court of Queen's Bench, the Lord Chief Justice of the Court of Common Pleas, and the Lord Chief Baron of the Court of Exchequer, or with any of them, or jointly with the President of the Queen's Bench, Common Pleas, and Exchequer Divisions of the High Court, or with any of them with reference to solicitors.

These enactments, however, have reference to the making of rules and regulations for the admission, &c., of solicitors, and have nothing to do with the power to take cognisance of any of their wrong doings which may come to the notice of any particular Court. The general principle upon which notice will be judicially taken of such wrong doings, and of what nature they must be to be so noticed, will here be generally pointed out. For example:—The Court will not allow suitors to be exposed to gross fraud and dishonesty at the hands of one of its officers, and will therefore punish misconduct which does not arise in a matter strictly between solicitor and client: In re *Blake*, 30 L. J. Q. B. 32. Gross fraud.

Blackburn, J., In re *Hill*, L. R. 3 Q. B. 547, said that, in his opinion, when judges are called upon in the exercise of their equitable jurisdiction to order an attorney to perform a contract to pay money, or to fulfil an undertaking, that there they have jurisdiction only if the undertaking or the contract was made in his character of attorney, or so connected with his character of attorney as to bring it within the power of the Court, to require that their officer should behave well as an officer. Re *Hill*.

The Court must see that the officers of the Court are proper persons to be trusted by the Court with regard to the interests of suitors, and must look to the character and position of the persons, and judge of the acts committed by them, upon the same principle as if it were considering whether or not a person is fit to become an attorney. The principle on which the Court acts is to see that its suitors are not exposed to improper officers of the Court.

It is not proposed to deal with the cases in which solicitors can be struck off the rolls or suspended. They are, fortunately, of somewhat rare occurrence. A few instances, however, of cases in which the application to strike a solicitor off the rolls was refused Striking off rolls.

Where application refused.

may not be considered here out of place. In re *Stewart*, L. R. 2 C. P. 88, by an order of the High Court of India, an attorney was struck off the rolls for inserting in a deed of conveyance a false recital as to the consideration money in it, knowing the same to be false at the time; and for attesting the execution of the deed, which contained a receipt for the consideration money; and for signing his name as a witness to such receipt, knowing that it had not passed, and was not intended to pass. The judicial committee discharged the order, because no fraudulent use of the instrument had been made or attempted, and no fraudulent motive was alleged, and no injury had been, directly or indirectly, occasioned by it.

Moneys misappropriated to be restored before re-admission.

If a solicitor is struck off the rolls for a fraudulent misappropriation of moneys of a client entrusted to him for investment, it is a condition precedent to his being restored that he should have made full restitution, or, at least, all the restitution in his power: In re *Poole*, L. R. 4 C. P. 350. Any application for re-admission must be by petition, and a copy of it served on the Registrar of Solicitors: Rules and Regulations, 1875, 2, 3.

Application for re-admission by petition.

Indictable offence or gross misconduct must be imputed.

The principle seems to be that in order to entertain an application to strike a solicitor off the rolls, an indictable offence or gross professional misconduct must have been committed by him; but the length of time since its commission does not appear material: Ex parte *Bromsall*, 2 Cowper, 829. When there are circumstances which mitigate the offence, the punishment will be reduced to suspension; but a solicitor when acting as clerk to another solicitor is equally liable to the punishment: In re *Hill*, quoted above, p. 13.

Suspension.

Clerk equally liable.

Answering matters of affidavit.

Where no conviction has taken place, an order is generally made to answer the matters of an affidavit. A primâ facie case of misconduct, fraud, or malpractice, should be shown and distinctly stated, that the solicitor may either answer or confess it: In re *King*, 3 Nev. & M. 716. It is not sufficient to set forth the mere facts of the misconduct alleged, without supporting them by an imputation by the deponent of their effect. The client, too, must have done all in his power: In the matter of *A Solicitor*, Solrs. Journal, Feb. 10, 1883, p. 235.

Heading.

The affidavits should be headed in the action in which the alleged malpractice arose, although judgment may have been signed in it, as well as in the matter of the solicitor; but if there was no action, they may be entitled in the matter of the solicitor only. Counsel can move only in one case at a time: In the matter of *A Solicitor* (Jan. 29), Solrs. Journal, Feb. 3, 1883, p. 216.

Where a solicitor has been suspended from practice in Chancery for a given time, the Common Law Courts used to grant a rule to suspend him for the like period. The practice in the Common Pleas was slightly different: In re *Turner*, L. R. 8 C. P. 103.

Summary Jurisdiction of Court.

There are, however, many other cases of a less serious nature in which the solicitor is amenable to the jurisdiction of the Court, quite apart from any liability he may be under to answer to his client for the offence he has committed, and it is of these that some notice will be taken here. For some of them he is liable to attachment, for others to the payment of costs,—for example, see *Upton* v. *Brown*, 20 Ch. D. 731,—and for the rest he is liable to be deprived of his own costs, and to be fined or censured.

In re *Rush*, a solicitor, decided by Lord Romilly

in 1870, and reported in L. R. 9 Eq. 147, is still good law. There default had been made by a solicitor in payment of a balance found due from him upon taxation of his bill of costs under the common order for the purpose. The Court held that this was default in payment of a sum of money ordered to be paid by him in his character of an officer of the Court, within the meaning of the Debtors Act, 1869, s. 4, sub-s. 4, and that an attachment might issue against him.

Non-payment of balance found due.

Debtors Act, 1869, s. 4, sub-s. 4.

This sub-section excepts such a case from non-imprisonment for debt. The words are: "Default by an attorney or solicitor in payment of costs, when ordered to pay costs for misconduct as such, or in payment of a sum of money when ordered to pay the same in his character of an officer of the Court making the order." It would seem from *Evans* v. *Bear*, L. R. 10 Ch. 76, and In re *A. & B.*, solicitors, W. N. 1877, 207, that the Court had not jurisdiction to refuse an attachment in such a case if applied for; but since the Debtors Act, 1878 (41 & 42 Vict. c. 54, s. 1), the Court has had full powers to deal with each case as to it seems right.

Debtors Act, 1878, s. 1.

The policy of this Act is explained by Bacon, V.-C., in *Barrett* v. *Hammond*, 10 Ch. D. 289. He said that, under the Debtors Act, 1869, the judge had no power to inquire, before allowing the writ of attachment to issue, whether the debtor had the means of satisfying the order or not; but that the Amendment Act of 1878 gives to the Court a jurisdiction, which it did not possess before, of inquiring into the case, and of either granting or refusing the application. The question then comes to this, whether it will serve any good purpose to send the defaulter to gaol. The law does not act vindictively; the

Court has no power to inflict any punishment upon him; and sending him to prison will not enable him to pay.

This seems also to have been the opinion of Malins, V.-C., in *Street* v. *Hope*, quoted in a note to *Barrett* v. *Hammond*. So that now, before the Court will order an attachment, it must be shown to it that the defaulting solicitor can pay and won't pay, or no order as to costs, or otherwise, will be made upon the motion. When attachment issues.

In no case can an attachment issue without notice: Jud. Act, 1875, O. XLIV., r. 2; In re *A Solicitor*, 1 Ch. D. 445. Not without notice.

But the notice may be served by leaving it at the place of residence of the party affected thereby: In re *A Solicitor*, 14 Ch. D. 152. Service.

The heading of the order, for the breach of which attachment is desired, must have been exact, and any omission will invalidate the motion for the attachment: In re *Holt*, 11 Ch. D. 1; see also Daniel's Practice, 6 ed. 1, p. 884, and Braithwaite's Practice, 167. Order.

But attachments issue against solicitors, not only for non-payment of moneys, but also for disobedience to orders made to deliver documents of title to clients. This order may be made on petition: 14 Ch. D. 152. Attachment issues for disobedience to other orders. The Judicature Act expressly provides attachment as a punishment for a solicitor in two cases: (1) Upon failing to enter an appearance in pursuance of a certain undertaking to do so on behalf of a defendant: O. XII., r. 14; and (2) if, when an order for discovery or inspection against any party is served upon him, he neglects without reasonable excuse to give notice thereof to his client. Attachment under Jud. Act.

The case of a solicitor who uses a client's name, without proper authority, to bring an action, is treated of at p. 29, in the chapter on "Retainer," and is a good instance of when he will be compelled to pay costs personally.

Payment of costs personally. Another instance in which he may have to pay costs personally is when he omits to deliver briefs, which he should do in good time. As to the time for delivery, see *Thomas* v. *Palin*, 21 Ch. D. 363. He is entitled to do so when the action has been entered for trial, and before it appears in the cause list. The result of this omission would be that it is heard as undefended. In such a case the Court grants an order for a new trial, after ordering him to pay the costs as between solicitor and client.

Tilney v. *Stansfield.* In the late case of *Tilney* v. *Stansfield*, W. N. 1880, 77, V.-C. H., an order having been made that proceedings should be stayed, and that the plaintiff's solicitor should pay to the defendants their costs in the action as between solicitor and client, it being considered that the action was frivolous, vexatious, and an abuse of the process of the Court, upon a motion for attachment for non-payment of such costs, which had been taxed, the following order was made:—Order upon this motion for non-payment of taxed costs, £52 14*s*., and £3 11*s*. 2*d*., costs of an application for substituted service, and an order for the payment of costs as between solicitor and client of the motion and of the attachment. Order not to be drawn up for a week, and respondent to have notice that it had been made, and that at the end of a week it would be drawn up and acted upon.

Solicitor acting without authority. In re *Savage*, 15 Ch. D. 557, the solicitor got the authority of all the petitioners, except two, to use their names as petitioners, and these two he did not even see; but he asserted that he was assured by the other parties that they were willing to concur. It appeared that he could have obtained their address, and could have written to them; and if they had refused to be petitioners he might have made them respondents. He did not write, preferring to make them co-petitioners, in order that expense might be saved. The Master of the Rolls said that, in an ordinary case like this, the solicitor who acts without authority should be made to pay the costs. More will be found upon this head in the chapter on "Retainer," at p. 29.

Non-attendance in Court when cause is called on.

Again, if a solicitor is not present in Court when a cause is called on, and it is found that it cannot conveniently proceed, by reason of his having neglected to attend personally or by some proper person on his behalf, or having omitted to deliver some paper necessary for the use of the Court, and which according to its usual practice ought to be delivered, he may be ordered to pay personally to all, or any, of the parties such costs as the Court thinks fit to award: Cons. Ord. XXI., r. 12. Or he can be the cause of his clients not getting their costs, if a paper or document which should have been in Court is not there when wanted: Knight Bruce, L.-J., in *Gillimore* v. *Gill*, 4 W. R. 774.

Schjott v. *Schjott.*

In *Schjott* v. *Schjott*, 19 Ch. D. 94, the solicitors of the next friend of a married woman were ordered by the Court of Appeal to pay personally the costs of an action which was dismissed with costs; because the next friend, when challenged to show his authority to commence the action, failed to do so.

Solicitor acting as advocate.

There are also certain things from which solicitors, as officers of the Court, as well as counsel engaged in the case, must abstain, which may require a passing notice in this place. For example, solicitors, when using their privileges as advocates, and conducting a case, must not use words which are irrelevant, malâ fide, and spoken with express malice: *Seaman* v. *Netherclift*, 1 C. P. D. 540; *Dawkins* v. *Rokeby*, L. R. 7 H. L. 744.

Writing to public press during action.

Moreover, they are prohibited from writing to the public press during the continuance of a case, or while a suit is pending, letters tending to influence the result. Lord Romilly, in *Daw* v. *Eley*, L. R. 7 Eq. 61, said, that it is highly important that the Court should not allow steps to be taken by the officers of the Court, in causes in which they are engaged, which possibly may have an effect favourable to their client, or unfavourable to the other side; and that it is impossible for the judge to go minutely into every sentence of a letter written in a public newspaper, to say this is questionable, and that is doubtful, and the like. They should, therefore, abstain entirely from discussing the merits of pending cases in public prints; and if they do it at all, they should certainly put their names to their communications.

In the case last quoted, where the solicitor had done so under an assumed name, he was held to have been guilty of a contempt of Court, and was committed for it. The order was not, however, to be drawn up for a fortnight, that he might appeal, if so advised, or in case he should desire to apologise, in which case he was to pay the costs of the motion.

Improper conduct during trial.

Before a solicitor or barrister is committed for contempt of Court for improper conduct or language during a trial, the specific offence should be stated, and an opportunity given him of answering it: In re *Pollard*, L. R. 2 C. P. 106.

Solicitors excepted when wit-

A solicitor to one of the parties not going out of Court when the witnesses in a case are ordered out of Court does not commit a contempt of Court, for where witnesses are ordered out of Court, and among those who are going to give evidence is the solicitor to one of the parties, if he states that his presence in Court is necessary for his client's interests, he will generally be allowed to remain: *Everett* v. *Lowdham*, 5 C. & P. 91.

nesses ordered out of Court.

In Oke's Mag. Syn., p. 124 (8th ed.), it is said that the attorneys for the respective parties are always excepted when witnesses are ordered out of Court by magistrates.

CHAPTER III.

RETAINER.

THE authority given a solicitor to act, which is generally called a retainer, must be proved in order to enable him to fix with his costs the party giving it, and also to prevent his repudiating anything properly done on his behalf. It may be evidenced by circumstances and by the conduct of the parties; nevertheless, a written appointment should be invariably procured whenever practicable, and it should come from the party engaging the solicitor, or from some one duly authorised to give it. This should be required by the solicitor, as much for his own sake as for that of the client. Lord Tenterden, in *Owen* v. *Ord*, 3 C. & P. 349, says that it is much better for him, because it gets rid of all difficulty about proving his retainer; and it would also be better for some clients, as it would put them on their guard, and prevent them from being drawn into law suits without their own express direction.

Written retainer.

That this is no less the case now may be learnt from V.-C. Bacon's remarks in *Bird* v. *Harris*, W. N. 1880, 166. He there says that the onus of proof lies upon the solicitor who has obtained leave to attend proceedings under a decree, without a written retainer, and whose authority is disputed, to show

Onus of proof lies on solicitor.

his authority to obtain the order made; and that, in the absence of a written retainer, he would be held to have been acting unauthorised. The fact of this case having been overruled by the Court of Appeal (W. N. 1881, 5) does not affect the value of these observations of the learned Vice-Chancellor.

Form of retainer.

The form in which the authority is given is immaterial. I, A B., of   , authorise Mr. Y. Z, solicitor, of   , to take such proceedings as he may think necessary and proper on my behalf in the High Court of Justice, or elsewhere, for [the object desired]. Perhaps even a simpler plan is to get the client to endorse the writ issued in the proposed action with some such authority as this:—I, the within-named A. B., authorise Mr. Y. Z, solicitor, to issue this writ, and to continue on my behalf the action it begins.

What constitutes a retainer

It has been held (*Tabram* v. *Horn*, 1 M. & Ry. 228) that not even the delivery of papers to a solicitor by a party stating that he was entitled to an estate, and that he would pay him if he recovered it, is sufficient to entitle him to recover the costs of an ejectment brought for the estate; and it is certainly not wise for the solicitor who has only a general authority to act as such to a private individual to bring an action for him without a written retainer: *Saffron Waldon Second Benefit Building Society* v. *Rayner*, 14 Ch. D. 406, 409, per James, L.J.

Although, if the client afterwards takes advantage of such action, or even of unnecessary doings (as, for instance, journeys of the solicitor unauthorised by him) in connection with it, and so ratifies the proceedings of the solicitor, he may be held to have adopted them.

Companies, retainer by.

And this is still more the case with public companies, which generally give formal sanction from time to time, or else take exception to the acts of their legal advisers. If these are passed over unnoticed, they will be taken to have been adopted by the company: In re *Snell*, 5 Ch. D. 815.

Client ratifying solicitor's actions.

If a client attends at the solicitor's office, and recognises his employment, or in some other way ratifies his actions, this may be sufficient to fix him with the costs of any proceedings that may have been instituted; but with a written retainer it would palpably be much easier to justify such proceedings, especially if disputed by his client's opponents.

In the case of *Eley* v. *The Positive Government Security Life Assurance Company*, 1 Ex. D. 20, it was stated by the judges of the Divisional Court, that the engagement of a solicitor by a company was a contract not to be performed within a year, and therefore bad, under the 4th section of the Statute of Frauds, if not in writing. When the case came before the Court of Appeal no decision upon this point was given, but it was held that a statement in the Articles of Association of a company, that A. B. should be the solicitor, did not create any contract between A. B. and the company, because Articles of Association were only a matter between the shareholders inter se or the shareholders and the directors. Solicitors, therefore, to companies incorporated under the Companies Acts should be appointed in writing, by some person acting under the express or implied authority of the company; and solicitors to corporations, under their common seal, except in the case of a corporation which has a special power under the instrument incorporating it of appointing a solicitor

Appointment in Articles of Association.

Appointment by companies.

Corporations.

in another way: *Reg.* v. *Justices of Cumberland*, 17 L. J. Q. B. 102.

Must be client's own retainer.

Furthermore, for the purpose of beginning an action, the solicitor must receive specific authority from his client himself; and it is not safe to rely upon the retainer of the near relations of the proposed plaintiff: *Hall* v. *Bennett*, 2 Sim. & Stu. 78. But although this applies also to co-plaintiffs (and pro formâ plaintiffs) the same necessity for special instructions, almost necessarily in writing, does not exist in the case of defending actions.

Though not necessarily for defending.

A general authority from the client is usually sufficient for this, but *Williams* v. *Preston*, 20 Ch. D. 672, shows how it may be abused and the proceedings of the solicitor set aside. And a general retainer would not enable the solicitor to bring a cross action, and probably not to set up a counter claim.

By a firm.

Where a retainer is given by a firm, it should be signed by all the partners of the firm. The acts of a solicitor appointed by one member only, may be easily adopted by the other partners, but that their adoption will take place should not be relied on: *Hambridge* v. *De la Crouée*, 3 C. B. 744. Speaking generally, the authority of the solicitor extends to the doing of all things necessary for the accomplishment of the work for which he is retained: *Reg.* v. *Lichfield Town Council*, 16 L. J. Q. B. 333; and a general retainer authorises him to defend any action brought against his client, but not to institute any proceedings in his name without his express direction.

Its extent.

If he receives his express direction to do so, he has free power to act for him in all points of doubt or discretion until judgment; but he is not bound to follow the instructions of his client to do what is meant merely for delay: *Johnston* v. *Alston*, 1 Camp.

May issue execution.

176; and he may issue execution for the amount of the judgment obtained, but he may not receive part of the debt and take security for the remainder, after judgment obtained, upon his own authority alone: *Connop* v. *Chattie*, 17 L. J. Exch. 319. Indeed, a solicitor may enter into a compromise without the consent of his client, if he acts bonâ fide and with reasonable skill, provided it be for his benefit, and not in defiance of him: *Fray* v. *Voules*, 7 W. R. 446; but if after judgment he compromises, when instructed not to do so by his client, even though he acts optimâ fide, and with the consent of the mother and brother-in-law of his client, with whom he principally communicated in the business relating to the action, he exceeds his duties: *Butler* v. *Knight*, L. R. 2 Ex. 110.

May compromise before judgment.

Compromise in defiance.

May not issue execution against his client's wish.

Moreover, he cannot sue out execution against his client's wish: *Barker* v. *St. Quentin*, 12 M. & W. 441. The true rule is that although technically the relation of solicitor and client ceases when judgment is recovered, yet still, that the slightest indication on the part of the client that he desires the solicitor to continue to act, or perhaps almost in the absence of any instructions from him that he does not, it will be taken to continue. The effect of this is that any compromise made with the solicitor might be pleaded by the defendant, if an attempt were made by the plaintiff to enforce judgment against him after a compromise was supposed to have been effected with the solicitor.

Joint and separate retainers.

For the purpose of seeing who may be charged with costs, it is sometimes important to determine whether the retainer is a joint or a separate one. In *Watson* v. *Row*, L. R. 18 Eq. 680, two executors, defendants in an administration suit, gave a joint retainer. The chief clerk found that one of them, who had since died insolvent, was indebted to the testator's estate. The surviving executor was held to be entitled to be paid out of the estate, all the costs for which he was liable; but the costs incurred by the other had to be set off against the debt due to the estate. In this case, had the retainer been separate, the solvent executor might only have been allowed half of the costs.

This case was dissented from however, to some extent, by the Master of the Rolls, in *Smith* v. *Dale*, 18 Ch. D. 577, which deals with the case of a defaulting executor who had become bankrupt, after having been a co-defendant in an administration action. It was held that the costs incurred by the executors prior to the bankruptcy should be distinguished, and that the solvent one should be allowed only his proportion out of the fund, the defaulter's proportion being set off against the debt due from him; but that the costs incurred by both subsequently to the bankruptcy should be allowed in full. *Smith* v. *Dale.*

Another recent case is In re *Allen Davies* v. *Chatwood*, 11 Ch. D. 244. The head note says that in a suit by a shareholder against the seven directors, the secretary, and the company, to restrain an action for calls, to be relieved of his shares on the ground of misrepresentation in the prospectus, and to be indemnified by the directors; the defendants, having all appeared by the same solicitor, put in a joint and several answer signed by one counsel, and joined in their defence, signing three separate retainers to the solicitors, all in these terms. You having up to the present time conducted the defence of this suit in behalf of all the defendants, and in pursuance of their instructions in that behalf, we the undersigned, In re *Allen Davies* v. *Chatwood.*

do hereby confirm such instructions, and request you to continue such defence, and to take such steps as you may consider necessary in the matter. And that it was held that the retainers were separate and not joint, and that the assets of the company (in liquidation) were liable for one ninth only of the costs. Here, had all the defendants given a joint retainer, it is quite possible that their solicitor would have got all their costs out of the estate of the company in liquidation.

When appearance entered without authority.

The Judicature Acts have prescribed the procedure in cases in which solicitors use the names of persons who have not retained them; but before these provisions are considered it may be well to notice one or two instances in which it has been decided that an appearance can be entered by a solicitor for a party without his authority. And, first, a general authority to act as solicitor gives power to defend actions brought against the client without any special authority from him on that behalf. In

Heinrich v. Sutton.

Heinrich v. *Sutton*, L. R. 6 Ch. 223, the deed of settlement of a banking company contained a proviso that where property was vested in trustees, the court of directors should have power to direct any action to be carried on on account of the property of the bank, and to direct the necessary parties to carry them on, and that they should be indemnified out of the funds of the bank. One of such trustees (who had executed the deed) was made a co-defendant along with two other trustees, in a suit by a person claiming property adversely to the bank, and the solicitors to the bank forthwith entered an appearance for him. He moved the Court that the appearance in his name might be expunged or varied, as having been entered without his authority, and that the solicitors of the bank might pay the costs as between solicitor and client, and indemnify him against all costs occasioned by the appearance. It was held, that as he had no real interest in the action, and was only a nominal defendant, the solicitors to the bank had acted rightly, as they had merely acted under the provisions of the deed of settlement. Here then, was an instance in which an individual had himself indirectly given authority to another to instruct a solicitor to use his name. The cases in which a third party, acting under a general authority, retains a solicitor are of the same class; and it need only be remarked further, with reference to them, that such third party only is liable for costs.

In the cases of an infant and of a married woman who applies to the Court by a next friend, although 15 & 16 Vict. c. 86, s. 11, enacts that a written authority from the next friend to use his name must be filed with the copy of the writ, there is no necessity for the solicitor to have a retainer from the infant or married woman themselves; sufficient guarantee for the bona fides of the transaction being given by the written authority of the next friend. See *Schjott* v. *Schjott*, 19 Ch. D. 94. However, the Court of Appeal dismissed an action brought by the next friend of a married woman, with costs, to be paid by the solicitors of the next friend, as he, when challenged to show his authority from his client, did not show any.

Infants.

Married woman.

The following are instances of the way in which a solicitor may be liable through not being properly retained.

Liability for acting without retainer.

In *Doe d. Davies* v. *Eyton*, 3 B. & Ald. 785, a solicitor innocently acted for an absent party under a forged authority. He was, however, held to be liable for the costs.

Innocently acting under a forged authority.

When employed by wrong set of directors.

Where a solicitor has been instructed to issue a writ by one set of directors for a company, a dispute having arisen in its governing body, and two sets of directors having been appointed, each claiming the right to represent the company, and the Court comes to the conclusion that the set of directors instructing him, not being the right one, could not authorise him to act for the company. This occurred in *New-biggin-by-the-Sea Gas Company* v. *Armstrong*, 13 Ch. D. 310; and the Court of Appeal held that although he had acted bonâ fide he had done so at his own risk and must pay the costs of the suit.

Nurse v. *Durnford.*

Another instance is the case of *Nurse* v. *Durnford*, 13 Ch. D. 765. There the solicitors on the record purported to act for a plaintiff, and were held liable to pay his costs of the motion to have his name struck out, as between solicitor and client, and also to pay the costs of the defendants of the action and all the motions therein.

The solicitors in that case were the London agents of one J. N., upon whose instructions they were accustomed to act as regards the institution and framing of suits without enquiry, assuming that they had proper retainers. In this particular instance they had taken instructions, according to their custom, from J. N. to institute an action in the joint names of three plaintiffs of whom he, J. N., was one; and, as he was so, they were further instructed to use their own names as the plaintiff's solicitors, and not as agents for J. N.

The London agents had, of course, a good claim against J. N. for the amount of all the costs they had to pay; but it is obvious that, in the case of a man of straw, this claim would be of but little value.

Measure of

The exact measure of the liability of a solicitor

inserting the name of a plaintiff on the record without his authority, was defined in these cases by the Court of Appeal to be: To pay the costs of the plaintiff, as between solicitor and client, of a motion by the defendants that the plaintiff be ordered to proceed with the action (wrongly instituted), or that the action might be dismissed with costs; and also of a motion by the plaintiff that his name might be struck out of the record as a plaintiff, on the ground that the same had been inserted therein without his knowledge, consent, or authority; and also the defendant's costs of the action, including in these costs all motions made in the action as between party and party.

Liability for using plaintiff's name without authority.

The direct provisions of the Judicature Acts relating to this subject are Order VII. r. 1. "Every solicitor, whose name shall be indorsed on any writ of summons, shall on demand in writing made by or on behalf of any defendant who has been served therewith, or has appeared thereto, declare forthwith whether such writ has been issued by him, or with his authority or privity; and if such solicitor shall declare that the writ was not issued by him, or with his authority or privity, all proceedings upon the same shall be stayed and no further proceedings shall be taken thereupon without leave of the Court or a judge." This rule as is stated in Wilson's Judicature Acts, is substantially the same as sec. 7 of the Common Law Procedure Act, 1852. It is not, however, there noticed that the words "who has been served therewith, or has appeared thereto" which were not in the former Act, make some difference as to the persons on whose behalf the demand may be made. It may further be remarked that the fact of appearing to a writ, does not exclude, but

O. VII. r. 1.

rather expressly gives, permission to a defendant to make this demand. The effect of this rule as seen from the cases of *Nurse* v. *Durnford* and *Newbiggin-by-the-Sea* v. *Armstrong*, referred to before in this chapter, is this, that it does not seem to throw any obligation on the defendant to ascertain whether the solicitor had authority to issue it; and its object, therefore, is simply to verify the name of the solicitor upon it, and to preserve to the defendant a right of action (whatever that may be worth), against such solicitor, if he has wrongly used the name of the plaintiff.

Defendant is not bound to inquire into authority to issue writ.

O. IX. r. 1. The next provisions in the Judicature Act, of a like character, have reference to the defendants' solicitor, and are contained in Order IX. r. 1. "No service of a writ shall be required when the defendant by his solicitor agrees to accept service and enter an appearance;" and Order XII. r. 14. "A solicitor not entering an appearance, in pursuance of his written undertaking so to do on behalf of any defendant, shall be liable to an attachment."

Undertaking to enter appearance.

A consideration of the case of non-appearance by the defendant's solicitor after agreeing so to do, hardly comes under the head of retainer, and, therefore, it need only be said that under The Common Law Procedure Act there was the same provision for attachment in a like case, and the reported case of *Jacob* v. *Magnay*, 12 L. J. Q. B. 93, illustrates it. In the case of a defendant's name being used without any authority, he could move to strike it out, and to be indemnified for all costs occasioned by the appearance; and costs, as between solicitor and client, as was asked for in *Heinrich* v. *Sutton*, would probably be granted.

Non-appearance afterwards.

Use of defendant's name without his authority.

Fraudulent defence by solicitor.

In a case in which a solicitor has put in a fraudulent defence for his client without the knowledge of the client, making admissions on which judgment is obtained against the client, the Court has jurisdiction to set aside the judgment, and to permit the client to withdraw the defence, and to put in a fresh defence; for his authority does not extend to the commission of a fraud. If there has been a bonâ fide mistake, his client may be bound by his act, though he may have a remedy over against the solicitor for such mistake; but the Court will always interfere to relieve the client against a fraud: *Williams* v. *Preston*, 20 Ch. D. 672.

Where bonâ fide mistake, client has remedy over against solicitor.

Retainer by trustee.

The effect of a retainer, however perfect, of a solicitor to a trustee, is not to give him as of necessity his costs out of an estate: he may have a right of action against his client, but his right to costs out of an estate is only the right of his client, and if either he or his client has been guilty of misconduct, the Court can refuse to allow his costs to be paid out of the estate, even though they have been taxed and an allocatur has been made by the master.

The payment of costs out of an estate is discretionary. Thus, when a trustee in bankruptcy and his solicitor had been engaged in purchasing debts due by a bankrupt, in order to procure the appointment of a trustee favourable to the bankrupt, the Court refused the solicitor costs to be paid out of the estate, and went behind the allocatur: Ex parte *Harper* in re *Pooley*, 20 Ch. D. 685, and see the judgment of Jessel, M.R., p. 688.

Turner v. *Hancock*.

But the mere fact that a trustee, who denies that he is indebted to the trust estate, is found, on taking the accounts, to be indebted in a small amount, is no ground for disallowing him his costs: *Turner* v.

Hancock, 51 L. J. Ch. 519. So that the solicitor to a trustee or a mortgagee will not be deprived of his costs out of the estate, except for the misconduct of his client, or for his own impropriety of conduct.

Employment must be legitimate.

The employment for which a solicitor has been retained must be legitimate, and he could not recover his costs for the negotiation of a corrupt contract of any kind; but if he prepares a document which is illegal, if there is any doubt of its illegality, he could recover. If he was retained by both the plaintiff and defendant in a suit he could recover costs from neither. In *Little* v. *Kingswood Collieries Company*, 20 Ch. D. 733, Hall, V.-C., restrained a solicitor from acting for the antagonist of his former client, upon the principle that a man ought to be restrained from doing any act contrary to the duty he owes to another, and that it will be exercised at the instance of the former client, whether the solicitor was discharged by him, or had discharged himself, whenever the transaction in reference to which the injunction is sought, is so connected with that in which he was formerly retained, that the same matter of dispute may probably arise; but on appeal the injunction was considered to have gone too far, and was dissolved by consent, the solicitor undertaking not to disclose his former client's secrets. See also In *re Birt*, *Birt* v. *Birt*, 1883, W. N. 18.

When restrained from acting for opposite party.

Must be qualified.

The solicitor himself must not only be a duly qualified practitioner, but must not be in partnership with any one who is not: *Richards* v. *Suffield*, L. R. 2 Exch. 616; and see also *Abercrombie* v. *Jordan*, 8 Q. B. D. 187. He must, if the business he is carrying on for the client be in London, and be of such a character as to make him act or practise in London, within the meaning of the statute 33 & 34 Vict.

c. 97, s. 59, take out a certificate for practising in London. In re *Horton*, 8 Q. B. D. 434, defines what practising is.

Duration of retainer.

The duration of the retainer of a solicitor must next be considered. And, first, it is put an end to by the death of either of the parties; and *Foster* v. *Elsley*, 20 Ch. D. 518, decides that a direction in a will, appointing a particular person solicitor to a trust estate, imposes no trust or duty on the trustees of the will to continue such person their solicitor in the management and affairs of the estate. The solicitor cannot suddenly give up his appointment until the completion of his work, even though funds are not provided by the client immediately they are required; but there is no necessity for him to provide himself for disbursements; and if the client does not provide funds in a reasonable time, when called upon to do so, he can cancel the retainer and claim costs up to date.

Foster v. *Elsley*.

Work must be completed before thrown up

Unless funds refused

Reasonable causes for retiring.

There are other reasonable causes owing to which he can give up his employment, as his desire to retire from business, or his leaving the country; but he must give his client due notice, so that he may not be hurt by his so doing. If he throws up his employment suddenly, and so damages his client, an action will lie for negligence against him.

Retainer by wife.

If a married woman instructs a solicitor to institute a suit for a judicial separation for her, before he can charge the husband with the costs the necessity for the proceedings must be made out in fact: *Taylor* v. *Harlstone*, Solrs. Journal, p. 39, Nov. 18, 1882. If a married woman retains a solicitor to do anything connected with her separate property, he will now, it seems, have to look to her for payment.

Married Women's Property Act, 1882, s. 1, s.-s. 3.

CHAPTER IV.

PRIVILEGE.

Foundation of privilege.

THE equity upon which privilege is founded is this:—That a person in a confidential relationship may not disclose the knowledge acquired by him in that relationship. The subject is treated of, among many other places, in the author's Hints on Practice, ed. 1, p. 130, and it will only be glanced at here. It affects solicitors generally, either when making an affidavit of documents, or giving evidence on the trial of an action; and it must be remembered that the privilege claimed is not that of the solicitor, but of his client: *Mayor of Swansea* v. *Quirk*, 5 C. P. D. 106, just as the right of the solicitor to a trustee in bankruptcy to be paid his costs out of the bankrupt's estate is only the right of his client the trustee. The solicitor has no independent right: Ex parte *Harper*, In re *Pooley*, 20 Ch. D. 685.

Privilege is that of client.

Law as to privileged communication. *Greenough v. Gaskell.*

The law as to the privilege which attaches to professional communications, is laid down at length by Lord Brougham in *Greenough* v. *Gaskell*, 1 M. & K. 98, which may perhaps be considered the leading case on the subject. What it comes to shortly is this. No legal adviser is allowed, without the authority of his client, to disclose anything the client has told him in professional confidence during his employment, either with reference to a matter in litigation or not in litigation; or to disclose any advice that he may have given his client. And this is so, whether or not the client is a party to the action in which the question is put to the solicitor. But this rule does not extend to any communication made in pursuance of a criminal purpose, or to any fact, to which the client may have drawn his attention, from which he may have gathered that a fraud has been committed by the client since his employment by him.

Does not extend to criminal matters.

These exceptions really only amount to instances in which the solicitor would in fact be an accessory to a crime if he continued to assist his client in the furtherance of his intentions. This subject will not be dealt with at further length here, but it is thoroughly discussed in Taylor on Evidence, ss. 832—9.

Fraud is an exception to rule.

Cases of fraud are exceptions to the rule that a person in a confidential relationship may not disclose the knowledge acquired by him in that relationship. If a man is employed as a solicitor in any unlawful act, his duty to the public obliges him to disclose it; for "no private obligation can dispense with that universal one which lies on every member of the society to discover every design which may be formed contrary to the laws of the society to destroy the public welfare." Thus, a solicitor's confidential clerk is not bound to keep secret irregular transactions in which his master is engaged, for if the Court compelled him to do so, it would be lending itself to the commission of fraud. Lord Hatherley in *Eastside* v. *Outram*, 5 W. R. 35.

Extension of principle to solicitor's clerk.

But in all proper cases, privilege can be enforced against a solicitor's clerk just as much as against his master: *R.* v. *Upper Boddington*, 5 L. J. o. s. M. C. 10. In an old case, *R.* v. *Avery*, 8 C. & P. 596, a solicitor who had been employed by a mortgagor and mortgagee to negotiate a loan between them, and had received from the former a forged will as part of his title deeds, was compelled to produce the will at a trial of the mortgagor for forgery. So when a solicitor acts for two parties in a suit, he cannot claim privilege for any documents relating to the suit in behalf of one of the parties as against the other: *Reynell* v. *Sprye*, 10 Beav. 51.

When acting for two parties privilege cannot be claimed.

Trustee acting for one of his cestuis que trust and against others.

And this is particularly the case if he places himself in a false position, however innocently; as for instance, where a solicitor being a trustee, acted professionally for one of his cestuis que trustent against another. In such a case, he would be bound to produce correspondence which had passed between his client and himself: *Tugwell* v. *Hooper*, 10 Beav. 351. The principle in such a case is that a solicitor must not put himself, inadvertently even, in a situation in which he cannot do his duty to all parties to whom he owes duties, if he desires to claim any other privileges of the situation. There he could not carry on communications respecting the trust matters clandestinely with one of his cestuis que trustent and keep them secret from the others.

Principle in such cases.

Mayor of Swansea v. *Quirk.*

In a case in which a corporation elected to answer by their town clerk, who was a solicitor, it was held that he could not claim the privilege of professional confidence, although he was acting as their solicitor in the action: *Mayor of Swansea* v. *Quirk*, 5 C. P. D. 106. The reason for the decision in this case (to judge from the decision of Lopes, J.) appears to have been, that if privilege had ever existed, it had been waived by the corporation having elected to answer by their solicitor. In the argument against privilege, the case of a litigant suing by himself as solicitor was put, and it was not denied that he could not avail himself of privilege.

Residence of ward must not be concealed.

Again, a solicitor, as an officer of the Court, is bound not to conceal any fact which will enable it to discover the residence of its ward, although such information may have been communicated to him by his client in the course of his professional employment: *Ramsbotham* v. *Senior*, L. R. 8 Eq. 575; and see also *Burton* v. *Earl of Darnley*, referred to in a note to that case.

Third parties.

But even in the case of third parties, answers to inquiries by a litigant solicitor with a view to and in contemplation of anticipated litigation, are privileged: *M'Corquodale* v. *Bell*, 1 C. P. D. 471; but they must be in anticipation of litigation or they cannot claim privilege, James, V.-C.: *Paddon* v. *Winch*, L. R. 9 Eq. 667. And as to the privilege attaching to correspondence in a suit between the plaintiff and a third party, including correspondence between them and their solicitor, see *Bullock* v. *Corry*, 3 Q. B. D. 356. That case decided, that an inspection of papers relating to any previous action by the defendants, is not allowed in an action by the plaintiff against them for not unloading a cargo purchased by them from the plaintiffs. The plaintiffs, having entered into a charter party upon terms as to the discharge of the ship, similar to those in the contract for sale to the defendants, had been sued by and had had to pay damages to the shipowners. And it appears from the case of *Heath* v. *Crealock*, L. R. 15 Eq. 259, decided by V.-C. Bacon, that a solicitor cannot be compelled to disclose the address of a client. *Turton* v. *Barber*, L. R. 17 Eq. 331, is an authority that a

Inspection of papers relating to previous action.

Address of client.

Bill of

Costs privileged at client's desire.

bill of costs is privileged from production, if the client desires that it should be so, and further, that a solicitor's making an affidavit as to documents, is no waiver of privilege.

Communications made to solicitors.

It was formerly doubted whether communications between solicitor and client must not have been made in view of approaching litigation for privilege to be claimed respecting them. Lord Cottenham, however, in *Nias* v. *Northern and Eastern Ry. Co.*, 3 My. & Cr. 355, said, that the real principle is, that parties are to be at liberty to communicate with their professional advisers, with respect to matters which become the subject of litigation, without restriction, and without the liability of being afterwards called upon to produce or discover what they should so have communicated. He said further, that it was not pretended that a solicitor could be compelled to answer as to what his client told him, with reference to an expected contest; and that it could not make any difference in principle, whether what was communicated, was communicated by word of mouth, or in the form of a case stated for advice. Lord

Minet v. *Morgan.*

Selborne, in *Minet* v. *Morgan*, L. R. 8 Ch. 361—(see also *Eadie* v. *Addison*, 31 W. R. 320)—finally settled the law in the form in which it remains, viz.: that a plaintiff will not be compelled to produce confidential correspondence between himself or his predecessors in title, and their respective solicitors, with respect to questions connected with matters in dispute in a suit, although made before any litigation was in contemplation; and certainly, documents prepared in relation to an intended action, whether at the request of a solicitor or not, and whether ultimately laid before the solicitor or not, are privileged, if prepared with a bonâ fide intention of being laid before him for the purpose of taking his advice; and an inspection of such documents cannot be enforced: *Southwark and Vauxhall Water Co.* v. *Quick*, 3 Q. B. D. 315: Contra, see *Paddon* v. *Winch*, L. R. 9 Eq. 61, 1870; and *Mason* v. *Cattley*, W. N. 18, 1883.

If, however, a solicitor learns anything by other means than confidential communications from his client, privilege does not extend to it. This was settled by the Master of the Rolls, in the case of *Lewis* v. *Pennington*, 8 W. R. 466, in which case, the present Lord Chancellor and Master of the Rolls were the counsel for the party objecting to the privilege.

Matters coming to solicitor's knowledge otherwise.

And with reference to documents in a solicitor's possession, it is clear that they must have come into his possession in professional confidence, and for the purpose of obtaining the advantage of his professional assistance, in order to claim protection: *Reynell* v. *Sprye*, 10 Beav. 56.

It is hardly necessary, perhaps, to say that a solicitor, like any other witness, cannot be compelled to produce his title deeds to any property, or any document which could criminate him; though he cannot refuse simply because such production might lay him open to an action, or because he has a lien on it: *Hope* v. *Liddell*, 7 De G. M. & G. 331. And a solicitor to a defendant in an action for recovery of land, though he must make an affidavit of his documents of title, may have a right to refuse production: *New British Mutual Investment Co.* v. *Peed*, 3 C. P. D. 196.

Title deeds. Incriminating documents.

Furthermore, if a solicitor acts for two parties, as for a mortgagor and mortgagee, he cannot set up professional privilege, as if he had acted confidentially for one only of the parties; and a mortgagor has always a right to call for the production of the mort-

Solicitor acting for two parties.

gage deed: *Patch* v. *Ward*, L. R. 1 Eq. 440; and see also Conveyancing Act, 1881, sec. 16.

There must be no question of retainer.

There must be no question of the solicitor having been properly retained, in order to claim privilege; see V.-C. Bacon's judgment in *Smith* v. *Daniell* L. R. 18 Eq. 654, where it was held that an opinion expressed by a lawyer, unless expressed in discharge of a professional duty, is not privileged.

Must be during time retainer operates. *Crawcour v. Salter.*

The communication must have been made to the solicitor during the time of his being retained. It has, however, been held by Malins, V.-C., in the case of *Crawcour* v. *Salter*, 18 Ch. D. 30, that a solicitor employed to obtain the execution of a deed, and who is one of the witnesses, is not precluded on the ground of a breach of professional confidence, from giving evidence as to what passed at the time of execution by which the deed may be proved invalid. As this case went to the Court of Appeal, and this dictum was not commented upon by the Lords Justices, it may, perhaps, be taken to have been approved, or, at all events, not disapproved of.

Inspection of confidential documents cannot be refused.

It is clear, that with regard to documents, inspection cannot be refused, even though the person who wrote them stipulated that they should be considered as private and confidential, and refuses to authorise their production. Brett, L.J., in *McCorquodale* v. *Bell*, 1 C. P. D. 476.

And this is so, even though the persons to whom they were written are solicitors.

How privilege claimed.

In answering interrogatories, privilege is claimed in the affidavit in answer, and vivâ voce, at a trial. As to the sufficiency of an affidavit of documents when privilege is claimed, see *Taylor* v. *Batten*, 4 Q. B. D. 85, and Hints on Practice, ed. 1, p. 131; and, for an instance of a solicitor refusing to answer in Court a question as to a communication made to him by a client: *Branford* v. *Branford*, 4 P. D. 73.

If a solicitor refuses to produce a document, on the ground of privilege, he lets in secondary evidence of it, if he has been served with a subpœna duces tecum, and has refused to produce it, or if he has been sworn as a witness and asked for the document, and admitted that it is in Court: Stephen on Evidence, ed. iii., p. 74.

Secondary evidence; when it can be given.

CHAPTER V.

GENERAL VIEW OF LIEN.

Safeguard to client.

LORD ROMILLY said in In re *Moss*, L. R. 2 Eq. 347:—"I think it of great importance to preserve the lien of solicitors. That is the real security for solicitors engaged in business. It is also beneficial to the suitor. It would frequently happen but for the lien which solicitors have upon papers and deeds, that a client, who is not able to advance money to enable them to carry on business, would be deprived of justice through inability to prosecute his claims in the Court, and therefore I regard it as a matter of great importance to the due preservation of rights in courts of justice, to preserve the lien of solicitors."

Different kinds of.

What is generally called solicitor's lien is of three kinds:—

Specific, sometimes called particular; general; and that on property recovered or preserved, given by the Solicitors' Act, 1860, sec. 28.

The specific lien was originally merely that which any workman has upon the subject of his handiwork.

Extent of.

This was, however, soon extended to any property of his clients which came into his hands for the purpose of being used in legal proceedings, for his charges therein; but it does not extend to charges which do not arise out of them. Such property he is entitled to hold until he is paid, except when public inconvenience would arise from his so doing. For instance, he is not entitled, on the ground of his lien on the documents of a bankrupt for his services before bankruptcy, to refuse to produce them for the inspection of the trustee. And see further as to the exceptions which are grounded upon the public inconvenience the exercise of lien would cause, the cases mentioned at the end of the chapter.

Duration of lien on will.

In an old case a solicitor prepared a will for a man which he duly executed, but did not pay for. It was held that his lien expired with the life of the testator; for that otherwise the proceedings of the then Court of Probate would have been intercepted. The solicitor would have had a lien on the will had he not allowed it to be executed until he was paid for it; but, having allowed it to be executed, his lien became thereby limited in duration to the life of the testator.

Peculiarity of solicitor's lien.

The way in which the simplest form of solicitor's lien differs from that of any other person will be apparent. A law stationer engrosses a deed; he has a lien on the parchment so engrossed for the cost of the engrossment. A solicitor is employed by a client to defend him in an action, and for this purpose obtains from him, in the course of his employment as such solicitor, various articles, as for example—securities, letters patent, and money—for the purpose of effecting a compromise. Upon all these, and, indeed, upon all property coming into his hands for the purposes of the defence, he would have a specific lien for the taxed costs and proper expenses incurred by him in such defence. This specific lien, however, would not cover any claim he had in respect of other legal proceedings, and would, of course, not extend to any

What it does not extend to.

property left with him for a specific purpose, and with a special stipulation earmarking that purpose; as, for instance, a deposit on a loan of money. Nor would it extend to property, the possession of which was acquired by him in a different capacity, as steward or agent; for example—*Champernown* v. *Scott*: 6 Madd. 93. If, however, a town clerk acts also as legal adviser to the corporation of the town, he is not, by the fact of being also town clerk, prevented from getting a lien upon any papers belonging to the coporation of such town as may come to his hands as their legal adviser: *Rex* v. *Sankey*, 5 Ad. & E. 423. In *Newington Local Board* v. *Eldridge*, 12 Ch. D. 349, the Court of Appeal held that his lien is not to be prejudiced by the order for production of documents in a suit by the solicitor, unless a sum sufficient to meet his claim against the defendant is paid into Court. In this case the solicitor was the former clerk of the plaintiffs. The same remark would probably apply to a solicitor who was also agent for a property to the owners of which he was the legal adviser.

Of town clerk on corporation papers.

How prejudiced by order for production.

General lien does not involve power of sale.

A general lien does not involve a power of sale, and is that which a solicitor has upon all documents belonging to a client not left with him for a specific purpose, and with a specific stipulation that they shall be returned when that purpose is accomplished, for the balance due to him from his client for professional services generally. If, however, the documents are left with him after this specific purpose is accomplished, his general lien will attach. Thus, when there is a change of solicitors, the first solicitor has a general lien extending to all costs due from the client to him upon whatever of the client's papers or property he has in his possession, which had not been

Lien in case of change of solicitors.

given him for a specific purpose, the time for the performance of which had not arrived: In re *Faithfull*; In re *London, Brighton, and South Coast Ry. Co.*, L. R. 6 Eq. 325. The incidents alluded to as affecting a specific lien, *i.e.*, as to the things to which it attaches, and the capacity in which the solicitor must obtain possession of them, apply equally to the general lien; and it may be remarked that it exists only for professional services properly incurred by the person retaining him. If a solicitor acts for a firm, and also for the partners composing the firm, no lien will attach to the documents of the individual partners for the bill owing by the firm: *Turner* v. *Deane*, 18 L. J. Ex. 343.

To what a specific lien attaches.

Solicitor to a firm.

Of course, this lien cannot be set up against third parties, whose title is paramount to that of the client. And it would not attach to deeds upon which a mortgage had been executed for the expenses of perusing the reconveyance, &c., as against the mortgagor, when he brought his principal and interest to redeem: *Wakefield* v. *Newton*, 6 Q. B. 276. Or to deeds sent to be investigated with a view to a mortgage, though the agreement was that the borrower was to pay expenses if the negotiations fell through. If the solicitor acts for mortgagee as well as for mortgagor, he loses his lien for previous costs on the deeds of the mortgagor comprised in the security. Indeed, the law does not favour the idea of one solicitor acting for two opposite parties; and not only is his doing so often against the interests of his clients, but also against his own; for by so doing he loses his right to those privileges, such as lien which appertain to his privileged profession.

To what not.

Solicitor acting for both mortgagee and mortgagor.

If, for example, the same solicitor acts for the mortgagor and mortgagee, he has no lien upon the deeds comprised in the mortgage against the mortgagee for his charges, unless by express agreement, the idea being that it was his duty to get him as good a security as possible.

Mortgagor borrowing deeds from equitable mortgagee.

It was held by Lord Langdale, M.R., in *Young* v. *English*, 7 Beav. 10, that a mortgagor who had borrowed title-deeds from an equitable mortgagee, to enable him to sell the property, could give his solicitor a lien by handing such deeds to him in order to complete if the mortgagee acquiesced in the sale. The mortgagor's solicitor, however, had only a lien for his cost of the transaction and not for his other claims for costs against the mortgagor.

Solicitor may act for two parties not antagonistic.

But there is no objection to a solicitor acting for two or more parties who are not antagonistic, and he will not lose his lien by so doing. In the case of a purchase, however, a solicitor may be placed in an awkward dilemma by acting for the vendor and also for the purchaser. See Sugden's Vendors and Purchasers, p. 7. In a case like the following, however, the same solicitor may well act for the two parties.

Solicitor acting for two parties.

See *Raymond* v. *Tapson*, 22 Ch. D. 434.

H. deposited shares with a solicitor to take proceedings alone. He incurred costs, and then sold the shares to X., with notice of the solicitor's lien. Afterwards X. employed the same solicitor to continue the proceedings; and he at length obtained cheques in exchange for the shares which X. claimed. It was held that he was entitled to retain the cheques as security for H.'s debts to him, notwithstanding his having taken a retainer from X.

And such lien will generally be respected by the Court, who will not prejudice it by ordering even production of the documents upon which it exists, without payment into Court of a sufficient sum to meet the amount claimed. Moreover, if a client has

When two bills.

got an order of course to tax a bill of costs in a suit with a view to a change of solicitors, and there has been more work done by the solicitor for the client after the delivery of the first bill, and a second bill has been delivered for it, he will not be ordered to deliver up the client's papers without payment of both bills: Ex parte *Jarman*, 4 Ch. D. 835.

General lien, unless by special agreement, cannot be lost.

Papers.

Moneys.

It may therefore be taken generally, that when a solicitor, from his position, has a general lien upon deeds or papers, he cannot lose that right unless there is some special agreement that he shall do so. And with regard to moneys of his client which have come to his hands, unless such moneys were placed in his hands for a specific purpose, he has also a lien upon these for his proper professional services, but for nothing else: In re *Clarke*, Ex parte *Newland*, 4 Ch. D. 518. The common law lien of a solicitor is not barred by the Statute of Limitations: Re *Murray*, W. N. 1867, 190; but the statutory lien arising from the Solicitors Act, 1860, s. 28, is not given for a debt which has become statute barred by the terms of the Act itself.

When statute barred.

While a receiver is in possession, however, and the name of the solicitor who has obtained the charge is on the record, the statute does not run: *Baile* v. *Baile*, L. R. 13 Eq. 497; *Harris* v. *Quine*, L. R. 4 Q. B. 653.

Besides his lien, a solicitor has a statutory right ancillary to, but co-existent with, it. The statute 23 & 24 Vict. c. 127, s. 28, has given him the right to call for a charge, whenever he thinks fit, for the taxed costs, charges, and expenses of or in reference to the suit, matter, or proceedings in which he has been engaged; and the only person who could possibly contest his claim would be a purchaser for

Right to statutory charge.

D

valuable consideration without notice. But it has been held that this lien (if lien it can be called), under section 28, has priority over all charges created by the client himself: *Haynes* v. *Cooper*, 23 Beav. 431. It is, of course, not easy to define what "property recovered or preserved through his instrumentality" is; but if the result of the proceedings instituted by him gives his client a right to the property, it is enough; and it is not necessary that he should absolutely obtain possession of it; and certainly, the persons who keep back the property will not be able to take advantage of their own wrong doing. Money paid by virtue of an award, or paid into Court in the course of an action, is money preserved. The Court will not, however, except in the case of a conspiracy, prevent a compromise, though the solicitor may be thereby deprived of all security for payment out of the funds or property in litigation.

See Chap. 24, p. 196.

Costs properly incurred.

The late case of *Emden* v. *Carte*, 19 Ch. D. 318, illustrates the meaning of the section; which enacts, in effect, that the judge shall have the power to declare the solicitor entitled to a charge on the property recovered or preserved through his instrumentality in a suit, matter, or proceeding for the taxed costs, charges, and expenses of such suit, matter, or proceeding. The judge's duty in making the order is to limit it to the costs properly incurred, and to direct taxation of them. The facts of the case were these:—An undischarged bankrupt, with the knowledge of his trustee, brought an action in respect of which the defendant, without admitting any liability, paid £360 into Court; and the plaintiff took out a summons to have the money paid out to him. The trustee, hearing of this, obtained an order

Emden v. *Carte.*

joining himself as a co-plaintiff, and ultimately obtained an order for the conduct of the proceedings. The bankrupt's solicitor then applied for a charge under section 28 in respect of his costs, charges, and expenses of or in reference to the action. These he was allowed to have up to the time when the trustee came into the suit; as the trustee had taken the benefit of his action by adopting it.

The subject of charges is, however, treated of at greater length in a separate chapter.

Questions often arise as to the priorities of charges upon property recovered. *Faithful* v. *Ewen*, 7 Ch. D. 495, was a case of this kind. There the plaintiffs in a suit by a deed charged funds, which were part of the funds sought to be recovered in the suit, with a payment to the defendants. The plaintiffs' solicitor prepared the deed, but nothing was said about his costs in reference to the suit. Afterwards the solicitor petitioned for a charging order, and he was held entitled to it in priority to the charge given to the defendants; upon the principle that they must be presumed to have known the rights of the plaintiffs' solicitor. This subject, too, is dealt with separately in another place.

Priorities of charges upon property recovered.

Chap. 25, p. 203.

A charging order under section 28 may be obtained on summons or on petition, and it need not be intituled in the action or proceeding in which the property is recovered or preserved: *Hamer* v. *Giles*, 11 Ch. D. 942.

Charging order, how obtained.

When a charging order has been obtained, and due time has elapsed, the solicitor takes out a summons calling upon his client to attend upon an application, that the amount of his taxed costs may be paid out of the sum upon which the charging order was obtained. It is not easy, if the client absconds, to get an order made upon the summons. But a notice

Next step.

Notice when client absconds.

is sometimes ordered to be put up in the Master's office, stating that the summons has been issued; and that if the client does not appear within one month, service will be dispensed with. Proper notice to the same effect must be given to the other parties to the suit in which the order was obtained, and it should be advertised once in the "Times": *Hunt* v. *Austin*, W. N. 1882, 80.

Change of solicitor.

Supposing a solicitor applies to his client for funds to carry on a suit, and the client fails to provide them, this is a discharge of a solicitor by himself; and he may have to hand over the papers relating to the suit to any new solicitors that the client might appoint, upon their undertaking to hold them without prejudice to his lien. The exact terms upon which such an arrangement was ordered will be found in *Robins* v. *Goldingham*, L. R. 13 Eq. 440; and the whole subject of change of solicitors is also dealt with in another place.

Chap. 7, p. 62.

Lien of town agent.

A town agent of a solicitor has a lien on any papers or property which have come into his hands in the regular course of his employment, for the amount of his proper costs and charges in such employment in a particular matter; but not a general lien upon them for any balance that may be due to him from his country client. And when the country solicitor has been paid by his client, the town agent cannot set up his lien as against the ultimate client's claim. A very late case upon this is Ex parte *Edwards*, 8 Q. B. D. 264. There the town agent of the solicitor of the plaintiff, in an action in which judgment had been recovered for a debt, refused to pay over to the plaintiff the amount of the debt which had been received by him from the sheriff under a writ of fi. fa. The ground of such refusal was that he was

Has not a general lien.

Ex parte *Edwards*.

entitled to retain such amount for a debt due to him from the country solicitor of equal amount. The country solicitor, however, had no lien on the proceeds of the fi. fa. against his client. It was held that the town agent had no lien, and that the Court, in the exercise of its summary jurisdiction over its officers, would order him to pay over the amount of the debt to the plaintiff.

London agent's lien.

Against client.

Against country solicitor.

The nature of the London agent's lien, as between him and his client, is such that it extends only to the costs of the particular action in which he is engaged; but, as against the country solicitor, he has a general lien upon any money recovered in an action for all costs for agency business and disbursements due from the country solicitor, whether in the particular action or in any other proceedings: *Lawrence* v. *Fletcher*, 12 Ch. D. 858.

Lien, only a right to embarrass.

Chap. 6, p. 56.

Chap. 24, p. 194.

The result of the cases upon lien, as was pointed out in an able article in the "Law Journal" of March 18th, 1882, is, that the more essential to a client the documents upon which the solicitor has a lien are, the greater the leverage it gives him; but that his lien is of imperfect value unless the documents are essential. The case there referred to was the *West of England Banking Co.* v. *Batchelor*, W. N. 1882, 11, in which Fry, J., showed that the lien in that case only gave the solicitor a right to embarrass the plaintiffs. Jessel, M. R.'s, remarks, in *Pringle* v. *Gloag*, 10 Ch. D. 680, demonstrate that because a solicitor has a lien he has not necessarily the means of ever paying himself; and, his lordship adds, that before he undertakes a particular business for a client, he should see that the client is able to pay. This is also the expressed opinion of Lord Blackburn, in In re *Sullivan* v. *Pearson*, Ex parte *Morrison*, L. R. 4 Q. B. 153.

Solicitor's lien is no bar to order upon client to produce.

A solicitor's lien upon papers is no bar to an order upon the client, though bankrupt, to produce them: *Rodick* v. *Gaudell*, 10 Beav. 270. And, in a winding-up, no lien bars the official liquidator's right to the production of documents relating to the company: In re *South Essex Estuary and Reclamation Co.*, Ex parte *Paine* v. *Layton*, L. R. 4 Ch. 215; see also In re *Union Cement and Brick Co.*, Ex parte *Pulbrook*, L. R. 4 Ch. 627. Also, in a bankruptcy there is no solicitor's lien which prevents the trustee from having production of the documents of the debtor: In re *Toleman and England*, Ex parte *Bramble*, 13 Ch. D. 885.

Lien no bar to official liquidator's right to production.

Nor to trustee's in bankruptcy.

See beginning of chapter.

Effect of not keeping undertaking given on waiver of a lien.

As a lien is often waived upon a satisfactory undertaking having been entered into in reference to the solicitor's claim, let us see what the effect of not keeping an undertaking is. In the case of an unconditional undertaking to do a certain thing by a solicitor, the Court has jurisdiction to enforce in a summary way that undertaking, though given out of Court: In re *Woodfin* v. *Wray*, L. J. 1882, Notes of Cases, p. 31. And an undertaking by the solicitors of a company with the petitioning creditor's solicitor, in a winding-up petition, to pay all proper costs under the petition if it be withdrawn, is a personal undertaking, and they are liable under it: In re *Grundy, Kershaw & Co.*, 17 Ch. D. 110. The reason being, that if solicitors undertake anything in their own name on behalf of their principal, they have pledged their own credit and made themselves liable. Thus, a solicitor is personally liable to the law stationer he employs, even though the work that is done is not for himself; and, if he undertakes anything in the course of legal proceedings, he does so as an officer of the Court, and the Court will see that he carries out his undertaking.

The subject of undertakings, however, appears to be of so important a character as to merit a separate place, and the reader is therefore referred for the further consideration of the subject to p. 79. In this chapter it has been thought well just to glance generally at the subject of lien, and to deal somewhat more thoroughly with some of its many ramifications one by one as they arise, in other parts of this book.

It is for this reason that much ground in this chapter will be gone over again; but, had it not come in here, a fair bird's-eye view of lien could hardly have been given in so short a space

CHAPTER VI.

LIEN II.

West of England Banking Co. v. Batchelor.

ONE of the latest cases in which the subject of lien has come before the Court is *West of England Banking Co. v. Batchelor*, W. N. 1882, 11, which was alluded to in the previous chapter. The material facts in that case were the following:—B. mortgaged a policy of assurance on his life to O. Notice thereof was given to the insurance company. The mortgage was paid off, and O. re-assigned the policy to B., who left it, together with the re-assignment, with his solicitor, to whom he owed some costs. Afterwards B., who who had forgotten what had become of the policy, applied to the plaintiffs to lend him some more money upon it, which they did upon a certified copy issued by the company. The plaintiffs did not inquire whether the policy was in the hands of B.'s solicitor, and knew nothing of this fact. The plaintiffs subsequently sold the policy, and after such sale the solicitor gave, for the first time, notice to the insurance company that he held the original policy, upon which he claimed a lien for costs due to him from Batchelor. The claim in the action was for a declaration that the plaintiffs' mortgage was the first charge on the policy, and had priority over the lien of the solicitor. It will be noticed in this case that the plaintiffs did wrong in making no inquiries into the possible existence of a solicitor's lien upon the original policy; but this appears to have been the only omission they made. The solicitor, on the other hand, had done nothing whatever to perfect his lien, by way of giving notice to the company, until after the sale of the policy to an innocent third party for value. Mr. Justice Fry, however, said a solicitor's lien was a merely passive right—a right to hold a piece of paper or a parchment until he was paid his costs. That the lien in the present case gave the solicitor no right to be paid out of the fund; the only right he had was to embarrass the plaintiff. He had no right by notice to make the company trustees of the fund for him. He had merely a right to the policy, the piece of paper; and the fact that he held the paper was of itself notice to all the world that it was held by someone other than B., and this was the only thing of which the solicitor was bound to give notice. No fraud could, therefore, be committed by his omission to give notice, and the plaintiffs chose to run the risk of the original policy being in the hands of someone who might have a lien on it. It was for this reason, then, that the claim against the solicitor failed. From this case it will be seen that the view the Courts now take of solicitor's liens is in harmony with the definition of it in *Hammond* v. *Barclay*, 2 East. 235. Lien is a right in one man to retain that which is in his possession belonging to another, till certain demands of him (the person in possession) are satisfied.

What a solicitor is bound to give notice of.

The way in which the lien of the solicitor differs from that of any other person is this, that whereas a law stationer, for example, has a lien upon the very piece of paper or parchment upon which he may have placed an engrossment, and upon nothing else belonging to his employer that he may have in his possession, the solicitor can retain any papers he may have belonging to his client to satisfy his claims against him, and, therefore, his power of embarrassing him is much greater than that of any other class, and so he has something which is of tangible value to him as a means of getting his costs.

Lien must be for professional services. This lien, however, must be for professional services, and does not extend to other claims, as, for instance, for money lent; and in no case can it be (as where a solicitor holds a client's moneys) for a larger amount than the client's debt: *Miller* v. *Atlee*, 3 Exch. 799. And therefore the lien in a suit may be said to be for "the taxed costs, charges, and expenses of or in reference to such suit": Solicitor's Act, 1860, s. 28. And that he is entitled to this he can obtain a declaration, upon application to the Court, as explained in the previous chapter.

When this application is made, affidavits in support of it should state the probable amount of the solicitor's claim: *Davies* v. *Lowndes*, 3 C. B. 828; as the object of lien is simply to adequately secure the payment of a debt due; and, therefore, if a solicitor has a number of deeds belonging to a client in his hands, and only a small claim against him, he may be ordered to give up some of the deeds, and permitted only to retain enough to secure effectually his debt: *Du Boison* v. *Maxwell*, W. N. 1876, 146. A lien only attaches to documents which are the client's property, and reasonableness is the foundation of all the legal doctrine of lien: therefore, if a client mortgages a property to a solicitor, and afterwards to someone else, and the solicitor prepares the first mortgage, he has no lien upon the deeds for the costs relative to the first mortgage. The deeds are the deeds of the solicitor as mortgagee, and are not in his possession as solicitor for the mortgagor. There is only a contingent right of redemption in the mortgagor, and it would be unreasonable to imply a lien from such a right: Thesiger, L.J., in *Sheffield* v. *Eden*, 10 Ch. D. 293. And there is no lien upon a client's letters to a solicitor and his copies of his answers thereto. They are the solicitor's own property, and he is entitled to retain them upon payment of his bill: In re *Wheatcroft*, 6 Ch. D. 97.

No lien upon a client's letters.

But there is a lien upon anything whatever belonging to the client which comes into his hands as his solicitor: as, for instance, upon money received by him on his client's behalf in a suit. For example, if a solicitor is retained by a married woman in a matrimonial suit, he has a lien for costs incurred on her behalf, including costs disallowed on taxation as between her and her husband, but allowed as between solicitor and client, upon all money, including alimony, received by him on her account in the course of the suit: Ex parte *S. Bremner*, in the matter of *Bremner* v. *Bremner and Brett*, L. R. 1 P. & D. 254.

On alimony.

If notice of a lien is given, the fact of taking a retainer from the person to whom such notice is given to recover a debt upon which the lien is claimed, does not necessarily amount to an abandonment of the claim, or give a right to the party so retaining the solicitor to have the whole of the debt recovered without satisfying his claim: *General Share Trusts Company* v. *Chapman*, 1 C. P. D. 771.

Retainer by person to whom notice of lien given.

How lien can be used.

Having now considered generally what a lien can be had for, and upon what it can be had, the practical question next suggests itself, How can it be used? It is a good defence in an action of trover or detinue by the client (*Lightfoot* v. *Keane*, 1 M. & W. 745), and a valid excuse for not producing deeds, &c., where subpœnaed to do so by his client, or those claiming under him (who cannot give secondary evidence of them), but not by third persons; and if the client is obliged to produce deeds, the solicitor is likewise: *Furlong* v. *Howman*, 2 Sch. & Lef. 115.

Excuse for not producing deeds.

How lien may be lost.

The ways in which a lien are lost will next be considered.

Acting for mortgagee and mortgagor.

(1.) If the solicitor acts for mortgagee and mortgagor, and if he has a bill of costs against the latter, he loses his lien upon the deeds relating to the mortgaged property, and holds them for the former, unless his lien is expressly reserved: Jessel, M.R., in In re *Snell*, 6 Ch. D. 107.

But where a solicitor was instructed to prepare a mortgage and the title deeds were deposited with him by the mortgagor, although he also acted for the mortgagee and afterwards continued to hold his deeds for him, when the mortgagor filed a petition and the trustee appointing another solicitor sold the equity of redemption, the first solicitor was held to have a lien for the costs due to him from the mortgagor: In re *Messenger*, Ex parte *Culvert*, 3 Ch. D. 317 (V. C. B).

Waiver of lien.

If the solicitor consents to waive his lien, it is of course gone. Thus, supposing he consents to go in with the other creditors of a bankrupt, and takes a dividend, he cannot afterwards fall back upon his lien: *Cowper* v. *Green*, 7 M. & W. 633.

By claim-

(2.) And though a lien is not lost by claiming

more than is due, it is by claiming some other right to detain documents than that of mere lien (*Weeks* v. *Goode*, 6 C. B. N. S. 367), or by denying his client's title to them.

ing some other right.

Lucas v. *Peacock.* *Bozon* v. *Bolland.*

In conclusion, two cases,—*Lucas* v. *Peacock*, 9 Beav. 177, and *Bozon* v. *Bolland*, 4 My. & Cr. 354,—seem to establish nearly all that remains to be said upon the subject of lien. From them it is clear that a lien upon a fund is not a general lien; and that what it extends to is only costs in the cause, and costs immediately connected with the costs in the cause: as, for instance, the costs of successfully protecting a solicitor's right to the costs in a cause; that such a lien he is entitled actively to enforce; but that the general lien upon a client's papers, which applies to all his bills of costs, cannot be actively enforced, and merely amounts to a right to retain the papers themselves for whatever they may be worth.

CHAPTER VII.

CHANGE OF SOLICITORS.

WHEN there is a change of the solicitors of a party in an action, it is plain that if the former ones are allowed to keep his papers to protect their lien, his new solicitors may have a difficulty in prosecuting the action satisfactorily; and also that the other side may not know on whom service of papers in the action may with safety be made. Consequently, an order of Court is necessary for this purpose, except in a very few instances, as where the solicitor on the record has died, or where a party, who originally had appeared without a solicitor, appoints one; in which cases notice to the records and writ clerk and to the solicitors of the other side is sufficient.

Where order necessary.

When not, what is necessary.

Where solicitor discharges himself.

The rule is different where a solicitor discharges himself and where he is discharged by his client. Where a solicitor discharges himself during an action, his client is entitled to an order for delivery up of his papers, upon an undertaking by the new solicitor to carry on the action vigorously, and to hold them without prejudice to the first solicitor's lien, and to return them after the action has been brought to an end. If it is brought to a conclusion by which the client gets anything, the first solicitor's lien is a first charge upon any payment to be made

First solicitor's lien.

to the client: *Wilson* v. *Emmett*, 19 Beav. 233. Where a solicitor places himself in such a position as to render himself incapable of performing his duty to his client, he discharges himself. A solicitor is taken to have discharged himself where he applies to his client for funds to carry on a suit, and upon the client not furnishing any, declines to continue it: *Robins* v. *Goldingham*, L. R. 13 Eq. 440 (V. C. M.). There the undertaking was to hold the papers without prejudice to the lien of the former solicitor, and to return them undefaced within twelve days after the conclusion of the suit, and to allow the former solicitor access to them for the purpose of carrying on an action for his costs.

Where solicitor discharges himself.

Client failing to find funds.

If a solicitor becomes bankrupt, this is a discharge by himself; but if a client becomes bankrupt, that is a discharge by the client: In re *Moss*, L. R. 2 Eq. 348. If the solicitor's principal becomes bankrupt, and his trustee appoints another solicitor, in such a case the solicitor is held to have discharged himself: *Simmonds* v. *Great Eastern Ry. Co.*, L. R. 3 Ch. 799. In the case of a deceased principal, his solicitor would probably be taken not to have discharged himself: Ex parte *Underwood*, 9 Jur. 632.

Bankruptcy.

The papers which the solicitor will be ordered to deliver up are only such as are necessary to enable the client to proceed with pending matters in litigation; and where he is ordered to deliver up all documents in his custody or power, such order does not extend to documents which are detained by third parties, and which the solicitor cannot obtain without bringing an action. In re *Williams*, 9 W. R. 393, a solicitor had been ordered to deliver up some papers which were in the chambers of counsel, who declined to part with them until his fees were paid,

Order for delivery of papers.

Papers in the hands of counsel.

as the solicitor had made an agreement with him that such papers should remain with him as a security for such fees. It was held that these documents were not in the solicitor's custody or power.

Counsel have no lien.

It was argued by Selwyn, then Q.C., in this case, that counsel had no lien for their fees on papers sent to their chambers, as they are not bound to take in papers without payment; and the payment of counsel not being a debt which could be established by any legal proceedings, that therefore no lien could possibly arise.

Principle where solicitor discharges himself.

The principle in such cases seems to be that if a solicitor chooses to discharge himself he must not leave his client in the lurch in the middle of a matter, even though his client cannot supply him with money, or by reason of any other difficulty; and if he does he must produce to the new solicitor all papers necessary to enable him to prosecute or defend the matter in litigation. In other words, if the solicitor refuses to act for his client, his lien may be of little value, as he cannot in that case deprive him of the full use of papers for the purposes of the suit.

Where solicitor discharged by client.

If, however, the client discharges or ceases to employ the solicitor, the case is now different. It was originally held by Lord Eldon, in *Ross* v. *Laughton*, 1 Ves. & B. 349, that even in such a case the solicitor was compelled to afford facilities for the continuance of the proceedings by the use of papers and documents; but afterwards, in *Lord* v. *Warmleighton*, reported in Jac. 580, he decided that a solicitor, if discharged by his client, could not be compelled to assist him by the delivery up of papers in a pending suit. And this has ever since been the established rule. Lord Cottenham gave effect to it in

Bozon v. *Bolland*, *Husband* v. *Bolland*, 4 My. & Cr. 358. In that case the client had ceased to employ C. as his solicitor in a cause; C. had a deed belonging to the client which was valuable evidence in the cause. The Lord Chancellor said that he might have withheld the use of this deed, and so, if it really was essential to his client, have compelled payment of his general professional demand; but that it would have been at the option of the client to purchase the use of the deed at that price or not. The solicitor did not tender this option, but he produced the deed as evidence in the cause; and then, contending that the decree, which was ultimately made in favour of his client, could not have been obtained without such production, asked the Court to declare him entitled to the same lien on the fund that he had on the deed. The Lord Chancellor pointed out that the lien he had on the deed was a passive lien, but that the one he asked for, a declaration of on the fund, was an active one; that the former lien was a general, and that the latter was a specific, one for his costs in and relating to the suit. He gave him, however, the costs of the suit out of the fund. The rule in this case was approved of, and acted upon, by Malins, V.-C., in In re *Faithfull*, In re *London, Brighton and South Coast Ry. Co.*, L. R. 6 Eq. 328. And the only case at all at variance with it is In re *Becan and Whitting*, decided by Lord Westbury, and reported in 33 Beav. 439. It is commented upon and distinguished In re *Faithfull*.

Rule in *Bozon* v. *Bolland*.

A solicitor, however, cannot embarrass a suit by keeping papers which belong to an estate which is being administered by the Court, and cannot use that means of obtaining payment, even though he has been discharged by the trustee of

In administration.

the estate: *Belaney* v. *Ffrench*, L. R. 8 Ch. 920 (James, L.J.).

What is discharge by the client.

If a woman, a party to an action, marries during the action, and her husband changes the solicitor, this was a discharge by the client; as may also be outrageous conduct on the part of a client, which makes it impossible for a solicitor to continue to act for him: *Steel* v. *Scott*, 2 Hog. 141. Where a client gets an order to change solicitors, this is a discharge by the client.

Solicitor must carry on suit to the end.

It must be observed that the power of a solicitor to discharge himself in the middle of an action is a very limited one. It exists if his client dies, or if, after reasonable notice from him, the client neglects to provide funds. In the case of *Whitehead* v. *Lord*, 7 Ex. 694, Park, B., said that this rule must not be extended to a case where a suit in Chancery had fallen into a state of sleep for a lengthened period, the rule being (subject to the two exceptions before mentioned) that a solicitor, when once retained to conduct a suit, is under the obligation to carry it on to its termination. This is expressly the case where a solicitor makes a bargain with a client to carry on an action for him on the chance of getting the costs out of the other side. In *Webster* v. *Le Hunt*, 9 W. R. 804, the agreement made was that the solicitor should carry on a suit without requiring to be supplied with funds up to hearing. The order then made was appealed from, and it was held by Kindersley, V.-C., that as the word "hearing" must be taken to have meant the original hearing, the solicitor had a right to refuse to go on after the original hearing without funds. But, with respect to the papers, he ordered the delivery over of them to the new solicitor, without prejudice to the lien of the

Speculative action.

first solicitor, upon an undertaking to restore them when the appeal was disposed of. The order was in the usual form.

Costs of affidavits and list of deeds.

A solicitor, if he makes an affidavit when he hands over papers, can, it appears, charge for it; but he cannot charge for a list of the deeds and documents which he hands over to his client: Re *Catlin*, 18 Beav. 514.

Grant v. *Holland.*

The present practice as to the form of the order for changing a solicitor is stated by Field, J., Huddleston, B., and Lindley, J., in *Grant* v. *Holland*, *Ross* v. *Grant*, 3 C. P. D. 180, to be the same in law as in equity—viz., that it will now be made without any provision as to the payment of the first solicitor's costs.

CHAPTER VIII.

DISABILITIES OF SOLICITORS.

Gifts and purchases from clients.

THE principle which puts restrictions upon the receipt of gifts and the purchase of property from clients by solicitors, is that the clients may have been acting under undue influence and without sufficient information in such transactions.

Dealings between solicitors and clients, principle.

It was said by Turner, L. J., in *Gresley* v. *Mousley*, 10 W. R. 224, that there is one principle which runs through all the cases on dealings between solicitor and client—viz., that the solicitor dealing with the client is bound to give him at least the same protection as he would be bound to give him if dealing with a stranger. It would be his duty to see that the client, if dealing with a stranger, did not commit himself to anything which would be to his prejudice. If, for example, he were dealing with the stranger for an advance of money upon security, or for the sale of an estate, he would have to see that the client did not acknowledge the advance, or give a receipt for the purchase money, unless it was actually paid. If he failed to advise the client acting in the transaction under his advice not to give the acknowledgment, or to sign the receipt, unless the money was actually paid, he could not be permitted to set up in justification of his own negligence that the client had done so without his advice; and if he could not do this in the case of a client dealing with a stranger, how could he be allowed to do so in the case of the client dealing with himself? From this consideration follows the necessity of independent proof of payment in the case of dealings between solicitor and client. The obligation which rests upon him to protect the client when dealing with him in matters of security or purchase would be of no value unless some independent proof of payment was required, and it is no hardship upon him to require such proof, for it is no less his duty than his interest to keep correct accounts, and to preserve the evidence of his dealings with his clients. In *Lewes* v. *Morgan*, 5 Price, 153, Lord Redesdale said:—"This is the case of an attorney, who acted as general agent and legal adviser of his principal and client, obtaining his bond. He is, therefore, bound by a very strict rule of law to prove by other evidence the actual advance of the whole consideration." So that on a purchase by a solicitor from his client, the onus of showing that the purchase money was actually paid cannot be shifted from the purchaser, and the receipt endorsed upon a conveyance or security made by a client to his solicitor is not sufficient for this purpose, nor is the defect cured by a lapse of twenty years: *Gresley* v. *Moulsey*.

Necessity of independent proof of payment.

Taking security.

In purchase from client, onus of proof of payment on solicitor.

Upon the same principle, in *Watson* v. *Rodwell*, 11 Ch. Div. 150, an account which had been settled between a client, who was an old lady, and her solicitor, including arranged bills of costs, was ordered to be re-opened, and the bills of costs taxed, after the lapse of nearly two years, although without actual proof of error or overcharge. The ground of the order was that the client had acted under undue

Account re-opened after nearly two years.

influence and without sufficient information, and that much of the business charged for was unnecessary and improper. In *Pisani* v. *A.-G. for Gibraltar*, L. R. 5 P. C. 536, it was said that the effect of previous decisions had been that the Courts do not hold that a solicitor is incapable of purchasing from his client, but watches such a transaction with jealousy, and throws on the solicitor the onus of showing that the bargain is, generally speaking, as good as any that could have been obtained by due diligence from any other purchaser. In the case last quoted it was held that the circumstance of the employment of the solicitor might be considered, and the amount of influence estimated; and it appeared from that case, too, that the opinion of the Court was, that a legal adviser purchasing from his client ought to insist on the intervention of another professional adviser. This would seem to be the view of the Courts in the case of taking security from a client, as well as in the case of a purchase.

Purchase must be a good one for client.

Client should have independent legal advice.

A strong example of this was *King* v. *Savery*, 1 Sm. & G. 276, where a mortgage given by a son to a family solicitor, to secure his father's debt, was not allowed to hold good, as he had had the advantage of no other professional assistance than that of the family solicitor himself.

Solicitor purchasing annuity from client.

Where a solicitor bought an annuity from his client, and paid for it by his personal bond, the transaction was set aside by Lord Eldon: *Gibson* v. *Jeyes*, 6 Ves. 266. In *Spenser* v. *Topham*, 22 Beav. 576, £100 was not thought by the Master of the Rolls a difference sufficient to set aside the sale of a property, the purchase money of which amounted to £1820.

Of course, the general principle stated by Turner,

L.J., in *Rhodes* v. *Bate*, L. R. 1 Ch. 257, to apply to persons standing in a confidential relation towards others, exists in the case of solicitors—viz., that they cannot entitle themselves to hold benefits (other than trifling ones) which those others may have conferred upon them unless they can show, to the satisfaction of the Court, that the persons by whom the benefits have been conferred had competent (see *Gibbs* v. *Daniel*, 10 W. R. 688) and independent advice in conferring them. Age and capacity afford but little protection in cases of influence founded upon confidence. Of course, a confidential relationship has to be established, and the existence of such a relationship will not be interfered with, without the strongest evidence, by the appointment of an agent: *Rhodes* v. *Bate*, L. R. 1 Ch. p. 259. Where a relation of confidence is once established, either some positive act, or some complete case of abandonment, must be shown in order to determine it. The mere fact that the relation is not called into action is not sufficient of itself to determine it, for this may well have arisen from there having been no occasion to resort to it. And with regard to gifts to solicitors by clients, the rule was that where the relation exists they are contrary to public policy, and void: *O'Brien* v. *Lewis*, 9 Jur. N. S. 521; *Walker* v. *Smith*, 29 Beav. 394; and to prevent the operation of the rule, there must not only be a total absence of fraud, misrepresentation, or even suspicion, but there must be a severance of the confidental relation: *Morgan* v. *Minett*, 6 Ch. D. 638 (V. C. B.). But in the case of *Mitchell* v. *Homfray*, 8 Q. B. D. 592, Lord Selborne decided that such a gift was voidable only, and cannot be impeached after the death of the donor; and it seems from this case, that where the influence which

Independent advice necessary when benefits conferred.

Relation of confidence not easy to determine.

Gifts to solicitors by clients contrary to public policy.

Cannot be impeached after death of donor.

a solicitor may be supposed to have exerted over his client has been removed, the solicitor may become the object of his client's bounty, and may receive from him a gift which will be valid both at law and in equity. See also In re *Holmes' Estate*, 3 Giff. 337.

Gifts by will.

As to gifts by will from clients to solicitors, one of the latest cases referring to them is *Morgan* v. *Minett*, 6 Ch. D. 647 (V. C. B.), quoted before. The Vice-Chancellor in his judgment states that a client inclined to bestow bounty upon his solicitor, can do so, and the solicitor can accept it; but both must act under circumstances which preclude the possibility of suspicion. Suspicion is the basis of the rule of influence, and is enough to upset the transaction. The relation of client and solicitor must cease before the gift is made. In that case a separate solicitor was called in, who explained to the client the effect of what he had done inter vivos, and of what he proposed to do for his solicitor by will, and the new solicitor expressed it as his opinion that the client thoroughly understood what he was doing, and that he expressed the strongest regard for his solicitor, as being a person to whom he was under the greatest obligation. If a new solicitor is called in, it is indispensably necessary that he should explain to the client the law upon the subject; and why the interference and advice of an independent person is necessary at such a time.

Suspicion must be impossible.

What new solicitor must explain.

While the relation of solicitor and client exists, the inference produced by that relation is such that it makes it almost impossible that the gift can prevail: Re *Holmes' Estate*, 3 Giff. 345. Above all things, there must be no concealment of the transaction at the time by the solicitor taking the benefit.

Therefore the case of the solicitor taking a gift by will is much the same as when taking it in the lifetime of his client. His conduct is viewed with great suspicion; and he can derive no advantage from his client's will, especially if drawn by himself, unless it is clearly shown to the Court that it was not made under any influence, direct or indirect, springing from their relation, exercised over the client by the solicitor; and unless the law on the subject and the nature of the transaction was explained to the client by another solicitor, who in every respect acted as solicitor to the client in the matter. The ignorance of the solicitor does not help him: *Bulkley* v. *Wilford*, 2 Cl. & F. 141.

Difference between gifts to and purchases from clients.

In conclusion, it may be observed that a purchase from or a security given to a client, or even a gift of leases which involved obligations (*Harris* v. *Tremenheere*, 15 Ves. 34), is not to be considered in the same light as a gift inter vivos or by will, from a client to a solicitor.

They stand on a different footing than that of mere bounty; and, yet, even in these, the onus lies on the solicitor to show that he dealt with his client exactly as a stranger would have done. This difference cannot, perhaps, be better illustrated than by the argument of the present Mr. Justice Kay in the case of *Morgan* v. *Minett*, quoted above; to which the reader is referred.

CHAPTER IX.

AGREEMENTS WITH AND UNDERTAKINGS BY SOLICITORS.

Agreement to be paid more than taxed costs.

BEFORE the Solicitors Act of 1870, although a solicitor might agree with a client to be paid less than his taxed costs in a proceeding, he could not enforce an agreement for payment to himself of more than his taxed costs; and if the client repudiated the agreement his only remedy against him was for his taxed costs. This also applied to arrangements between country solicitors and their town agents, although the question might arise whether the special agreement constituted the relation of agency or that of partnership between the parties: Lord Selborne in *Ward* v. *Lawson*, L. R. 8 Ch. 70.

Between country solicitors and agents.

In *Jones* v. *Read*, 5 A. & E. 531, it was held that work done in the character of an attorney could be done upon a contract to take costs out of pocket which should not exceed a sum named. As the Act of 1870 only applies to agreements in writing, the same rule still holds good as to all parol agreements between solicitor and client. Thus, in *Jennings* v. *Johnson*, L. R. 8 C. P. 426, the following verbal agreement by the solicitor was upheld. To act as attorney for the plaintiff in an action, to charge him nothing if he lost the action, and to take nothing for

Solicitors Act, 1870, applies to agreements in writing only.

costs out of any money that might be awarded to him in such action. The only way in which such an agreement could be impeached under the statute is under section 11, which provides against champerty. But this agreement not to charge anything for costs is not champerty (Bovill, C.J.). Therefore, though a solicitor may still agree with a client verbally to charge him less than his taxed costs, he cannot make an agreement with him which will bind the client to pay him more. If he desires to do this, he must do it in writing. The proper way to object to a claim by the solicitor in such a case is to plead no signed bill delivered: *Scarth* v. *Rutland*, L. R. 1 C. P. 642; then, upon delivery of such bill and taxation of it by the client, he may be entitled to less, but he cannot recover more, than the agreed sum.

Champerty.

Solicitor charging more than taxed costs.

No third person can, however, benefit by a private arrangement between a client and his solicitor. For example, a company who employed standing solicitors at a fixed salary purchased property under a sale by order of the Court. The biddings were opened on payment by the applicant of the costs of the company. The arrangement between the company and their solicitors did not affect the amount of costs payable by the applicant to the company's solicitors: *Raymond* v. *Lakeman*, 34 Beav. 584.

Third parties cannot benefit by private arrangements between solicitor and client.

Under the Act of 1870, however, the remuneration of a solicitor for the whole or any part of any past or future services or disbursements may be fixed by agreement in writing to be signed by the solicitor and the client. Lord Coleridge says In re *Lewis*, Ex parte *Munro*, 1 Q. B. D. 724, that an agreement in writing, to come within the provisions of this Act, must be an agreement by both parties, and both parties must sign their names upon the agreement. The object of

Alteration by Solicitors Act, 1870.

Both parties must sign the agreement.

this was that no discussion might occur as to what was really understood by either party, and that the solicitor might not be able to place before the client a document containing favourable terms for himself signed by himself alone, and then to contend that the client was bound by it. See also Re *Fernandez*, 1878, W. N. 57.

Solicitors' Remuneration Act, 1881. See Appendix.

The Solicitors' Remuneration Act, 1881 (44 & 45 Vict. c. 44), which will be found together with the orders made under it in the Appendix, regulates the remuneration of solicitors in respect of business connected with sales, purchases, leases, mortgages, settlements, and other matters of conveyancing, and in respect of other business, not being business in any action, or transacted in any court, or in the chambers of any judge or master, and not being otherwise contentious business, and to this extent restricts the operation of the Solicitors Act of 1870. Its scope, however, being limited to non-contentious business, it will not materially affect the provisions of this Act (Solicitors Act of 1870), which will here be considered alone.

Agreement to be examined by taxing master.

Section 4 goes on to say that when any written agreement signed by solicitor and client shall be made in respect of business done or to be done in any action at law or suit in equity, the amount payable under the agreement shall not be received by the solicitor until the agreement has been examined and allowed by a taxing officer of the Court having power to enforce the agreement. From the words of the section it would appear that the amount agreed to be paid for business other than that done or to be done in any action at law or suit in equity could not be adjudged to be unfair or unreasonable. However, In re Attorney and Solicitors Act, 1870 (1 Ch. Div.

575) Jessel, M.R., says that the meaning of section 4 is that a solicitor may make what agreement he likes with his clients, but that he is not to receive any payment under it unless the taxing master considers it fair and reasonable, and if he does not consider it so that he may require the opinion of the Court or a judge to be taken upon it.

Charges must appear reasonable.

This opinion, however, cannot be taken until something is payable under the agreement (same case), although attempts have been made on the part of solicitors who have obtained their clients' signatures to agreements to get the opinion of the Court upon them before anything was done under the agreements as to whether they would be considered on taxation fair and reasonable or not.

Opinion of Court cannot be taken till something due under agreement.

An agreement which gave the solicitor in the event of success what was equivalent to a tenth part of the property to be recovered, was in the opinion of Jessel, M.R., pure champerty, 1 Ch. Div. 575.

Champerty.

A bill of costs, in proceedings before magistrates, can be taxed before the master of the Crown Office: Re *Lewis*, 1 Q. B. Div. 726, Lord Coleridge and Quain, J.

Costs in proceedings before magistrates.

Agreements only bind the solicitor and the client, and do not affect the amount recoverable from the client by any third person; and any provision in them limiting the responsibility of the solicitor is void. An action cannot be brought upon the agreement for remuneration due under it; but any question respecting it can be determined and the agreement enforced or set aside on motion or petition by any person, or the representative of any person, who is alleged to be liable to pay, or entitled to be paid, the costs in respect of which the agreement was made. The provision that an action may not be brought under

Agreements do not affect third parties.

Agreement set aside on motion or petition by any person interested.

such an agreement means upon the particular stipulation for the remuneration of the solicitor, not the entire contract between the parties. The agreement often is in effect that the client will employ the solicitor to act as his solicitor in a certain transaction, and then if the allegation is that the client has refused to employ him damages can be claimed by reason of that refusal: Kelly, C.B., and Bramwell, B., in *Rees* v. *Williams*, L. R. 10 Exch. 206 and 209.

Client refusing to employ solicitor under agreement.

Improper agreements.

Section 9 enacts that improper agreements may be set aside upon motion or petition, and that the matters referred to may be taxed as if no such agreement existed, and the Court may make what order it thinks fit as to the costs of such motion or petition. Upon a petition for taxation, In re *Thompson*, 8 Beav. 240, Lord Langdale said, as to the costs, that in some cases circumstances arise which create a modification of the rule, that a petition if dismissed should be dismissed with costs; as, for instance, if pressure has been used. See In re *Whitcombe*, 8 Beav. 144, where the conduct of the solicitor was exposed to suspicion. Where there was ambiguity as to the mode of payment: In re *Carew*, 8 Beav. 153. Where the items were probably not correct: In re *Drake*, 8 Beav. 123. All these cases were petitions for taxation which were dismissed without costs, for the reasons given above. It may, therefore, now well be that a petition under this section of the Act may be dismissed, but without costs, as the notion of the Court is that the solicitor has all the knowledge on his side, and that therefore the agreement should contain nothing not fair and reasonable upon the face of it. Therefore, great care should be taken in drawing such agreements to avoid a petition or motion for the setting aside of an

Costs of petition for taxation.

agreement, which, even though dismissed, may be dismissed without costs.

Section 10 permits agreements to be re-opened under special circumstances within twelve months, and the money paid under them to be repaid. This section merely gives powers to the Courts with reference to agreements analogous to those they have with reference to solicitors' bills under 6 & 7 Vict. c. 73, s. 37. The section, however, goes on to enact that in the case of agreements made by trustees, guardians, or committees, such agreements must be before payment examined and approved by the taxing officers, under the penalty of their having to account for any moneys paid without such examination, and in the case of the solicitor having, if so ordered, to refund the same. The effect of this section is illustrated by the remarks of Lord Romilly (In re *Brown*, a solicitor, L. R. 4 Eq. 465 and 466), upon the taxation of a bill under the third party clause (6 & 7 Vict. c. 73, s. 38), which, however, only applies to costs between solicitor and client, and not to party and party costs: Jessel, M.R., in *Grundy, Kershaw & Co.*, 17 Ch. Div. 112.

Agreements re-opened within twelve months.

Agreements by trustees, &c.

The prohibition of dealings analogous to champerty has been alluded to before, and is expressly forbidden by section 11.

This is not, perhaps, an inappropriate place for a few words upon the undertakings of solicitors, as the consideration of undertakings by solicitors may not unnaturally follow that of agreements by the same persons.

Undertakings of solicitors.

The rules of law which apply here are the same as those which apply in all cases of agency, and they are, perhaps, as carefully stated in Chitty on Contracts, 10th ed., p. 205 and 206, as in any other treatise. But

Instances of liability of solicitor as agent. a few instances of the liability of a solicitor in his capacity as an agent, will be given here. Thus, where, on an indictment against a parish for not repairing a road, the solicitors on either side entered into an agreement by which the one agreed, "on the part of the parish, to pay the costs," this was held to be a personal undertaking: *Watson* v. *Murrell*, 1 C. & P. 307. In like manner, where the solicitors to the assignees of a bankrupt tenant, upon whom the landlord had distrained, gave an undertaking in the following words, they were held personally liable: "We, as solicitors to the assignees, undertake to pay to the landlord his rent": *Burrell* v. *Jones*, 3 B. & Ald. 47.

To pay costs.

To pay rent on part of assignees of bankrupt.

Use of previous decisions here.

The use of previous decisions in the case of undertakings is only to show the weight to be allowed to any particular fact which may be found in any one of them and the case under consideration. Where the evidence has to be got from documents or letters, too much stress must not be laid on single expressions; the real question, which can only be extracted from the whole of the documents, or the correspondence in its entirety, being what was the real intention and understanding of the parties; and evidence of intention dehors the instrument creating the liability may be given: *Wake* v. *Harrop*, 6 H. & N. 768.

Evidence of intention of parties.

And a solicitor may be liable on his undertaking, not only if he voluntarily intervenes as a solicitor to one of the parties to a quarrel which is settled by such undertaking, but also if the parties have each at the time another solicitor, and the interference of the solicitor is not that of the solicitor in a cause: Denman, C.J., in *Harper* v. *Williams*, 4 Q. B. 231.

Where undertaking doubtful in form.

An undertaking may be in such a form and framed on such terms as to make it impossible to ascertain with certainty from its language alone whether it creates a personal liability or not, or it may point rather to a promise made by one person as agent for another, than as intended to bind the party writing in the character of a principal. This is especially the case where reference is made to a third party by name. An instance of this is *Downam* v. *Williams*, L. R. 8 Q. B. 103, where the solicitor was held not to have made himself personally liable.

Where solicitor has only limited authority.

If the solicitor has only a special authority as an agent, clearly limited in its extent by his principals, and falling short of sanctioning the particular undertaking into which he entered, so that no action would lie on the undertaking against the principals, and the want of authority is not known to the other party, he makes himself personally liable. See Story on Agency, 1839, p. 226.

Where solicitors agree.

Where an agreement between the solicitors to plaintiff and defendant contains by implication a promise to pay costs when taxed, if they have personally undertaken that the stipulations contained in the agreement shall be performed, it is not a question of suretyship, because the principals are not bound, and therefore an action is not premature because no demand has been made upon the client: *Iceson* v. *Conington*, 1 B. & C. 162.

Not as sureties.

Undertaking in professional character.

But besides the liability to which a solicitor subjects himself, in common with other agents, in entering into an undertaking, namely, that of being held personally liable in damages under such undertaking, there is another, which has been previously noticed at p. 17, namely, where an undertaking to do something as an officer of the Court is implied.

In order, however, to subject him to this liability, he must have been acting in his professional character, and the principle upon which it is enforced is that of the trust and confidence which is necessarily reposed in solicitors in such professional character.

If, therefore, a solicitor, when acting professionally for a client, undertakes to do anything, and he is trusted in consequence of his professional character, unless he can show any sufficient excuse for not fulfilling the trust, he is compellable to fulfil his undertaking forthwith. And it is no objection to his being so compelled to perform it, that the proceedings in respect of which the obligation was incurred took place in another Court to that in which application is made for its enforcement: Ex parte *Bodenham*, In re *Jephson*, 8 A. & E. 962. Although, where practicable, the application should be made to the Court in respect of the proceedings of which the obligation was incurred.

Court in which such undertakings will be enforced.

Gilbert v. *Cooper*.

The undertaking must be a personal one, and supposing it to consist of several provisions, one of which, for instance, is that one solicitor shall pay costs to the other solicitor, it must be clearly shown to the Court, upon an application for an order that he do pay such costs, what has been done under the other provisions: The Lord Chancellor, reversing the V.-C. of England, *Gilbert* v. *Cooper*, 11 L. T. 169.

Construction of order for solicitor to give undertaking.

Hill v. *Fletcher*.

Where there is a difficulty as to the construction of an order under which a solicitor has to give an undertaking, it appears that he will have the benefit of such difficulty. Thus, in *Hill* v. *Fletcher*, 4 Ex. 470, a judge's order was made in these terms. "The plaintiff to forthwith give security for costs to the satisfaction of the master. No stay of proceedings in the meantime. The attorney for the plaintiff hereby undertaking to find such security." No further proceedings were taken, and no security given. This was held to mean that the undertaking was the price of proceeding, not of the liberty to proceed.

The Courts will enforce an undertaking on which an action would be prevented by the operation of the Statute of Frauds or Limitations, because the rules of law applicable to contracts do not apply to their summary jurisdiction over solicitors as their own officers; but they will not interfere with respect to contracts or promises, as to pay over the balance of the purchase money of an estate, or to guarantee a loan to, a client: Pulling, 3rd ed., p. 431. Statute of Frauds or Limitations no bar.

The way in which such enforcement takes place, is by an order to do whatever the solicitor has undertaken to do, and if this order is not complied with, a motion for the attachment of the defaulting solicitor must then be made, on the ground of his having committed a contempt of Court in having disregarded such order. The practice in applications for attachment is treated of, among other places, in the writer's "Hints on Practice," 1st ed., 179. Some other observations upon this head, especially as to the penalties for failure to enter an appearance for a client after undertaking so to do, and for neglect to give notice of an order for discovery to a client (there being an implied undertaking in the acceptance of the retainer to do so), will be found in the chapter upon Solicitors as Officers of the Court. How enforced. Attachment on non-compliance with order. See p. 81.

CHAPTER X.

TOWN AGENTS.

Solicitor is liable for negligence of his agent.

ALTHOUGH it is quite discretionary with a solicitor whom he shall employ to do any act not in itself prohibited to be done by anyone not a solicitor, yet, as he, being directly retained, is liable for the negligence of his agent, it has been found to be safer that town agents for all purposes should be regularly admitted solicitors. There is no summary process by which the jurisdiction of the Court can be set at work in the case of an agent not being a solicitor, even though money has been received by him in that capacity: *Cole* v. *Grove*, 1 Scott, N. S. 30. Persons without any qualifications are, however, often appointed to serve writs and notices, to make demands, and to collect debts and rent. Moreover, of late, London law stationers have been employed by country solicitors to do work of a ministerial character, such as to take to the registry original wills, and the engrossments of them, together with the proper affidavits, and if these are in order, to fetch away the probate. It has been decided that this work may be done by persons not solicitors, provided that if any question arises as to the sufficiency of the documents, they communicate it to the country solicitor, and that they leave the papers in the names

Law stationers acting as agents.

of the latter, and charge only for their clerk's time, and for the engrossing and copying of the documents when required. If law stationers, however, act for themselves, and not as agents for solicitors whose names they give, and with whose authority they act, and if they undertake to prepare affidavits or to prepare documents which could be used for the purpose of obtaining probate, they might then come within 40 & 41 Vict. c. 62. The test is whether or not they do something which anyone may do, although solicitors generally do it; and whether they get a share in the profits made by solicitors, or indeed act in any way so as to get, in the name of the solicitors, the solicitor's profit: *Law Society* v. *Shaw; The same* v. *Waterlow*, 9 Q. B. D. 15.

Test of law stationers acting ultra vires.

The name and place of business of the agent, as well as of the country solicitor, must appear on the writ and pleadings: Orders IV., r. 1, XII., r. 7, XIX., r. 7. If a solicitor has not a London certificate he exposes himself to penalties by practising in London, within the meaning of the Stamp Act, 1870, s. 59. To fall within its meaning, however, he must do a series of acts, and not one isolated transaction. He must carry on business with a quasi-permanent habitat within the proscribed locality: In re *Horton*, 8 Q. B. D. 436.

Name of agent must appear on writ.

Doing London business without London certificate.

Attending a taxation is not within the section: In re *Horton*; and if the costs of a country solicitor attending a bankruptcy appeal are allowed in a proper case (In re *Foster*, Ex parte *Dickens*, 8 Ch. D. 598), à fortiori, such attendance does not come within the meaning of the statute. The town agent should not take any steps which he is not expressly directed to take, and he has not the same privilege as a solicitor who, for the benefit of his

What is not.

Agent should not take steps unless expressly

directed to do so. client, outsteps his authority: *Malins* v. *Greenway*, 17 L. J. Ch. 26.

Work done by town agent must be in ordinary course of business.

In order to bind the client, that which the town agent does in an action must be done in the ordinary course of business as such town agent, and his authority as an agent does not extend beyond the proceedings in the cause entrusted to him: *Hanley* v. *Casson*, 11 Jur. 1088.

No privity between client and London agent; right of action between.

There is no privity between the client and the London agent, and the client cannot bring an action against him, for instance, for moneys had or received; except on the ground of his having improperly received them. Where moneys do not come to the hands of the London agents in their character of London agents, but by what amounts to mistake, as when sent to them by the under-sheriff out of the regular course of business, and they attempt to apply it to a debt owing from the country solicitor, the Court will interfere summarily. The test is simply whether they obtained the money in their character of solicitors: *Robbins* v. *Heath*, 11 Q. B. 258. The country solicitor is liable to the client for money improperly received by his agent: *Gray* v. *Kirby*, 2 Dow. P. C. 601.

Money improperly received by town agent.

Robbins v. *Fennell*, *Child* v. *Kelly*, 11 Q. B. 248, decided that where a country solicitor, who is employed in a cause, employs an agent, there is not in general such privity between the client and the agent as entitles the client to recover against the agent for money had and received in respect of the proceeds of the cause, which the agent has received in the ordinary course of his business.

Money received by agent in ordinary course of business.

Summary jurisdiction of Court.

The proper course, therefore, is to appeal to the summary jurisdiction of the Court, and the London agent will be ordered to pay the money over, even though the country solicitor is indebted to the London agent in a greater sum on his account.

No right of action by town agent against client for fees; nor by client against agent for negligence.

The town agent cannot maintain an action against the client for his fees, nor the client against the town agent for negligence: Lord Denman, in *Cobb* v. *Becke*, 6 Q. B. 935. The same case decided that where A., being defendant in an action brought by B., paid the debt and costs to his own country solicitor for transmission to B., who sent a cheque exceeding the amount to his town agent, telling him to pay the debt and costs out of it; and the agent acknowledged the letter and promised to do so, but in fact retained the money in reduction of a debt due to him from the solicitor, there was no sufficient privity to support an action for money had and received by A. against the agent. In Ex parte *Jones*, 2 Dow. P. C. 161, it was held that where a plaintiff obtained a verdict in consequence of the defendant's agent not having informed the defendant of his having been served with notice of trial, that the solicitor was liable for the neglect of his agent. In fact the country solicitor is responsible to his client for all the acts and representations of his London agent: Re *Ward*, 31 Beav. 1.

Country solicitor is liable to his client for negligence of his agent.

Town agent accountable to country solicitor for negligence.

The agent is, of course, accountable to the country solicitor, and may be sued by him for negligence or for any other default. The late case of Ex parte *Edwards*, 8 Q. B. D. 262 (C. A.), decided that the Court, in the exercise of its summary jurisdiction over its own officers, will order the town agent to pay over the amount of a debt received from the sheriff under a fi. fa. to the plaintiff, though there is no fraud imputed, unless the country solicitor has a lien upon it for a greater amount; thus giving expression to the principle that a town agent has no right to retain money, the proceeds of a judgment, in order to satisfy a debt due to him from the country solicitor. An injunction would be granted at the instance of a client to restrain a London agent from paying over a debt received by him to the country solicitor, if the latter were suddenly discovered to be in a state of hopeless insolvency, and commanding him to pay it into Court or to pay it over to the client: Manisty, J., in Ex parte *Edwards*, 7 Q. B. D. p. 159.

Insolvency of country solicitor.

Lien of town agent on deeds as against country solicitor.

Same agent employed by two solicitors.

As against client.

Extent of town agent's lien.

The lien of the town agent on deeds is, as against the country solicitor, general: *Bray* v. *Hine*, 6 Price, 203, 210. Where there have been two country solicitors who have each employed the same town agent, his lien extends to what is due to him for each: *Ward* v. *Kepple*, 15 Ves. 297. As between the town agent and the client, the lien of the former extends only to the costs of the particular proceeding in which he has been engaged: *Lawrence* v. *Fletcher*, 12 Ch. D. 860. A town agent's lien extends to a charging lien upon a fund: *Farewell* v. *Coker*, 2 P. Wms. 460. In *Stevens* v. *Avery*, 1 Dick. 224, a defendant was restrained from paying fees to the representatives of a deceased solicitor until the costs of his agent were paid. But notice must be given to the client by the London agent.

In a case in which a country solicitor has moneys of his clients exceeding the amount of costs in his hands, and an order in the suit is made to pay the client's costs to the country solicitor's London agent, if the country solicitor take advantage of the Bankruptcy Act, the costs must be handed over by the London agent to the client, at least up to the amount that was in the country solicitor's hands: *Peatfield* v. *Barlow*, L. R. 8 Eq. 61.

As between the town agent and the client, the lien of the former extends only to the costs of the particular action in which he is engaged: *Lawrence* v. *Fletcher*, 12 Ch. D. 860.

Lien of town agent extends to costs of particular action.

V.-C. Malins, in *Peatfield* v. *Barlow*, L. R. 8 Eq. 61, said that he assumed that if the town agent had given the client notice not to pay any money to the country solicitor without providing for his costs, that this would disentitle him to pay the country solicitor anything after the date of such notice; but it would not have deprived the client of the right of treating any moneys in his hands as part of the costs due to him, for this is simply a right of set-off.

Notice by town agent to client not to pay money to country solicitor.

The costs of a town agent, if employed by a country solicitor trustee in ordinary business, will be allowed, and can be charged to the trust estate: *Burge* v. *Burton*, 2 Har. 373.

Town agent employed by country solicitor trustee.

The Solicitors Act, 1870 (33 & 34 Vict. c. 28), does not apply to dealings between town agents and country solicitors. Interest cannot, therefore, be allowed on disbursements made prior to the passing of the Act: *Ward* v. *Eyre*, 15 Ch. D. 130.

Ward v. *Eyre*.

CHAPTER XI.

SOLICITORS AS TRUSTEES.

It is not proposed here to do more than mention briefly that, although a solicitor is the agent of his client and not a trustee for him, except in special cases, as where he receives money to invest for him, and acts under a power of attorney,—*Burdick* v. *Garrick*, L. R. 5 Ch. 233,—he may become constructively liable as a trustee under certain circumstances.

Acting as agent to trustee who has committed breach of trust. He is not liable to the cestuis que trustent for acting as an agent to a trustee who has committed breaches of trust, unless he is cognisant of a dishonest design on the part of the trustee: *Barnes* v. *Addy*, L. R. 9 Ch. 244; **Paying money to one of two trustees.** but if he pays trust money to one of two trustees only, and it is lost, he practically constitutes himself a trustee for the parties beneficially entitled: *Lee* v. *Sankey*, L. R. 15 Eq. 204. The object of this chapter is rather to touch upon the duties and disabilities of a solicitor who has allowed himself to be appointed a trustee.

He cannot act as solicitor for one of his cestuis que trustent against another of them: *Ingwell* v. *Hooper*, 10 Beav. 349.

Cannot charge trust estate unless He cannot, unless allowed by the instrument creating the trust, charge the trust estate with more than costs out of pocket for work done in or out of

Court: *Broughton* v. *Broughton*, 25 L. J. Ch. 250; or the costs of his own defence to a suit regarding the trust estate.

specially authorised.

A deed executed by his cestui que trust for securing a solicitor trustee his costs, was set aside without costs: *Gomley* v. *Wood*, 3 J. & L. 678.

Member of a firm being trustee.

A firm of solicitors, of whom one member is a trustee, cannot charge more than costs out of pocket for work done for the trust estate. But the trustee could employ the firm as his solicitors, provided he took no share of profits out of the transaction, and in fact, to all intents and purposes, was not a partner in the firm pro ea vice: *Clack* v. *Carlon*, 9 W. R. 568.

From this case it would also seem that two firms can come to an arrangement for conducting each other's trust business; for the Courts consider that the rule that a solicitor trustee shall have only his costs out of pocket, is a severe one: *Gomley* v. *Wood*.

Town agent's charges to solicitor trustee.

A town agent's charges to a solicitor trustee are chargeable to the trust estate: *Burge* v. *Burton*, 2 Hare, 373.

Solicitor appearing for himself and a co-trustee.

A solicitor trustee appearing for himself and his co-trustee in a suit, is entitled to full costs, as if he were not a party, except so far as the costs are increased by his being a party: *Cradock* v. *Piper*, 1 Mac. & G. 664. And no special direction is made in the decree giving him his costs. This decision was questioned in *Broughton* v. *Broughton*, 1 Jur. N. S. 965, and it might not be safe to act upon it.

Acting for mortgagor and also for trust estate as mortgagee.

Where a solicitor who is a trustee acts for a mortgagor, and also for the trust estate as mortgagee, he can charge the mortgagor the ordinary costs: *Whitney* v. *Smith*, L. R. 4 Ch. 513. The same case is also an authority that a solicitor may derive some profit, and yet not have to account for it, in consequence of the employment of part of the mortgaged estates for building purposes. And he can get his costs out of the other side: *Pearce* v. *Beattie*, 11 W. R. 979.

Clause in trust deed.

Even supposing there is in the trust deed a provision for the retainer by the trustees of costs "incurred, sustained, or borne" by them, or which they might sustain or be put to, this will not give ordinary costs to a solicitor trustee: *Moore* v. *Frowd*, 3 My. & C. 45. If the clause enables him to make the ordinary charges for professional services, this clause will be construed strictly against him, and he will not, if appointed also executor, be thereby enabled to charge for the work ordinarily done by an executor; as, for example, attending at the Bank making transfers and selling stock: *Harbin* v. *Darby*, 28 Beav. 325.

Cannot charge for work ordinarily done by an executor, when acting as such.

Trustee in bankruptcy.

In the same way, a trustee in bankruptcy, when a solicitor, can contract to be remunerated for acting as a solicitor, and the petitioning creditor may act as solicitor to the trustee: Ex parte *Chamberlayne*, 19 L. J. Bank. 10.

Rule.

Perhaps a fair way to put the law relating to solicitor trustees is this;—that a trustee to a trust estate is the trustee of any profits he may make out of the trust estate for the benefit of those beneficially entitled to the trust estate; and that, therefore, a solicitor trustee must not by getting himself appointed solicitor to the trust estate get costs (other than out of pocket costs, which are not profit) out of it for his own benefit. But if a solicitor, being a trustee, employs the trust funds in loans, charging no costs other than out of pocket costs, to the estate, even though his so doing puts him in the way of getting business, he is not liable to the trust estate for remote profits of this kind.

Such profit is not fairly the produce or profit of the trust estate, or a matter with which the cestuis que trustent have anything to do: Giffard, L.J., in *Whitney* v. *Smith*, L. R. 4 Ch. 573.

CHAPTER XII.

SOLICITORS AS ADVOCATES.

THE true rule would appear to be that at the trial of any action, when it is not the invariable custom, according to the practice of that Court, for counsel only to be heard, the actual solicitor of either or both parties may conduct the case on their behalf before any Court of Justice in this country.

Preliminary inquiry.

At a preliminary inquiry to decide whether there is sufficient ground to commit a prisoner for trial, it is optional with the magistrates conducting it whether any advocate for the prisoner may attend on his behalf: *Cox* v. *Coleridge*, 1 B. & C. 50. The proceedings before the grand jury are of the same nature; and it would be difficult if the right exists in the one case to deny it in the other.

Proceedings before grand jury

Trial before magistrate.

At a trial before a magistrate it is different, for either party is allowed to plead by attorney (11 & 12 Vict. c. 43, s. 129); but a prisoner has no right to require his case to be adjourned in order that he may procure the attendance of a solicitor on his behalf: *R.* v. *Biggins*, 5 L. T. N. S. 605.

In Bankruptcy Court solicitor to the parties may be heard.

In the Bankruptcy Court the actual solicitor to the parties can be heard, but not a solicitor retained as an advocate by another solicitor.

The object of allowing the appearance of a solicitor

as representing another person is, that the Court should have before it a person who, on the one hand, is under an obligation to the Court, because he is one of its officers; and, on the other hand, is under an obligation to the suitor, because he is in privity with him, and is the actual person who represents him. Unless that chain of connection is maintained and kept complete, the object of allowing solicitors to appear on behalf of other parties is entirely defeated: Lord Cairns, in Ex parte *Broadhouse*, L. R. 2 Ch. 659. And although these remarks of his lordship apply primarily to the Court of Bankruptcy, it is submitted that they apply also to proceedings in all other Courts where solicitors are heard.

Object of the Court allowing solicitor to appear.

That this view is correct as regards County Courts can be gathered from *Bookham* v. *Potter*, Ex parte *Rogers*, L. R. 3 C. P. 490, where it was held that the only attorney who is entitled to be there heard is the one who is acting generally in the action for the party; and that the County Court judge is bound to determine the question; and unless he did not decide upon the question when submitted to him, a superior Court, in the opinion of Bovill, C.J., and Willes, J. (although it does not so clearly appear to have been that of Montague Smith, J.), cannot interfere.

County Courts.

It ought, however, to be observed that there is the following provision with regard to County Court practice and solicitors. 15 & 16 Vict. c. 54, s. 10, enacts, that an attorney of a Superior Court, being an attorney acting generally in the action for the party, but not retained as advocate by the acting attorney, may appear for a suitor in the County Court.

Probably this does not mean that an admitted

solicitor acting as the clerk to the solicitor to the suitor may not be heard.

This appears to have been the opinion of the Court in the case last cited, but there is in it no direct authority to that effect.

Solicitor's clerk.

A clerk to a solicitor who is not himself a solicitor, has no right to act as an advocate in Court, or to cross-examine a witness, and a Registrar in Bankruptcy can decline to hear him; but he must not decide against the client without having heard him personally, or by an advocate. He ought to adjourn the hearing in such a case, that the client may be properly represented: Ex parte *Streeter*, In re *Morris*, 19 Ch. D. 222.

Who may be heard before magistrates.

From Oke's Magisterial Synopsis it would appear that police magistrates in the metropolis permit articled clerks to be heard before them; and, quoting Cockburn, C.J., in Ex parte *The Local Board of Health of Leamington*, 5 L. T. N. S. 637, that justices may permit a police superintendent to appear, and hear him on a case before them, if they think fit.

Privilege.

Certain Acts too, as 7 & 8 Vict. c. 101, s. 68, sanction the conduct of cases by persons not solicitors, as, for instance, by the officer of a union.

When a solicitor is acting as advocate he has the same privilege as to the statements he may make to the Court as counsel: *Mackay* v. *Ford*, 5 H. & N. 792. What the nature and extent of that privilege is has been glanced at in the chapter upon Solicitors as Officers of the Court, p. 19.

CHAPTER XIII

SOLICITORS AS DRAFTSMEN.

ONLY a few words will be necessary upon the duties of the profession in this capacity.

The subject could not, however, be passed over entirely, in consequence of the passing of the Solitors' Remuneration Act and Order, which will be found given at length in the appendix to this book. This Act has made the payment of solicitors, in conveyancing matters and other non-contentious business, independent of the length of the documents drawn by them, and, indeed, in conjunction with the Conveyancing Acts, created a new era in the history of drafting.

Effect of Remuneration Act.

Before 6 & 7 Vict. c. 73, s. 37 (the Solicitors' Act of 1843), the charges of a solicitor for business relating entirely to conveyancing were not taxable, except upon bills filed, or possibly under the summary jurisdiction of the Court over solicitors; but the effect of that statute was to render them liable to taxation, or reduction to the established scale which is regulated only by length. That scale was one shilling for seventy-two words. Stat. 8 & 9 Vict. c 119, s. 4, and 8 & 9 Vict. c. 124, s. 3, as well as the Solicitors' Act of 1870, contain provisions that in taxing bills the taxing officer should consider the skill

Provision of Solicitors' Act.

Recent changes.

and responsibility attending the preparation of deeds; but the Remuneration Act has changed the basis of taxation and substituted value for length. Mr. Joshua Williams says, in his chapter on a modern conveyance (Real Property, 11th ed. p. 196), that the labour of a lawyer is very different from that of a copyist or printer. That it consists, first and chiefly in acquiring a minute acquaintance with the principles of the law, then in obtaining a knowledge of the facts of any particular case which may be brought before him; and lastly, in practically applying to such case the principles he has previously learnt; but that for the last and least of these claims alone has he obtained any direct remuneration. This is no longer true, and the reform which has been initiated by the Act is a thorough one which goes to the root of the matter.

Principles of drafting.

But although the method of remuneration has been changed, the principles upon which drafts should be drawn have not. Mr. Davidson's remarks (Precedents, chap. ii., Principles upon which Legal Instruments are framed) are as applicable now as they ever were. "It seems to be often considered," he writes, "that the business of the draftsman is a very easy one; that he has little more to do than to find an appropriate precedent, and then, by changing names and dates, to construct the new instrument required; and there is a class of draftsmen who draw from the precedents without knowing why or wherefore, who have little or no acquaintance with the commonest practical rules of their art, and not an idea of those general rules or principles on which it depends. But though men who trust thus implicitly to their precedents and remain in ignorance of the rules of their art, may, by good fortune, avoid doing any material mischief as long as they are confined to everyday matters, yet, when new combinations of circumstances arise, of which precedents afford no example, they are either unable to proceed without assistance or fall into pernicious mistakes."

Some few of these mistakes will now be noticed. An agreement between a solicitor and his client may be bad for champerty, as, for instance, where an agreement, under the Solicitors' Act, 1870, gave a solicitor, in the event of success, a tenth part of the property recovered: In re *Attorneys and Solicitors Act*, 1870, 1 Ch. D. 575. It may, perhaps, be broadly stated that any agreement to pay a share of, or a fixed commission on property recovered, is very likely to be bad for champerty. In *Earle* v. *Hopwood*, 9 W. R. 272, a contract that a part of the thing recovered should be given to the solicitor who supplied funds for an action, and also one by which the solicitor was to receive a sum proportioned to the estate recovered, were both stated to be illegal.

Agreements bad for champerty

This would have been known to a person acquainted with the principles of the law, and he would not have drawn such a draft.

But an agreement between several persons to maintain one another in defending a claim against them may be also an illegal negotiation: *Findon* v. *Parker*, 11 M. & W. 675.

If a solicitor drew such an agreement he could not recover the cost of so doing, nor, indeed, the cost of a corrupt contract of any kind. Where, however, a solicitor, under the advice of counsel, drew and sued on for a client an agreement bad for champerty, he was held not liable to an action for negligence: *Potts* v. *Sparrow*, 5 C. & P. 749.

Acting under counsel's advice.

Again, it is expressly said in *Ireson* v. *Pearman*, 3 B. & C. 812, that although it may not be part of

Wrong conclusions.

the duty of an attorney (*i.e.*, if he employs counsel) to know the legal operation of conveyances, yet that if he draws wrong conclusions from the deeds laid before him he does so at his peril.

If, therefore, a conclusion of law which was not correct were drawn from the perusal of an abstract of title, and a draft drawn in consequence, acting on such mistake, the solicitor would be liable to an action for negligence.

Counsel's fees.

It may here be remarked that under r. 4 of the Order (of 1882) made under the Solicitors' Remuneration Act, counsel's fees, stamps, and other disbursements, reasonably or properly paid will be allowed as out of pocket expenses, although clerk's and law stationers charges will not.

Precedents in Acts of Parliament.

Any draft, however, for which there is a precedent, in any Act of Parliament, as, for example, those in the schedule to the Conveyancing Act, 1881, should not, except in very special cases, be settled by counsel, as there can be but little doubt as to the form it must take.

Mistakes.

But it is the preparation of wills and settlements that the draftsman finds his most difficult task ; and it is probable that if a solicitor made such a mistake as that made by Mr. Butler, a conveyancer of great eminence—viz., the striking out, by mistake, of the word "Gloucester," in a devise of the testator's "estates in the counties of Sussex and Gloucester" (which was followed by the alteration by the copyist of counties into county), which resulted in a trial as to what the devisee took (5 Had. 364), he would be liable for it ; and it is arguable, even in this case, whether he would not be liable for not seeing that counsel followed out his instructions. Cases illustrative of this principle are: *Parker* v. *Rolls*, 14 C. B. 691 ; *Stannard* v.

Ullithorne, 10 Bing. 491; and *Taylor* v. *Gorman*, 4 Ir. Eq. Rep. 550.

The real difficulty is to know whether a case is one of difficulty or not, as this requires a sound knowledge of law: Introduction to Conveyancing, Elphinstone, 1st ed. p. 2.

All that has been said hitherto in this chapter has had reference to non-litigious business, and a few words are necessary with reference to drafts of notices and other things in an action.

Endorsements of writ, costs.

It is a matter of surprise why the endorsement on a writ should not always be settled by counsel, as it is surely the most important step in the action; and yet it is only sometimes allowed for on taxation between party and party. For example, if a writ is issued for an injunction and some other relief, and all that is required is obtained on the granting of an interlocutory injunction, and so the action is settled, when the bill is taxed, the rule in some taxing-master's offices appears to be this: The writ may have been endorsed by counsel unless a statement of claim has been delivered in the action; but, if a statement of claim is charged for, the allowance for the writ is withheld. It is not necessary to point out that at the time of the issuing of the writ it could hardly be foreseen whether or not a statement of claim would be required, and, therefore, the rationale of this custom is difficult to understand.

Another uncertainty which exists is that with reference to the allowance or non-allowance of notices of motion.

Notice of motion.

It appears that some taxing-masters rule that if a precedent for a notice of motion can be found in the books—as, for instance, in "Daniel's Forms"—that the solicitor should draw it himself. This is surely throwing responsibility upon him which is scarcely reasonable, as the same remark might apply to a pleading, a precedent for which probably exists if it can only be found and rightly applied.

Special summonses.

With reference to special summonses, it would appear that any reference in the summons to a particular rule and order makes it at once an ordinary one, and one for which counsel's fees for settling cannot be allowed.

It is true that the result of any ordinary interlocutory application is too often costs, costs in the cause, and that, therefore, the party who is right in the main gets his costs, and that therefore, it does not much matter if he makes a mistake in the form of a notice of an interlocutory motion or summons; but this custom does not conduce to the cultivation of exactness or style in such proceedings, and costs may, of course, not be costs in the cause, but plaintiff's or defendant's in any event.

Drawing pleadings.

This uncertainty as to when the fee to counsel will be allowed in settling notices of motion and summonses makes it easily to be understood why they are often settled by the solicitor; but it is not easy to see why pleadings, which are always allowed for, should not invariably be the work of counsel alone. It is apprehended that a solicitor drawing a pleading to which a demurrer was sustained, would be answerable to his client for the costs of his false step; and it is difficult to see how he would escape having to pay the costs himself of any successful attempt to strike out paragraphs, if the costs were given against his client.

Interrogatories.

The same remark applies to interrogatories, which, as well as the answers thereto, will always, if needed, be allowed for.

With reference to affidavits, it may be remarked that the Court has lately made the party filing unnecessary ones pay the costs of the same: *Hirst* v. *Procter*, W. H. 12, 1882: and see Hints on Practice, 1st ed. 143. It is difficult to see why a client, who had been ordered to pay his opponent's costs of answering an unnecessary affidavit by himself, would not have a remedy over against his solicitor for such costs if the solicitor had drawn it himself. Unnecessary affidavits.

It only remains to be said that in all drafts in litigious business the greatest care should be taken, and that the responsibility for the consequences of drawing a pleading, interrogatories, or the answers thereto, lies upon the solicitor (who takes upon himself what is not his province), except in so far as he may have acted under the advice of counsel.

CHAPTER XIV.

NEGLIGENCE.

No privity between client and counsel

No action can be brought against counsel, because there is no privity of contract between the client and the counsel, and the counsel cannot recover his fees from the client: *Swinfen* v. *Chelmsford*, 5 H. & N. 890. Therefore, in all proper cases, if a solicitor employs counsel, and fairly states a case to him and acts under his advice, he relieves himself from responsibility; but where the law would presume him to have the knowledge he proposes to get from counsel himself, he cannot shelter himself in this way: *Godefroy* v. *Dalton*, 6 Bing. 469. And where the opinion from counsel is not obtained bonâ fide, he is no shield: *Andrew* v. *Hawley*, 26 L. J. Ex. 323. As to what the true meaning of "instructing counsel" is, see Pollock, C. B.'s judgment in *Hawkins* v. *Harwood*, 4 Ex. 503. In a difficult case, and where some new point crops up, the solicitor should lay a full case before counsel and follow his advice thoroughly: *Manning* v. *Wilkin*, 12 L. T. 249; but in matters which he should know all about himself he cannot transfer his liability to counsel nor shift the responsibility on to any one else. Mere questions of law, the form of pleadings, and the kind of evidence to be adduced, are questions for counsel; but if the

Instructing counsel.

See p. 107.

Cannot transfer his own liability.

solicitor undertake to determine questions of law and acts upon his own opinion, he will, if wrong, be answerable for the consequences: *Stevenson* v. *Rowland*, 2 Dow. & Clark, 119. What are questions for counsel.

Solicitors are liable if they draw wrong conclusions from deeds laid before them, though it seems not to be part of their duty to know their legal operation. They should here consult counsel: Bayley, J., in *Ireson* v. *Pearman*, 3 B. & A. 799. If a solicitor undertakes to act without employing counsel he is liable if he makes a mistake in the principles of real property law. For example, if he prepares an instrument not under seal, where a deed is necessary: *Parker* v. *Rolls*, 14 C. B. 691; or if he permits a client to execute a deed which contains improper covenants: *Stannard* v. *Ullithorne*, 10 Bing. 491. Liability of solicitors for mistakes.

But a solicitor is liable both for the results of having exceeded his duty and also for negligence. Thus, if he be directed not to compromise an action, and he does so, he is liable to an action for damages for having so done, although he asserts that he has done so under the advice of counsel: *Fray* v. *Voules*, 7 W. R. 446. This is a breach of duty arising out of the relation of the parties for which the client is entitled to bring an action, even though it has been in the result beneficial to him. In such a case, however, the damages would probably be nominal: Crompton, J. Where special directions are given an attorney, he is bound to follow them: *Thomas* v. *Harris*, 27 L. J. Ex. 353. Exceeding his duty. Compromising action contrary to instruction; effect. Solicitor must follow special directions.

But a solicitor acting under a general retainer has power to compromise an action in which he is retained, unless the client, by giving him express directions not to do so, remains thus himself dominus litis. The compromise, however, in any case is good Acting under general retainer.

as between the client and the third party: *Fray* v. *Vowles.* If a client directs his solicitor to compromise for a certain sum, this means the sum mentioned clear after payment of costs: *Churchyard* v. *Watkins,* 30 L. T. 154.

Compromise for "certain" sum.

Extent of liability for negligence.

Where a solicitor has been guilty of negligence he is liable in damages to the extent of the injury sustained by the client; and the solicitor, if he relies upon the absence of actual damage, must prove that none accrued: *Godefroy* v. *Jay,* 7 Bing. 413. If the negligence complained of is in an action, the client has not to show that but for it he would have won the action. All that he has to show is, that there has been what amounts to negligence sufficient to entitle him to nominal damages; and to these he is entitled if there has been anything amounting to negligence which might operate to produce the loss of the cause.

Remedy of client is by action at law for loss sustained.

But, certainly, unless the solicitor acts fraudulently and improperly, as when he gives his client a worthless security: *Smith* v. *Pococke,* 2 Drew. 197; and not even then, possibly now, can a declaration be obtained in equity that the solicitor, for negligence in investigating a title, is liable to make good to his client the loss which he has sustained through his negligent and unskilful management on his behalf of the matter referred to him by the client, and that he be ordered to take the security off the hands of the client. The reason is, that the appropriate remedy is an action-at-law for the actual loss (when ascertained) that the client has sustained. And the fact that Courts of Equity have a concurrent jurisdiction with Courts of Law over their own officers, even in a case of culpable negligence, which is only one of non feasance, does not help the client, because of the appropriate remedy he has at law: *British Mutual Investment Co.* v. *Cobbold*, L. R. 19 Eq. 629. When there are abundant materials before the Court to show to what extent the client has been damnified by his solicitor's negligence, the solicitor cannot be permitted to measure the damages resulting from his own wrong: *Whiteman* v. *Hawkins*, 4 C. P. D. 20. The Statute of Limitations runs from the date of the act of negligence, not from the time when the injury accrues: *Howell* v. *Young*, 5 B. & C. 259, 266. The client is entitled to be placed in the same position as if the solicitor had done his duty, but to nothing more; and, consequently, when his client has no case, unless his solicitor by his negligence has caused him loss independent of the necessary result of the action the solicitor is not liable: *Harrington* v. *Binns*, 3 F. & F. 942. The amount of loss the client is likely to suffer may be taken into consideration by the jury in assessing damages: Mayne on Damages, 3rd ed. 414, commenting on *Howell* v. *Young*, 5 B. & C. 259, 266. Where a solicitor did not attend a trial with the witnesses, and the record was withdrawn, he was held liable for the expense so incurred, but not for more: *Hawkins* v. *Harwood*, 4 Ex. 503. This case is also an authority that the true meaning of "instructing counsel" is not putting a brief into his hands professing to be instructions in the cause in which he is to appear, but that it means putting him into such a situation, both with respect to the information which is given him and the means of making that information available, as will enable him to conduct the case properly. The links in the chain of instructions necessary to make the chain available must be there.

Statute of Limitations runs from date of act of negligence.

Right of client.

Probable loss may be assessed.

Instructing counsel.

See beginning of chapter.

Where the misconduct of the solicitor has forced

the client to take legal proceedings, it is conceived that, by analogy to what is done in the case of a sheriff's misconduct, only the taxed costs of such proceedings as between party and party can be recovered, and not the extra costs as between solicitor and client: *Jenkins* v. *Biddulph*, 4 Bing. 160. But where a cause in which a solicitor was acting for the defendant was taken as undefended, and a verdict given against the defendant in consequence, the Court ordered a new trial, the solicitor to pay all costs as between solicitor and client: *De Roufigny* v. *Peale*, 3 Taunton, 484. However, the Court has since refused to act in this way; but in such a case the jury might give the whole value of the subject-matter of the action as damages, as they did in *Hoby* v. *Built*, 3 B. & A. 350.

Neglect to defend.

Amount of negligence.

It is difficult to state what is the smallest amount of negligence for which a solicitor will be held liable; but it is certain that the ordinary idea that he will only be liable for gross negligence is an incorrect one. It has been pointed out in text books on negligence that more than ordinary care is required and presumed to have been taken by solicitors and other learned men. If this is so, ordinary neglect, where so great care is required, becomes in the eye of the law gross negligence. An error into which any careful man might have fallen is not negligence: *Laidler* v. *Elliot*, 3 B. & C. 738. But the dividing line between the necessary amount of care and negligence is not strongly marked: *Godefroy* v. *Dalton*, 6 Bing. 461. Want of care of a client's title deeds and losing them and mixing his papers with others, if the cause of any loss, is actionable: *Reeve* v. *Palmer*, 5 Jur. N. S. 916; *N. W. Ry. Co.* v. *Sharp*, 10 Ex. 451.

Client's deeds and papers.

Inattention to any fact of which he has received notice affecting his client in any pending matter, and in respect of which he should have taken precautions, is negligence: *Jacand* v. *French*, 12 East, 317. He is liable for the negligence of any agent employed by him as his town agent, agent for a particular purpose, clerk or partner, and whether he is acting gratuitously or not: *Donaldson* v. *Holdane*, 7 Cl. & F. 762. But if a clerk of the solicitor to an execution creditor were asked by the sheriff's officer what goods he was to seize under an execution, and the clerk refused to tell him, although he knew at the time that there were goods which might be seized, no action would lie at the suit of the client: *Smith* v. *Keal*, 9 Q. B. D. 348. His liability, however, is only to his own client, and does not extend to third parties, although such third parties may have been damnified by his negligence: *Fish* v. *Kelly*, 17 C. B. N. S. 194. But if he acts without authority for any person, he is liable to such person for the consequences of such misconduct, and even, it appears, to the person against whom he may have so acted wrongfully: *Hubbard* v. *Phillips*, 13 M. & W. 702. This branch of the subject is touched upon in the chapter upon Retainer.

Notices affecting client.

Negligence of agent or partner.

Third parties cannot sue.

Acting without authority.

A few instances will now be given of cases in which a solicitor is liable, and of cases in which he is not liable for negligence, from which it may, perhaps, be inferred, that if he properly states a case for counsel, and carries out his advice accurately, he is not responsible for any mistake made as to the effect of any principle of law, or as to the general course to be adopted in an action; but that he is liable for the neglect of any professional duty of a ministerial character, whether he employs counsel or not; and,

Employment of counsel.

of course, for any mistake he may make in the instructions he gives to counsel; as also for the results of ignorance upon any point of thoroughly ordinary law.

Champerty.

Thus, a solicitor was held not liable where, under the advice of counsel, he drew and sued on for a client an agreement bad for champerty: *Potts* v. *Sparrow*, 5 C. & P. 749. In this case had he not employed counsel he would have been liable.

Employing surveyor.

In the same way, if he takes the advice of competent surveyors as to the nature of a property upon which his client advances money, especially if he consults his client upon the transaction, although the security proves insufficient, he is not liable; for it is not a matter which requires professional skill: *Chapman* v. *Chapman*, L. R. 9 Eq. 276. In this case, the conduct of the solicitors complained of is described by V.-C. Stuart as being rather to be described as imprudent or indiscreet than as negligent.

Providing evidence.

Again, a solicitor, if he employs counsel, is not liable for a mistake as to the evidence required at the trial of an action; but he is liable for neglecting to provide it. For example, if he fails to have the necessary witnesses in Court at the trial: *Reece* v. *Rigby*, 4 B. & Ald. 202, or employs a surveyor who is a notorious drunkard, and who does not do the work entrusted to him to be done: *Mercer* v. *King*, 1 F. & F. 490.

Non-registry of lis pendens.

He is liable if he does not register a lis pendens, though not specially instructed so to do by the client; for this is an ordinary duty of a solicitor: *Plant* v. *Pearman*, 26 L. T. N. S. 313. He is not liable for error in judgment on points of rare occurrence, or such as are usually entrusted to men in the higher branch of the profession: *Godefroy* v. *Dalton*, 6 Bing. 460. Indeed, even when that case was decided, it appears that solicitors were liable for the consequences of the non-observance of rules of practice; want of preparation of a cause for trial, and for the mismanagement of that part of the conduct of the case which is ordinarily the business of the solicitors; but not for error in judgment upon points not belonging to their department of the profession, or upon points of rare occurrence.

It would, however, appear to be the safer course for him to adopt in order to limit his responsibility, to point out to his client when asked to advise upon a point of the latter kind, that it does not come within his province, and that the client must take his opinion for what it is worth, as it is a case proper to be sent to counsel. He is not liable for advice upon the facts, but only upon the law of a case: *Hill* v. *Finney*, 4 F. & F. 625.

Failure of action through improper advice.

It may be further added that if an action fails through being wrongly investigated and improperly advised the costs of it cannot be recovered from the client by the solicitor who advised it: *Dax* v. *Ward*, 1 Stark, 409. Such a course is derogatory to the dignity of a solicitor: *Ottley* v. *Gilby*, 8 Beav. 603. If a solicitor's services, which were at first of use to his client, are afterwards rendered useless by his negligence, he cannot claim costs: *Bracey* v. *Carter*, 12 A. & E. 373.

Abandoning cause.

If a solicitor abandons a cause without reasonable notice, as four days before assizes, he is liable: *Hoby* v. *Built*, 4 B. & A. 350.

When a solicitor takes upon himself to do an act for which his client has to answer, as for instance when a fi. fa. is set aside for being irregular: *Collett*

v. *Foster*, 2 H. & F. 356; the client will have an action over against the solicitor for having been the cause. Where, however, the act done by the solicitor is not necessary to the performance of his duty the client is not liable, and the solicitor only must answer for it. For example, it is not within a solicitor's authority to tell the sheriff how to perform his duty: *Smith* v. *Keal*, 9 Q. B. D. 354.

Acting as solicitor without certificate.

A person acting as a solicitor is liable for negligence whether in fact certificated or not, and even if he employs a certificated solicitor: *Brown* v. *Tolley*, 31 L. T. N. S. 485.

Where monies given for investment.

As the liabilities of a solicitor with respect to monies of his client handed to him for investment, and not so invested, are not treated of in this book, it may be mentioned here that there have been several late cases bearing upon this subject. As to the liability of a partner: *Cooper* v. *Pritchard*, Solicitor's Journal, p. 40, Nov. 18, 1882. For cases of fraud, see Solicitor's Journal, p. 236, Feb. 10, 1883, and p. 216, Feb. 3, 1883. As to what is sufficient segregation where there is a deposit of deeds, see *Hills* v. *Reeves*, 31 W. R. 209. Where the security is specified the solicitor is a trustee for the client: *Harpham* v. *Shacklock*, 19 Ch. D. 207.

See p. 256.

Further cases of negligence are collected in the Appendix.

CHAPTER XV.

UNQUALIFIED PRACTITIONERS.

Costs. Solicitors Act, 1874.

THE Solicitors Act of 1874 (37 & 38 Vict. c. 68, s. 12), enacts that no costs or disbursements relating to anything done (in or out of Court) by an uncertificated solicitor, shall be recoverable by any person or persons whomsoever. The effect of this section is to extend the operation of former Acts, and it prevents not merely the solicitor, but even the client from recovering such costs. A case like that of *Reeder* v. *Bloom*, 3 Bing. 9, which decided that the fact of his attorney being uncertificated, does not deprive the client of his right to costs against the opposite party to the extent of advances made by the client, if he did not know of this want of qualification, is therefore not still law.

Change in the law.

The construction of the section may in certain instances operate harshly, but the policy of the Act is clear: *Fowler* v. *Monmouthshire Canal Co.*, 4 Q. B. D. 336. This case in effect overruled In re *Jones*, L. R. 9 Eq. 63, which decided that a solicitor's want of a certificate did not extinguish the debt for costs incurred while so uncertificated, but merely the remedy; for example, that the solicitor had still a right of set-off in respect of them, and therefore, that costs, if even for work done when uncertificated, should not be struck out of a bill by the taxing master.

Now, as no person can recover in respect of such items, it would seem that there could be no use in their remaining in the bill. The case of In re *Hope*, L. R. 7 Ch. 776, also is now no longer law. It decided that a person who has been ordered to pay costs, cannot, on the ground that the solicitor on the other side was uncertificated, refuse to pay such costs. The section also enacts that persons pretending falsely to be qualified solicitors are to be liable to a penalty not exceeding £10 for each offence, and the offence may be prosecuted summarily.

Stamp Act.

The Stamp Act of 1870, enacts that an uncertificated solicitor who practises in Court, or who draws a deed for fee or reward, shall forfeit £50, and be incapable of maintaining an action for fees.

Legal accountants.

By 6 & 7 Vict. c. 73, s. 2, an unqualified person who acts as a solicitor commits an indictable offence; and he does so although he acts in the name and with the consent of a duly qualified solicitor: *Abercrombie* v. *Jordan*, In re *Hunt*, 8 Q. B. D. 187. And 23 & 24 Vict. c. 127, s. 26, extends the remedy by making such an offence contempt of Court, and by disenabling him from suing for fees, and also by rendering him liable to forfeit £50 with full costs of suit.

Penalty.

And by the Legal Practitioners Act, 1877, s. 2, (40 & 41 Vict. c. 62), surrogates or unqualified practitioners who, for reward alone, or as agents for others, prepare papers for probate forfeit £10. Such are some of the enactments under which an unqualified person acting as a solicitor can be reached; and with regard to them, it need only be said that the acts intended to be prohibited are those which are legally incident to the office of a solicitor, and not those which though usually performed by him are not of right incident to his office (compare the case of Proctors in *Stephenson* v. *Higginson*, 3 H. L. C. 638). And mere negotiations as to purchases, mortgages, or settlements are not strictly within the exclusive province of solicitors. The Acts use the expression drawing or preparing deeds relating to real or personal property.

Again, except in litigious business in which apparently the mere intermeddling of an unqualified person, unless himself a party to the action, would be a contempt of Court, it would seem that some "gain" must be anticipated by the person preparing any legal instrument or else he will not be amenable to the fines before-mentioned. This is particularly noticeable in the Stamp Act, 1870, and the Legal Practitioners Act, 1877. But these enactments not only impose penalties upon unqualified persons acting as solicitors in litigious business, or for reward doing such work as a solicitor only can do in non-litigious business; but some of them also deal with the case of a qualified solicitor who acts as an agent for an unqualified person, or who has allowed his name to be used by such an one (6 & 7 Vict. c. 73, s. 32). It in fact imposes a penalty on a solicitor who keeps an unqualified person to act as a solicitor. This section is directed primarily against the solicitor, but also in common with sect. 2 against the unqualified person. This class of case is of much more common occurrence than that of unqualified persons acting as solicitors without some shield; and in reference to them it must be premised that the affidavits setting out this offence must be sufficient.

Litigious business.

Gain must be anticipated.

Agent of unqualified person.

Solicitor employing unqualified person.

In an old case in 1834—In the matter of *King*,

In re *King.* 1 A. & E. 560—on an application to strike an attorney off the rolls for suffering an unprofessional person to carry on business for him as his clerk in the country (he living in London), it was decided that the affidavits must not only present to the Court facts from which it could draw its own conclusions, but that they were insufficient if they did not state the belief of the deponents that the parties moved against had acted from a corrupt motive; unless the facts sworn to were such as could by possibility lead to only that one conclusion. For instance, they should state that the profits were participated in, or at least sufficient grounds for that belief. From the judgment of Lord Denman, in the matter of *King*, it would appear that the fact of an attorney having stationed a jackal at a particular place was not within the statute then in force; although, as his Lordship then observed, such conduct is more within its mischief than a mere participation in profits.

Affidavits.

"Jackal."

Taunton J. also observed in the same case, that an attorney residing in London ought not to employ an auctioneer at a distant place to carry on business as his clerk. In such a case now, if the clerk attempted to conduct litigious business, he would come under the statute making such conduct contempt of Court; and if he participated in the profits of non-litigious business, he would transgress the enactments last referred to: the latest case of the kind is *Abercrombie* v. *Jordan*, 8 Q. B. D. 193.

Without certificate. Furthermore, a solicitor who has not a certificate in force at the time he does work for a client cannot recover his costs for such work.

Certificate. A curious case was In re the *Duke of Brunswick, and the Trustees of Crowl, and Another*, 4 Exch. 492. There the solicitor had a certificate which purported to be for the time during which the work was done; but it was shewn that there was a mistake, and that it had reference to the year before, and the Court held that the taxation must be set aside, as a solicitor could not recover his costs, having at the time the business was done, no certificate "in force."

The case of In re *Horton* has been referred to in another place, p. 85. See also p. 34.

CHAPTER XVI.

COSTS GENERALLY.

Costs in discretion of the Court.

SINCE the passing of the Judicature Acts, costs have practically been in the discretion of the Court, thus in effect adopting the old Chancery rules. And so, what was done in 1845, by Lord Langdale, M.R. in *Ottley* v. *Gilby*, 8 Beav. 604, may be done again now. In that case he said that on the whole he thought the plaintiff was not entitled to his costs; that the defendants were only entitled to such costs as they could retain out of a fund which was in their hands; and that the costs of their co-defendants must be borne by the plaintiff, and this, although the plaintiff had a technical right to part of his claim, viz., being a legatee, to an explanation of the state of his testators assets. He was told before the suit was brought that these were barely sufficient to pay the testator's debts, but it turned out that there was a very small balance in the defendants hands. Lord Langdale added to his decision as to the costs:—"This suit has been perfectly useless to every party concerned in it. Solicitors ought out of regard to the interests of their clients and to their own status and character to prevent such a course of useless litigation."

Useless litigation.

In the case of *Walford* v. *Walford*, quoted in a note to *Burdick* v. *Garrick*, L. R. 5 Ch. 455, which was an application to stay the execution of a decree pending an appeal. Lord Justice Selwyn, in reply to an observation of V.-C. Hall, who was then at the bar, to the effect that it is the settled practice of the Court of Chancery, that if you come for an indulgence you must pay the costs of the application for it, states it to be his opinion that costs even in such a case were in the direction of the Court, though the course suggested was a usual one. In that particular case as also in *Burdick* v. *Garrick*, they were ordered to abide the result of the appeal. From these instances it will appear that, according to the Chancery practice, it did not at all follow that obtaining a decree and getting costs went of necessity together, and the judgment of the Court was in fact taken upon both of these questions in every case. That this practice has been adopted by Courts of Common Law, the case of *Harnett* v. *Vise*, decided by the Court of Appeal, in 1880, and reported 5 Ex. D. 307, is a clear authority. It decided that a judge is not confined to the consideration of the conduct of the successful party merely during the progress of the action. If he thinks that although the plaintiff is legally entitled to a verdict, he has caused the litigation by his imprudent or vexatious conduct, or that there are any other equitable reasons owing to anything the plaintiff does, either before or after the litigation has commenced, why he should not be favoured by the Court, he has the discretion to refuse him his costs.

Indulgence.

Harnett v. *Vise*.

This being so, it will be apparent that a consideration of the general rules regarding costs is now most essential, and almost a necessary introduction to those which regulate solicitor and client, and party and party costs. When costs are ordered, the taxation of

Power to order solicitor and client costs.

costs as between party and party is intended; yet the Courts have power to give costs to be taxed between solicitor and client, and also to add to the latter all charges and expenses properly incurred. This chapter deals only with costs when given as between party and party, except where it is otherwise expressly pointed out.

First general rule as to costs.

The first general rule as to costs is that in the Chancery Division, the old Chancery practice as to costs will, except when expressly altered, remain in force: *Pringle* v. *Gloag*, 10 Ch. D. 676, because in the Chancery Division a case cannot be tried with a jury: *Warner* v. *Murdock*, 4 Ch. D. 756. This means that the judge of first instance has a large discretion as to costs, and that as long as he acts upon his discretion alone, it is uncontrolled. He may make the defendant pay the costs of some of the issues in which he failed, even though he have succeeded on the whole action. Or, he may say that both parties are wrong, and that if he cannot apportion the blame, the claim must be dismissed without costs. He may say that the plaintiff shall have half the costs of the action or some other aliquot part. The best course to adopt, according to Jessel, M.R., in *Willmott* v. *Barber*, 17 Ch. D. 774, is to fix a definite sum for one party to pay to the other, so as to avoid the expense of taxation, taking care in doing so to fix a smaller sum than the party would have to pay if the costs were taxed.

Second general rule.

The second general rule is, that in the Common Law Courts, where the trial is before a judge alone, costs are absolutely in his discretion. Upon this head more will be found later on in this chapter.

Third rule.

The third rule is, that when there is a jury, costs follow the event, even though the judge refuses to certify for them: *Garnett* v. *Bradley*, L. R. 3 App. Cases, 944, except when sec. 5 of the County Courts Act, 1867, or Order LV., r. 1, take effect.

Sec. 5 of County Courts Act, 1867.

The former of these sections in effect enacts that costs are not recoverable in a Superior Court when less than £20 in an action on contract, or £10 in an action founded on tort are recovered, unless the judge certifies on the record, that there was sufficient reason for bringing such action in a Superior Court.

Order LV., r. 1.

Order LV., r. 1, makes costs of and incident to all proceedings in the High Court in the discretion of the Court; although nothing is to deprive a trustee, mortgagee, or other person to any right to costs out of a particular fund according to the former rules of Equity.

Jury cases.

But where any action or issue is tried by a jury, costs are to follow the event, unless upon application made at the trial for good cause shown, the judge before whom it is tried otherwise orders.

There have been many decisions upon the effect of this section, which will be noticed in this chapter; but the general effect of it is to repeal all previous enactments directing costs to follow certain rules, and so to unfetter the discretion of the Court, which is no longer bound by any provision or omission in any Act before the Judicature Act, as to costs: Ex parte *The Mercers' Company*, 10 Ch. D. 481; though on appeal as a general rule, the successful party will get his costs; Memorandum, 1 Ch. D. 41.

Costs on appeal.

Time for application.

The words "upon application made at the trial for good cause shown" have been decided to be capable of a broad meaning. Thus, an application made an hour after verdict is good: *Kynaston* v. *Mackinder*, 47 L. T. Q. B. 76, but four days afterwards, is not: *Tyne Alkali Company* v. *Lawson*, 36 L. T. 100.

Judge can deprive successful party of his costs, mero motu.

The application must be made to the same judge, and not to him when at Chambers: *Baker* v. *Oakes*, 2 Q. B. D. 171; and from this case it would appear that a judge can mero motu, and without the application of the defendant, deprive the successful plaintiff of costs; and the same may perhaps, be gathered from *Turner* v. *Heyland*, 4 C. P. D. 432, where Grove, J., observed that in his opinion the decision of the Court of Appeal in *Baker* v. *Oakes* (see especially that of Brett, L.J.), was not to the effect, that a substantial application is necessary before the power of the judge, to make an order which would prevent the costs from following the event, can be exercised.

Power of Divisional Court.

And the Divisional Court has, under Order LV., an original jurisdiction to deprive a successful party of the costs of an action tried before a jury. *Myers* v. *Defries and Others*; *Siddons* v. *Lawrence*, 4 Ex. D. 179. In the latter case judgmentwas signed, the costs taxed, and the plaintiff had obtained the Master's allocatur.

Baker v. *Oakes*.

And not only can a judge in a jury case mero motu, and without the application of the defendant, deprive the successful party of costs: *Baker* v. *Oakes*, if he considers his conduct bad in the course of the litigation, but even if he disapproves of it previous to and as conducing to the litigation: *Harnett* v. *Vise*, 5 Ex. D. 307. Further, he can make a plaintiff who recovered in an action, two sums of £85 and 6s., and in a second trial recovered the 6s. and lost the £85, pay the costs of both trials: *Harris* v. *Petherick*, 4 Q. B. D. 6, 110. How his discretion may probably be exercised will be considered further on. And see *Foster* v. *Great Western Ry. Co.*, 55 L. J. Q. B. 233.

Where

Where there are two trials, the second is the event

which decides costs: *Field* v. *Great Northern Ry. Co.*, 3 Ex. D. 261. This word "event" must be read distributively when in the same action the jury find for the plaintiff with damages as to one cause of action, and for the defendant as to other and distinct causes of action; and the defendant is entitled to tax the costs of the issues found for him if no order otherwise is made: *Myers* v. *Defries*, quoted above.

there are two trials.

Though a Master cannot award costs other than the costs of any proceeding before him, Order LIV., r. 2, yet he can decide who shall pay the costs of the examination of a party before a special examiner, in consequence of his answers to interrogatories being insufficient: *Vicary* v. *Great Northern Ry. Co.*, 9 Q. B. D. 168.

Proceedings before a Master.

See also pp. 130 and 212.

The Queen's Bench Division however, intimated that in some cases it was better that the question of costs should be reserved until the trial.

There is always an appeal from a Master as to costs, or from a District Registrar, as sec. 49, Judicature Act, 1873, does not apply in such cases: *Foster* v. *Edwards*, 48 L. J. C. P. 749.

Appeal from Master as to costs.

In a libel case, where a jury gave nominal costs and a verdict for plaintiff, and the judge refused to certify for costs, the plaintiff was held to be entitled to them: *Parsons* v. *Tinling*, 2 C. P. D. 119; and also in a slander case: *Garnett* v. *Bradley*, which has been before cited. Indeed, the case of *Parsons* v. *Tinling*, decides that all previous statutes as to costs, with the sole exception of such of the provisions of the County Courts Act, 1867, as are expressly preserved by sec. 67 of the Judicature Act, 1873, are repealed.

Libel and slander.

The chief provision of the County Courts Act we have to consider here, is the rule that a plaintiff

Costs in County Court.

cannot recover costs upon the scale allowed in the High Court (lower scale), unless in an action of contract he recover £20, or in an action of tort £10 or more. The County Courts Amendment Bill to be introduced next session proposes, as it is understood, to extend these sums to £50 and £20 respectively. It is doubtful, however, whether the costs in actions for large sums are much less in the County Court than in the High Court.

When actions are remitted to County Court.

The other provisions are, that claims for sums below, or which have been reduced below £50, can be remitted upon the application of the defendant to the County Court; that equitable claims which come within the limit (£500) of County Court actions can be referred to it upon the application of any of the parties interested, and that the defendant against whom an action is brought in a Superior Court for malicious prosecution, illegal arrest, or distress, assault, false imprisonment, libel, slander, seduction, or other action of tort, may, upon an affidavit that the plaintiff has no visible means of paying the costs if he loses, make him either give security for costs, or have his action remitted to the County Court.

In an action remitted under 19 & 20 Vict. c. 108, s. 26, the Superior Court has power over costs: *Farmer* v. *May*, 30 L. J. R. C. P. 295.

Costs in actions remitted to High Court.

It has been held, as was shown in *Parsons* v. *Tinling*, and *Garnett* v. *Bradley*, that in libel or slander, costs follow the event; and that a verdict of one farthing will carry costs where the judge declines to make any order. Also, where a plaintiff commences a suit in a County Court, which, at the hearing is transferred to the High Court, because the subject matter exceeds the amount of £500, though he succeeds and obtains the general costs of the suit, he must pay the costs of

Where amount £500.

the hearing before the County Court: *Ward* v. *Wyld*, 5 Ch. D. 779.

Contract or tort? Difficulties frequently occur as to whether an action is an action founded on tort or on contract, and consequently whether a plaintiff must recover £20 or £10, in order to get costs in the Supreme Court. Instances. A claim alleges that the plaintiffs caused to be delivered to defendants, as common carriers, a parcel, but that they did not safely carry it, and that it was lost. The defendants paid into Court £12 3*s*. 4*d*. which the plaintiffs accepted; and in this case it was held that the action was founded on contract: *Fleming* v. *Manchester, Sheffield and Lincolnshire Ry. Co.*, 4 Q. B. D. 81. On the other hand, in *Pontifex* v. *Midland Ry. Co.*, 3 Q. B. D. 28, it was held that the following action was founded on tort, and that, therefore, the plaintiff was entitled to his costs. The plaintiff entrusted goods to the defendants as carriers, consigned to intending purchasers. Before the goods were delivered or claimed, the plaintiff discovered that the consignees were insolvent, and as an unpaid vendor gave notice to the defendants not to deliver the goods to the consignees, but to hold them to the defendants order; and before they were delivered, the plaintiff required the defendants to re-deliver them to him, which they refused to do; but delivered them to the consignees, who absconded and never paid for them. The plaintiff claimed £12 16*s*. 6*d*., which was paid by the defendants into Court, and was taken out by the plaintiffs in satisfaction. *Bryant* v. *Herbert*. An action claiming the return of a picture, or its value, and damages for its detention, is an action founded on tort: *Bryant* v. *Herbert*, 3 C. P. D. 389. Costs on a reference. If an action is referred by consent to an arbitrator upon the terms that the costs of the cause shall abide the event, but the costs of the award shall be in the discretion of the arbitrator; if he decides in favour of the plaintiff he can give him the costs of the reference and award, though he is deprived of his costs of the action under the County Court Act: *Galatti* v. *Wakefield*, 4 Ex. D. 249. Where an action is referred by consent, the costs to abide the event; the plaintiff recovering less than £20 in contract, does not obtain costs without an order: *Fergusson* v. *Davison*, 51 L. J. R. Q. B. 266.

Cases.

Where amount reduced by counterclaim.

Where difficulties generally arise, is when the amount recovered by the plaintiff is reduced by the amount recovered by the defendant upon his counterclaim to a sum which brings it apparently under the County Court Acts; and these difficulties are further complicated if they arise out of a reference, as then the exact terms of the reference and of the finding have to be carefully considered. See *Lowe* v. *Holme*, 31 W R. 400.

Action and counterclaim referred to arbitrator

Thus, in *Stooke* v. *Taylor*, 5 Q. B. D. 569, to which the reader is referred, the Court was divided. This was an action for more than £50, to which there was a counterclaim, which was referred by consent upon the terms that the costs of the action should abide the event of the award, and that the costs of the reference and the award should be in the discretion of the arbitrator. The arbitrator found for the plaintiff for £35 and for the defendant for £20. Cockburn, C.J. and Manisty, J., held that the provision in the order of reference as to costs, did not alter the rights of the parties, and that the plaintiff was entitled to the costs of his claim, and the defendant to his costs of the counterclaim; but Field, J., was of opinion that the case was governed by the provision as to costs in the order of reference,

Stooke v. *Taylor.*

and that the plaintiff was entitled to the costs of the action, and that the defendant was not entitled to any costs.

In *Cole* v. *Frith*, 4 Ex. D. 301, an action with claim, defence, and counterclaim, was referred upon the terms "costs of the cause and counterclaim to follow the event, costs of the reference and award, to be in the discretion of the arbitrator." The arbitrator awarded the plaintiffs £371, and the defendants £375, and ordered the plaintiffs to pay to the defendants £4, and the costs of the reference and award. It was held that the plaintiffs were entitled to the costs of the action and the defendants to the costs of the counterclaim. Where an order of reference is silent as to costs, the Court under Order LV., may refuse an application for costs in favour of the party in whose favour the reference was decided: *Wilmshurst, Hollock and Co.* v. *Barrow Shipbuilding Co.*, 2 Q. B. D. 335.

Where order of reference is silent as to costs.

But perhaps it may be advantageous to consider further the costs of a counterclaim. Difficulties as to the apportionment of costs often arise with reference to counterclaims, as for instance, where both the claim and the counterclaim are dismissed with costs.

Costs of claim and counter-claim, where both dismissed with costs.

Here the plaintiff pays the defendant the general costs of the action, and the defendant pays the plaintiff only the amount by which the costs have been increased by reason of the counterclaim: *Mason* v. *Brentini*, 15 Ch. D. 287.

Where, by reason of a defendant gaining on his counterclaim, the claim of a plaintiff (in an action of contract and originally above £50) is reduced below £20, he is not deprived of his costs under the County Court Act, 1867, sec. 5, because he could not have

Potter v. *Chambers.*

got his relief in the County Court: *Potter* v. *Chambers*, 4 C. P. D. 457. If, however, in such an action, although the plaintiff got a verdict for £16, the defendants succeed upon their counterclaim to the extent of £23, so as to leave a balance in their favour of £7 due to them from the plaintiff; the defendants are entitled to their costs: *Chatfield* v. *Sedgwick*, 4 C. P. D. 459. It does not appear that the County Court Act applies to counterclaims; so where a defendant wins upon his counterclaim £10, though the plaintiff gets £40 on his claim, he is, in the absence of any order as to costs, entitled to the costs of proving it and the issue relating to it: *Blake* v. *Appleyard*, 3 Ex. D. 195.

Chatfield v. *Sedgwick.*

County Court Act does not apply to counterclaim.

If a plaintiff's claim is bonâ fide over £50, but by reason of a counterclaim he fails to recover £20 in an action on contract, he is entitled both to the general costs of the action and also to his costs of the issues upon which he succeeds, while the defendant is in like manner entitled to the costs of the issues upon which he succeeds. In fact, the general costs follow the judgment, but the costs of the particular issues must be respectively taxed in favour of the party who has succeeded on them. (This is the effect of cases collected in Andrews and Stoney's Jud. Acts, at p. 242, in nearly their own words, and the reader is referred there for many other isolated cases upon the subject). Order XXII., r. 10, says that where there is a counterclaim, if the balance is in favour of the defendant (*i.e.*, upon the hearing of the action)—*Rolfe* v. *Maclaren*, 3 Ch. D. 106,—the Court may give him judgment, or such other relief as he may be entitled to on the merits.

Where balance is in favour of defendant.

It may be noticed that a claim must not be made for a fictitious amount so as to get costs and take

Claim must not be for ficti-

the case out of the County Court Act: *Chatfield* v. *Sedgwick*, *ante*, and also that when the case does not fall under any of the rules given above, and difficulties appear likely to arise, a special order as to costs should be asked for at the time. Then the discretion of the judge seems to be almost absolute, although in the case of *Collins* v. *Welsh*, 5 C. P. D. 27, the reasons given by the Divisional Court and the Court of Appeal were not the same, although the result was. The facts of that case were these as given in the head note:—At the trial of an action of tort the jury found for the plaintiff for £12; the counsel for defendant was about to apply to deprive plaintiff of costs, when before he did so, the judge made that order, although the plaintiff's counsel objected. Grove and Lopes, J.J., held that the judge might, under Order LV., make the order without any application being made to him; and the Court of Appeal held that what occurred at the trial was equivalent to an application by the defendant, and to showing good cause why the order depriving the plaintiff of his costs should be made.

tions amount to get costs.

Collins v. *Welsh*.

In the Chancery Division, too, in the case of an unnecessary application to the Court, the successful party may not only be deprived of his costs, but made to pay those of the other side. In *Fane* v. *Fane*, 13 Ch. D. 228, the plaintiff was held to be entitled to judgment for the execution of the trusts of a settlement against the surviving trustee of which settlement he had made, but abandoned at the trial, charges of breach of trust, and for whose removal he had wrongly asked; but as the action was unnecessary he was made to pay the costs of it up to and including trial.

Unnecessary application in Chancery Division.

Money paid into Court taken out.

When a plaintiff takes out money paid into Court and confesses the defence under Order XX., r. 3, if not entitled to costs under this rule, he may be under Order LV.; or if the amount is small, under the County Courts Act.

Power to order costs on higher scale.

Again, a judge has power to order costs upon the higher scale under Rules of the Supreme Court (costs) Order VI., r. 3, in the case of the whole or any part of an action which would otherwise come under the lower scale set out in the schedule to that order. Jessel, M.R., did so in an action on a bill of exchange which was properly brought in the Chancery Division; *Pooley* v. *Driver*, 5 Ch. D. 494; but the authority to allow costs on the higher or lower scale as he may think fit cannot be delegated by a judge to the taxing master (*Corticine Floor Co.* v. *Jull*, 27 W. R. 373.)

Pooley v. *Driver.*

As an instance of a late case in which the lower scale only was allowed, *Chapman* v. *Midland Ry. Co.*, 5 Q. B. D. 431, may be referred to.

Where higher scale may be charged.

Under Order VI., r. 2 (costs), the higher scale may be charged in all actions for special injunctions, where procuring such injunctions is the principal relief sought, and in all cases other than those to which the lower scale is thereby made applicable. The case above referred to was an action for trespass, and in addition to damages for the trespass, an injunction was obtained. The Court of Appeal, however, held that this was not the kind of injunction referred to in rule 2.

Costs, Order VI. r. 2.

In the *Duke of Norfolk* v. *Arbuthnot*, 50 L. J. 384, it was held that though rule 2 does not apply to the Chancery Division alone but to all actions, yet that in that case, notwithstanding that the trial had lasted a long time, and the evidence had been voluminous, costs on the higher scale could not be allowed. An injunction to carry costs on the higher scale must be to restrain an injury to the soil: see *Goodhand* v. *Ayscough*, 10 Q. B. D. 71.

From the foregoing observations it will be seen that the discretion of the judge is almost unlimited, and that he will exercise it not only when asked to do so, but of his own accord. Indeed, the tendency of the courts has been to repress in every way unnecessary expense. For example in *Slack* v. *The Midland Ry. Co.*, 50 L. J. R. Ch. 196, the costs of an inquiry were reserved in order to keep the control over undue expense with the judge; and in *Fritz* v. *Hobson*, 14 Ch. D. 542, it was distinctly stated that in every order of the Court, liberty to apply is implied, so that an application as to costs may be made; as, for instance, when a motion for an interim injunction was adjourned to the trial, and no costs were at the trial asked for in respect of it. Courts discourage unnecessary expense.

Where a notice of appeal is given, but the appeal is not put in the paper by the party giving the notice, the other party ought not to appear, but may make a substantive application for the costs of his motion: *Webb* v. *Mansel*, 2 Q. B. D. 117. Costs of abandoned motion.

This tendency to repress expense has been shown as against solicitors in two late cases. From what the Master of the Rolls said, In re *Grundy, Kershaw & Co.*, 50 L. J. Ch. 467, it appears, that if on a party and party taxation, where the party taking the taxation pays the costs, the solicitor, whose bill is being taxed, delivers an exorbitant one to increase the costs of taxation, the Court can not only deprive the solicitor of such costs, but also make him pay the costs of taxation. Tendency to repress expense.

The other case is *Mildmay* v. *Quicke*, 6 Ch. D. *Mildmay* v. *Quicke*.

553, where the solicitors of a married woman in an action obtained a charging order, and afterwards a stop order. Having been served with the minutes of order, on further consideration, they appeared by counsel, and asked for their costs of obtaining the stop order and their appearance at the further hearing. Both were refused.

Costs of production of documents. It was not decided till the end of 1880 (*Brown* v. *Sewell*, 16 Ch. D. 517), that when an order is made in an action in the Chancery Division for the production of documents at the office of the producing party's solicitor, that that party, if ultimately successful in the action, is not entitled as between party and party to his solicitor's costs of the production, nor to his own costs of inspecting the documents of the other party.

Upon a notice of withdrawal. A good case illustrating what costs will be allowed when a notice of withdrawal is allowed, is *Harrison* v. *Leutner*, 50 L. J. Ch. D. 264, which shows that the test is whether the time for doing the work charged had arrived, and that the Judicature Acts had not altered the practice in this respect.

Objections to allowance of taxing master. Any party dissatisfied with the allowances of the taxing master, makes an objection in writing to his certificate, stating the items to which he objects, but not his reasons for so doing. Then the master reviews his taxation, and may receive further evidence; and if he refuses to entertain the objections, he states the reasons for his refusal. An application to a judge may be made to review any items which have been thus objected to but no other; yet sections

Secs. 30 & 32, costs. 30 & 32 (costs), the authority for these propositions, do not apply, where the general principle of the taxation is challenged. *Sparrow* v. *Hill*, 7 Q. P. D. 362, which apply only where specific objections are made to particular items. This point was not touched upon when this case came before the Court of Appeal, 8 Q. B. D. 479.

Time for taxation.

The time for taxation of costs is the termination of the action; but where the Court of Appeal has given costs in an interlocutory appeal in the ordinary way, "the judgment of the Court below to be reversed with costs of this appeal and of the proceedings in the Court below," the party to whom they are ordered to be paid is entitled to have them taxed and paid forthwith: *Phillipps* v. *Phillipps*, 5 Q. B. D. 60.

Appeal to Lords.

Payment of costs will not be stayed pending an appeal to the House of Lords if the solicitors to whom they are payable give their personal undertaking to refund them if the order is reversed, and payment will not be stayed on the ground that another proceeding in the same action is pending, upon which costs may become payable to the applicant: *Grant* v. *Banque Franco-Egyptienne*, 3 C. P. D. 202; *Morgan* v. *Elford*, 4 Ch. D. 388.

Set-off.

Though in the case of a party entitled to receive costs, but liable to pay some to the other party, the taxing-master may adjust them by way of set-off, yet such set-off is strictly limited to costs due to either party in respect of the same action, and cannot be enforced in respect of the costs of any separate proceedings between the same parties: *Barker* v. *Hemming*, 5 Q. B. D. 609.

Costs of third parties.

With regard to the costs of third parties, if an order has been made that a third party shall pay the costs of interlocutory proceedings taken to bring him before the Court, and yet by the judgment he is dismissed with costs, to be paid by the defendants, the Court cannot annul this order: *Beynon* v. *Godden*,

4 Ex. D. 246. But a party bringing in a third party can be ordered to pay his costs: *Dawson* v. *Shepherd*, 49 L. J. Ex. 548, explaining *Yorkshire Wagon Co.* v. *Newport and Abercorne Coal Co.*, 5 Q. B. D. 268. It may, perhaps, be taken generally from the above cases (subject, however, to *Hornby* v. *Cardwell*, 8 Q. B. D. 329, from which it would appear that a third party can be ordered to pay the plaintiff's costs), that the only discretion as to the costs of third parties that the Court has, is to impose them or not upon the party coming in, and in certain cases to make the party bringing him in pay his costs. But before the case last cited, the third party could not get his costs out of the plaintiff; but the plaintiff can out of him: *Piller* v. *Roberts*, 21 Ch. D. 198.

Hornby v. Cardwell.

Adjournment for parties to be added.

When the hearing of an action is adjourned for parties to be added, the party applying must pay not only the costs of the day, but also all costs occasioned by the action having been in the paper: *Lydall* v. *Martinson*, 5 Ch. D. 780.

Where unnecessary parties served.

If, in a motion for judgment against one of two defendants for default in pleading, the other be served with the notice of motion, he will be entitled to his costs if he attend at the hearing, such costs to be paid by the plaintiff: *Read* v. *Bailey*, Fry, J., Dec. 1st, 1882 (1881, R. No. 1581). See, however, Ex parte *Webster*, In re *Morris*, 22 Ch. D. 136, and Ex parte *Izard*, In re *Moir*, 20 Ch. D. 704.

Security for costs when ordered.

A few words as to security for costs will, perhaps, be expected in this place. Security will be ordered, though the matter is one of discretion, in the case of the insolvency or liquidation of the plaintiff, and in the case of a suit by a foreign government, but not of a foreign plaintiff if actually in England at the time of the application; but a defendant, though out of the jurisdiction, cannot be ordered to give security, even though he sets up a counterclaim overriding the plaintiff's claim in the action.

And the Court has had discretion to allow a married woman to sue alone or with a next friend, and with or without giving security, and to direct a next friend to give security at any time. If a married woman is suing alone she must give security if she has no available means to pay the costs if she loses, but not where she has such means: *Brown* v. *North*, 9 Q. B. D. 52, C. A. Under the Married Women's Property Act, 1882, a woman can sue, though married, as if she were a feme sole. When, however, the plaintiffs set up amendments which really raise a fresh case, security will be ordered: *Northampton Coal, Iron and Wagon Co.* v. *Midland Wagon Co.*, 7 Ch. D. 500.

Amendments set up by plaintiff.

And on an application for security for costs of appeal, for serving which no leave is necessary: *Grills* v. *Dillon*, 2 Ch. D. 325, the insolvency, though not the apparent poverty of the appellant, is a special circumstance which may cause the Court to order security; and now, *Harlock* v. *Ashberry*, 19 Ch. D. 84, the fact that an appellant would be unable, through poverty, to pay the costs of the respondent if the appeal should be unsuccessful, is in itself sufficient ground for requiring security for costs; also, the appellant being a foreigner, and having no property in this country. A good reason for ordering security will be if the appellant appears to be vexatiously and unreasonably appealing; but the time within which it must be given will not generally be fixed. If not given within a reasonable time, the respondent may move to dismiss for want of prosecution: *Polini* v. *Gray*,

Poverty of appellant.

Vexatious appeals.

5 Ch. D. 741. The judge has a discretionary power here: *La Grange* v. *McAndrew*, 4 Q. B. D. 210.

Costs of application. The costs of an application for security are costs of the appeal, and if the appeal is dismissed for want of prosecution, these costs will be included: *Judd* v. *Green*, 4 Ch. D. 784.

With regard to the rule that costs are in the discretion of the judge of first instance in the Chancery Division, it may be remarked that if an order dismissing an action without costs is appealed by the plaintiff, the defendant cannot get the Court to vary the decree by dismissing it with costs: *Harris* v. *Aaron*, 4 Ch. D. 749, for Judicature Act, 1873, s. 49, is imperative. No order made by the High Court of Justice, or any judge thereof, by the consent of the parties, or as to costs only, which by law are left to the discretion of the Court, shall be subject to any appeal except by leave of the Court, or the judge making such order.

Orders by consent and as to costs.

Interpleader. An interpleader tried by consent by a judge at Chambers is covered by this provision: *Edd* v. *Winsor*, W. N. 88, 1878; but not the order of a master or district registrar: *Foster* v. *Edwards*, 48 L. J. 767. See p. 212.

Appeals for costs. It is often very difficult to say what is an appeal for costs. Thus, where a judge held that the defendant had committed a breach of an injunction, but, as his committal was not pressed for, made no order except that he should pay the costs, this was held to be appealable: *Witt* v. *Corcoran*, 2 Ch. D. 69; but where a judge refused to commit for contempt, and made the costs costs in the cause, it was held that no appeal lay: *Ashworth* v. *Outram*, 5 Ch. D. 943

Decision Where a refusal or a giving of costs is put upon

principle, and not as a matter of discretion, an appeal lies: *City of Manchester*, 5 P. D. 221. If a judge is wrong in point of law, an appeal lies to the Court of Appeal: *Manders* v. *Lancashire and Yorkshire Ry. Co.*, 7 Q. B. D. 64. on principle not as an act of discretion.

Where a plaintiff had obtained a verdict in an action, and a new trial had been refused by the Divisional Court, but allowed by the Court of Appeal, which Court also ordered the plaintiff to pay the costs of the application; upon his failure to do so it was held by Mathew and Cave, J.J., in *Morton* v. *Palmer*, 9 Q. B. D. 90, that the defendant was not entitled to an order to stay the proceedings until the costs were paid. New trial granted by Court of Appeal.

Where an application is made against a solicitor, either to strike him off the roll or to show cause why he should not answer the matters of an affidavit, the same rules as to costs apply as in other cases, and an improper application is punished by the applicant having to pay the costs of it. Application against solicitors.

Moreover, where the Incorporated Law Society have been requested to intervene unnecessarily, their costs, also, may be ordered to be paid by the applicant: In the matter of *Mr. A. S. Jonas*, Solicitors' Journal, p. 56, Nov. 25, 1882. Law Society's Costs.

As to the costs of a mortgage, see Ex parte *Firth*, In re *Cowburn*, 19 Ch. D. 427, which explains the reason of the usual undertaking by the intended borrower's solicitor to pay expenses. Costs of mortgage.

CHAPTER XVII.

TAXATION OF COSTS.

The 37th section of the Solicitors Act, 1843, which prevents a solicitor from commencing an action for his costs until one month after he has delivered a signed bill, is given at length in an Appendix to this book; and with reference to that section it must be premised that the bill to be liable to taxation must be for the ordinary work of a solicitor done by a duly qualified solicitor. Thus, where a solicitor was employed as an electioneering agent, his bill was held not to be liable to taxation: Re *Oliver*, 15 W. R. 331; see also In re *Parker*, 21 Ch. D. 408. The fees of the steward of a manor who is a solicitor, but who has acted in the character of steward only, are not taxable: In re *Ward*, 5 Beav. 401. Where a solicitor, who was appointed returning officer for the election of a School Board, under the Elementary Education Act, 1870, sent in the bill of his charges in the usual form of a solicitor's bill, including both the election charges proper, and also those for attendance at the Board after the election was over: Lord Romilly, M.R., In re *Jones*, L. R. 13 Eq. 338, said that as he had constituted himself the solicitor to the School Board, his bill was taxable. It would appear from the arguments

Bill must be for solicitor's costs.

Electioneering agent.

Steward of a manor.

in that case that the Court has no jurisdiction over the performance of any duties but those of a solicitor, and that if the solicitor had then charged a lump sum, and had not constituted himself the solicitor to the Board his bill would not have been taxable.

Bill of town agent.

As a London agent is employed by a solicitor in the country, solely because he is a solicitor, he is bound to deliver his bill for such agency, and liable to have it taxed; for such bill is for business done by a solicitor in respect of an employment in his professional character as such. The taxing master, when the bill was for conveyancing and business not done in Court, was obliged to ascertain the proper amount of remuneration, as well as he could, according to the contract between the parties, express or implied: *Smith* v. *Dimes*, 4 Exch. 40; but, now, see Solicitor's Remuneration Act, 1881, and rules in Appendix, pp. 215, et seq.

For non-litigious business

Married woman employing solicitor.

Where a married woman employs a solicitor and makes her separate estate liable, she was, though not personally liable, a party chargeable under this section: *Waugh* v. *Waddell*, 16 Beav. 521. And probably the Married Woman's Property Act, 1882, now makes her liable as well.

Under the common order for taxation, an account has not to be taken of the pecuniary matters between the parties, which are foreign to the bill of costs; except where monies are paid on account of the bill of costs, or where, by agreement, the monies which come to the hands of the solicitor, are to be applicable to the payment of the bill: *Jones* v. *James*, 1 Beav. 307.

Solicitor refusing to produce his bill.

If a solicitor refuses to produce his bill it is presumed to be taxable: In re *Loughborough*, 23 Beav.

439; and the bill should be delivered, and not merely shown to the party chargeable.

Time for bringing action for costs.

The month, until the expiration of which, no action in respect of a solicitors's bill can be brought, was under the Act, 2 Geo. II., c. 23, s. 23, which was replaced by the 37th section of the Solicitors Act of 1843, a lunar month; but it is expressly enacted by section 48 of the same Act that the word month in this Act means calendar month. And *Blunt* v. *Heslop*, 8 A. & E. 581, is an authority that under the old Act no action could be brought until after twenty-eight days and so many hours over, as there might happen to have been of the day on which the bill was delivered, after such delivery. The words of the section in both Acts are similar, "until the expiration of one month;" but in the older Act the words "or more" follow. In the later Act, these words "or more" are excluded, and whereas *Blunt* v. *Heslop* is a direct authority that a lunar month is intended in the older Act, the Act of 1843 itself says that a calendar month is meant by that enactment. This being so, it is arguable whether the month must now be calculated exclusively of the days on which the bill is delivered and the action brought, as it had to be under the older Act. Messrs. Morgan and Wurtzburg (2nd. ed. p. 428) state positively that it is to be so calculated, relying, probably, upon *Englehcart* v. *Moore*, 15 M. & W. 548, which decides that the Act is to be construed liberally for the client.

Calendar month.

Mode of delivery of bill.

If the bill has been properly delivered after the month has elapsed, the solicitor, or his representative, or the party chargeable can get the bill taxed; and the solicitor can choose any method of delivery prescribed by the Act in delivering the bill to the party chargeable, or an agent authorised to receive it; or in the alternative by sending it by the post to, or leaving it for him at his counting house or last known place of abode. Parke, B., says in *Macgregor* v. *Keily*, 3 Ex. 797, that having selected his mode of delivery the solicitor must prove to the satisfaction of the jury an actual delivery by himself, or his agent, or some one authorised by him; and he has to satisfy them that the bill reached the party chargeable. In that case the bill was delivered to a man servant; this was evidence of a delivery of the bill to the party chargeable, and the onus was then upon that party to show that he had not received it. The solicitor, or his representative, must, however, prove, unless any informality is waived, that it was signed with the proper hand of the solicitor, or, in the case of a partnership, by one of the partners, or of the executor, administrator or assignee of such solicitor, or that it was accompanied by a letter so subscribed. Whether in the flap of the envelope "with compliments" and the name is sufficient, has never been decided. Although such an enclosure does not comply with the letter of the Act, it appears to satisfy its spirit. "With compliments" and the initials of the firm would not satisfy the requirements of the Act: see *Penley* v. *Anstruther*, W. N. 1883, 48.

Delivery of bill must be proved.

What constitutes delivery.

Must be signed by solicitor.

A judge's order must be obtained for the delivery of a bill, and this is obtained by summons at chambers. Afterwards a four day order to enforce the order previously made is a usual course to adopt. This order is as of course, and upon it there is no argument as to the propriety of the original order; and the order and the common order to tax may be enforced by attachment: In re *Gregg*; In re *Prance*, L. R. 9 Eq. 141, which is also an authority

Order for delivery of bill.

Enforced by attachment.

that an order for delivery improperly endorsed may be properly endorsed and served again. In ex parte *Alcock*, 1 C. P. D. 68, the rule for attachment was made absolute without an affidavit of personal service when the arguing of the rule had been put off by consent; upon the principle that the appearance of counsel, and his consenting to the rule being enlarged, was a waiver of personal service.

Where waiver of personal service.

In re *Dendy*, 21 Beav. 565, on payment of the costs of the motion the solicitor had further time for delivering his bill.

Cannot be altered after delivery.

After a bill has been delivered it cannot be altered, although the party chargeable send back the bill with suggested alterations which are partially acquiesced in. James, L.J., In re *Heather*, L. R. 5 Ch. 697, shows the danger of allowing alterations. He puts the case of the client through his new solicitor, saying, "I have looked through the bill, and I find many improper charges in it; but if you are satisfied to take so much in full payment, I will advise my client to pay that sum, and not to have the bill taxed." And the solicitor, saying to himself: "If I can so alter the bill as just to avoid taxation, I will do so. I know now what objections will be made. I cannot sustain all the charges of the original bill, but I am sure of the amount offered. I will put on so much more as will leave me safe against the costs of taxation; and if it is attempted, I shall have the profit of conducting the business."

The reason.

Special circumstances, however, such as fraud or mistake, may enable a solicitor to avoid taxation of a bill by withdrawing it, and delivering an amended bill: In re *Holroyd and Smith*, W. N. 6, 1881.

Taxation is not the only way in which a client

is entitled to protect himself. In an ordinary case a judge and jury would not go through the items of a solicitor's bill; but if a solicitor tenders a proof in the bankruptcy of his client in respect of his bill, the registrar can determine the amount due to him, taking assistance if he thinks necessary, and the solicitor cannot insist on taxation: Ex parte *Ditton* In re *Woods*, 13 Ch. D. 320.

Solicitor proving in bankruptcy for his bill.

Cannot insist on taxation.

No account stated, or admission by the client, defeats the provisions of the statute, and dispenses with taxation: Lord Denman in *Brooks* v. *Bockett*, 9 Q. B. 857.

Brooks v. *Bockett*.

Before the statutory enactments as to taxing bills of costs, a bill for an account and taxation by a client against his solicitor could be maintained in equity, and the jurisdiction was not taken away by those enactments.

Jurisdiction in equity.

Such a bill could not, however, be maintained by a person out of whose estate such a bill was to be paid, where a solicitor had not been employed by himself: *In re Spencer; Spencer* v. *Hart*, W. N. 170, 1881.

A solicitor may sue on a promissory note given on account of his costs before delivering his bill: *Jeffreys* v. *Evans*, 14 M. & W. 210.

May sue on promissory note given for costs.

Pending a reference for taxation against a married woman, the solicitor could not maintain a suit to enforce a lien for his bill of costs on her separate estate: *Waugh* v. *Waddell*, 16 Beav. 521.

When a sum is found due from a solicitor on taxation, he will be ordered to pay all the costs of the proceedings to compel payment, as, for instance, of substituted service of a copy of the certificate of the taxing master, a motion for a

Costs of taxation.

short order for payment, and delivery up of deeds and papers, and also all the subsequent costs: In re *Dufaur and Blakeney*, 16 Beav. 114; In re *Bambrigge*, 13 Beav. 108, and 14 Beav. 645.

Where mistake in order—time.

As to the time at which a motion should be made that the taxing master be directed to tax the bill in a particular way, see In re *Tibbitts*, a solicitor, W. N. 168, 1881.

Attendance by letter.

A solicitor cannot object to items in his opponent's bill at a taxation by writing to the taxing master. He must attend: In re *Upperton*, 30 W. R. 840.

Person not party dissatisfied

Where a person not a party to the order is dissatisfied with a taxation he should apply to discharge the order for taxation: *Charlton* v. *Charlton*, 31 W. R. 237.

CHAPTER XVIII.

TAXATION BETWEEN SOLICITOR AND CLIENT.

Party and party costs.

PARTY and party costs are such only as were necessary to enable the party entitled to them to conduct the litigation, in respect of which they have been incurred, successfully. These are the costs to which he is entitled upon a simple order for taxation of costs, even though, according to the practice of the Court, he would from his position (*i.e.*, as a trustee) be entitled to costs as between solicitor and client. The decree should specify that costs are to be so taxed, or that any special expenses are to be allowed whenever anything but party and party costs are to be given. Besides party and party costs and solicitor and client costs, there is a third method of taxation, namely, that by which there is allowed besides costs of suit all other costs, charges and expenses properly incurred. This is for the most part given to trustees, executors and administrators in the execution of their trust or the administration of their estate. These are not, strictly speaking, costs, and therefore the order giving or refusing them is subject to appeal: In re *Chennell, Jones* v. *Chennell*, 8 Ch. D. 502.

Costs of trustees, &c. right of appeal.

Solicitor and client costs not given as damages.

In *Cockburn* v. *Edwards*, 18 Ch. D. 459, Jessel, M.R., says: "I am of opinion that it is not according to law to give to a party by way of damages the costs as between solicitor and client of the litigation in which the damages are recovered." And Brett, L.J. added: "The damages in an action of tort must have been incurred when the action is brought, except in some cases where they include everything up to the time of trial, and they cannot include any expenses incurred in the action itself. The law considers the extra costs which are disallowed on taxation between party and party, as a luxury for which the other party ought in no case to be liable, and they cannot be allowed by way of damages."

Equity practice.

Sir R. Malins, V.-C., in *Turner* v. *Collins*, L. R. 12 Eq. 440, says that it is not the course of the Court to give other than party and party costs in dismissing a bill, except where the parties are in a fiduciary position, or where there is something in the nature of scandal, such as gross charges of fraud which are not sustained.

When solicitor and client costs given.

Where there was a fiduciary relation between the parties, solicitor and client costs were given in *Mordue* v. *Palmer*, L. R. 6 Ch. 22.

Stand alone charges.

In *Kevan* v. *Crawford*, 6 Ch. D. 35, the plaintiff was ordered by the Vice-Chancellor of the Palatinate Court to pay so much of the costs of the suit as had been occasioned by charges of immorality against the defendants, Mr. and Mrs. Crawford, between solicitor and client, and this decree was upheld on appeal.

Of gifts to charities.

Where there is a fund about which the contention is whether it has been given to charity or not the costs of all parties have been given between solicitor and client, but in *Wilkinson* v. *Barber*, L. R. 14 Ex. 99, Lord Romilly, M.R., said that he knew of no rule that this should be so, and that he could not act upon it. *Carter* v. *Green*, 3 K. & J. 591, was quoted in the argument in favour of the existence of such rule. In *Attorney-General* v. *Stewart*, L. R. 14 Eq. 25, Malins, V.-C., gave the Caledonian Asylum and the Attorney-General their costs as between solicitor and client out of the fund, though he dismissed the petition without costs. No Rule but the custom.

In the case of a relator in a charity information who has obtained a decree, although he has been allowed his costs, charges, and expenses of, incidental, and even preparatory to the cause itself, he ought only to be allowed his costs of the cause as between solicitor and client; and to be paid the difference between the amount thereof and that portion recovered from the defendants out of the charity estate. Relator's costs.

The extra costs of a charity information, instituted in respect of one only of several gifts belonging to the charity, should, in the first instance at least, fall on the property which is the subject of the information. It may happen that justice to the relator, and even the interest of the charity, might require a different provision which would be made when the circumstances require it, but not otherwise. Lord Langdale in the *Attorney-General* v. *Kerr*, 4 Beav. 303 & 304. In administration suits, too, costs as between solicitor and client are given in the following cases. The costs of the heir-at-law, where the real estate had been exhausted by creditors, were given as between solicitor and client, upon the principle of his being in the position of a trustee in *Tardrew* v. *Howell*, *Shitler* v. *Shitler*, 4 N. R. 485. But in *James* v. *James*, 11 Beav. 397, we find the general statement that the heir-at-law is only allowed costs as between solicitor and client in charity cases, and where he is a trustee. Also the costs of a plaintiff in a legatee's action on behalf of himself and all In administration suits. Costs of heir-at-law.

Of plaintiff in legatee's action.

other the legatees where there was a surplus after the payment of the creditors, although there was not enough to pay the legacies in full, were given as between solicitor and client in *Cross* v. *Kennington*, 11 Beav. 89. The Master of the Rolls said that if the assets were deficient, the plaintiff was entitled to costs between solicitor and client; and he ordered the master to tax the costs of the plaintiff and one defendant between solicitor and client including the costs, charges, and expenses properly incurred in certain sales and in making out the bill, and directed the amount to be paid out of the fund in Court; and he further directed the master to apportion the residue among the plaintiff and the other legatees mentioned in the master's report. See also 18 Beavan 216.

Costs in creditors administration suit.

The rule as to costs in a creditor's suit to administer the realty, where there was no personalty, and the realty was deficient is clearly laid down by Kindersley, V.-C., in *Henderson* v. *Dodds*, L. R. 2 Eq. 533, and has been subsequently approved and followed.

The plaintiff's costs are taxed between party and party, and not as between solicitor and client. The plaintiffs and the defendants, the beneficial devisees, have their costs as between party and party pari passu out of the fund, and any surplus of the fund has to be paid to creditors towards satisfaction of their debts. If such surplus is insufficient to pay the debts in full, the plaintiffs are entitled as between themselves and other creditors to have their extra costs as between solicitor and client out of such

In re *Richardson.*

surplus. In re *Richardson, Richardson* v. *Richardson*, 14 Ch. D. 612, Jessel, M. R., referring to *Thomas* v. *Jones*, 1 De Gex & Smale, 134, says that the principle was well laid down there by V.-C. Kindersley, that where the fund administered is a creditors' fund, it is extremely unreasonable that the general body of creditors should take advantage of the exertions of the particular creditor through whose instrumentality the fund has been recovered without paying all his costs. In this case the estate being insolvent, the creditors who had the conduct of an administration action against the sole next-of-kin had their costs as between solicitor and client. The rule therefore, shortly is—a creditor who brings an action on behalf of himself, and all other creditors for the administration of an estate which turns out to be insufficient to pay debts is entitled to solicitor and client costs, as is also a creditor who obtains the conduct of an action originally commenced by a legatee or next-of-kin. Rule

The Court may direct an unsuccessful party to pay the costs of a trustee as between solicitor and client when there is not any fund out of which they may be paid: *Turner* v. *Collins*, L. R. 12 Eq. 438. In *Poole* v. *Pass*, 1 Beav. 604, the master was ordered to tax the defendant his costs of the suit as between solicitor and client, and to tax him his charges and expenses properly incurred to be paid by the plaintiff, Lord Longdale, M. R., remarking, that no trustee would be safe unless such costs were allowed. Trustee's costs where there is no fund.

A trustee is not only entitled to his costs between solicitor and client, but also to his charges and expenses. He has a lien for them on the trust fund, and he is only deprived of them in a singular and extraordinary case: In re *Chennell Jones* v. *Chennell*, 8 Ch. D. 502. Trustee's charges and expenses.

The same rule applies to executors, and adminis- Executors

And administrators. trators as to the kind of costs to which they are in the absence of misconduct entitled. But it is determined by the Judge in Chambers, who under a general order shall attend the taking of the accounts at the cost of the estate. As a rule one solicitor has leave to attend on one side, and one on the other.

Who may attend. When the residuary legatees come in, one solicitor takes the accounts for them on one side, and one solicitor takes the accounts for the executors on the other: *Sharp* v. *Lush*, 10 Ch. D. 474. *Sharp v. Lush.* The costs of a residuary legatee in a suit for administering an insufficient estate were allowed as between solicitor and client: In re *Burrell*, L. R. 9 Eq. 443; but the rule is that in a next-of-kin's suit, or in a legatee's suit, where the estate is insufficient for payment of debts, the plaintiff is not entitled to solicitor and client costs: In re *Richardson Richardson* v. *Richardson*, 14 Ch. D. 613

In suit by next-of-kin or legatees where estate is insufficient.

Cost of next friend. Other cases in which solicitor and client costs are frequently allowed are a next friend's costs. In *Palmer* v. *Jones*, 22 W. R. 909, costs, charges, and expenses of a next friend properly incurred before suit, relative to its institution, were also ordered to be paid out of a fund recovered by the suit.

The costs of a plaintiff on a motion to commit the defendant for the breach of an undertaking, embodied in an order where the circumstances of the case would justify an order for committal which was not pressed for, were ordered by Jessel, M. R., in *Steele* v. *Hutchins* (1879, W. N. 18) to be paid as between solicitor and client.

Where a solicitor takes proceedings though unauthorised; see ante, page 30, and *Nurse* v. *Durnford*, 13 Ch. D. 964. There are also certain Acts under which such costs are given; viz., the Patent

Law Amendment Act, 1852, s. 43, which is explained by Lord Hatherley, in *Penn* v. *Bibby*, *Penn* v. *Jack*, *Penn* v. *Fernie*, L. R. 3 Eq. 311, 312. This section means that where, when a second trial for an infringement of a patent takes place, the certificate by the judge of the first action is produced in evidence on the second trial, the full costs, charges, and expenses as between solicitor and client are given the plaintiff on obtaining a decree upon such second trial, unless the judge certify that he ought not to have such full costs; and such extra costs are given to afford a full indemnity. These costs are costs of the second trial only, and the section does not apply to the costs of the first trial.

Patent Act, 1852, s. 43.

In suits for infringement of patents.

The Merchandise Marks Act, 1862, 25 & 26 Vict. c. 88, s. 23, also gives similar costs.

Merchandise Mark Act, 1862, s. 23.

Three late cases affect the subject of solicitor and client costs: In re *Emanuel*, 9 Q. B. D. 408, decides that a solicitor can recover charges other than those specified in the scale (38 & 39 Vict. c. 50, s. 8), in actions in the County Court under £20, for work done out of Court before and after the commencement of an action. This applies of course to solicitor and client costs to be paid by his own client.

Actions in County Court under £20.

In re *Worth*, 18 Ch. D. 521, shows that costs as between solicitor and client in a County Court administration action may be taxed in the Chancery Division.

Taxation of costs of administration action in County Court.

In re *Chapman*, 10 Q. B. D. 54, C. A., it was decided that the costs of counsel for attending judges' chambers would not be allowed even between solicitor and client, without their allowance being mentioned in the order made by the judge upon the hearing of the summons.

Costs of counsel attending judges' chambers

CHAPTER XIX.

WHERE TAXING MASTER'S OPINION FINAL.

THE taxing master's opinion is final not only on a question of quantum, but on a question of quoties. For instance, whether 3*s*. 4*d*. or 6*s*. 8*d*. be allowed for an interview; or whether ten or twelve interviews shall be allowed: Lord Romilly, M.R., In re *Brown*, L. R. 4 Eq. 466.

But if there has been a charge of a very exorbitant character, the Court will, even in a question of quantum, go into detail: Malins, V.-C., *Smith* v. *Buller*, L. R. 19 Eq. 474.

The question whether costs should be taxed on the higher or lower scale is also appealable: In re *Ferrell*, 31 W. R. 208.

Appeals on questions raised on taxation.

The Courts set themselves against appeals upon questions raised on taxation involving small amounts; and in no case will re-taxation be ordered when the overcharge does not amount to £2 in all: *Newton* v. *Boodle*, 4 C. B. 359.

Where amount small.

Where, however, a general rule is made by the masters, as for instance, that copies of pleadings are not to be allowed on interlocutory applications, it is different. If in any particular case where the taxing master has inquired into the question, and it is thought that he has come to an erroneous view, even if the Court be of a contrary opinion to the master, it will be very loth indeed to allow the appeal: Brett, L.J., in *Warner* v. *Mosses*, 19 Ch. D. 76. If the taxing master has exercised his discretion upon the facts of the case, and has not merely acted on a general rule, the judge will not, without very strong reasons, differ from the conclusion of the taxing master: *Midland Railway Co.* v. *Brown*, 10 Hare, App. 44; *Kirkwood* v. *Webster*, 9 Ch. D. 241, Fry, J.

When master has acted on a general rule.

In *Sparrow* v. *Hill*, 8 Q. B. D. 481, Brett, L.J., says:—"I agree with Bramwell, L.J., and I should have allowed something more to the defendant than the master has done; but in this he has not done anything so wrong that we should interfere."

Master must make a gross mistake.

On the taxation of the costs of a petition under the Parliamentary Elections Act, 1868 (31 & 32 Vic. c. 125), the number of witnesses to be allowed, the lengths of the briefs and proofs, the number of counsel, and the amount of fees, together with the incidental expenses of the trial, are matters in the master's discretion, subject to the control of the Court, where a proper case is shown for its interference: *Tillett* v. *Stracey*, L. R. 5 C. P. 185.

Matters in the master's discretion.

As to the amount of fees, the master's discretion will not be interfered with unless unreasonable: *Hargreaves* v. *Scott*, 4 C. P. D. 21; or unless a gross mistake has been made: *Brown* v. *Sewell* (see below). Grove, J., said in the former case:—"I do not see that the master has been so wrong as to warrant us in interfering." As a rule the junior counsel will receive two-thirds the amount allowed the leader, and two counsel in all but simple cases have generally been allowed, whether both juniors, or one leader and one junior. In *Stephens*

6 Ch. D. 520.

Counsel's fees allowed.

v. *Lord Newborough*, 11 Beav. 403, briefs to two counsel in an unopposed motion by a trustee to pay money into Court were allowed. In the Chancery Division the fees of counsel on an appeal are generally the same as on the original hearing; but in *Brown* v. *Sewell*, the taxing master was held to have the power of allowing a larger fee on the appeal than on the trial. In the Common Law Division, the practice as to refreshers is not quite the same as in Chancery. On both sides in actions with witnesses refreshers are allowed in the case of actions which have taken up more than one entire day for each day afterwards; but where the action is tried on affidavit no refreshers are allowed. Their amount is in the discretion of the master, and depends upon the fee originally marked on the brief and the nature of the case: *Harrison* v. *Wearing*, 11 Ch. D. 296. In *Smith* v. *Daniell*, 34 L. T. 897, refreshers were said to be within the discretion of the master. The true rule is stated by Jessel, M.R., in *Brown* v. *Sewell*, 16 Ch. D. 520. A taxing master has no discretion to allow refreshers unless the case has occupied more than six hours; when it has done so then the discretion arises. When a case, the brief of which was delivered in one term, is not reached until another, a refresher is generally allowed. The costs of brief copies of the notes in a reference will not be allowed unless by agreement: *Wells* v. *Mitcham Gas Co.*, 4 Ex. D. 1.

Refreshers. 16 Ch. D. 520. Term fee. Costs of brief copies of notes in a reference.

The master can disallow costs of abortive garnishee summonses under Rules of Court, 1875, Costs Order, 6, R. 26; *Simmons* v. *Storer*, 14 Ch. D. 156; but his decision can be reviewed. The rule, therefore, is that it lies on the party who impeaches what the master has done, to show that he has done wrong. And the master must have made a considerable mis-

Garnishee summonses.

take for the Court to interfere where he has acted upon his discretion, and has not acted upon some supposed rule which was not a correct one. When Court will interfere.

A master must not strike off all the specific items under a particular head without going into the separate items, otherwise the matter will be sent back to him: Brett, J., in *Tillett* v. *Stracey*, L. R. 5 C. P. 189. Such a consideration (in the absence of any order, or of any agreement by the parties) as that the losing party might have had to pay a sum equivalent to that charged (*i.e.*, for brief copies of shorthand writers' notes) must not weigh with a master, and ought not to be taken into account on determining their liability to these costs: *Wells* v. *Mitcham Gas Light Co.*, 4 Ex. D. 3; Kelly, C.B., and Cleasby, B. What master must not do.

Rule 29 of Order 6, Rules of the Supreme Court (costs) states what is in the discretion of the taxing master. It is:—"As to all fees and allowances which are discretionary, the same are, unless otherwise provided, to be allowed at the discretion of the taxing officer, who, in the exercise of such discretion, is to take into consideration the other fees and allowances to the solicitor and counsel, if any, in respect of the work to which any such allowance applies, the nature and importance of the cause or matter, the amount involved, the interest of the parties, the fund or persons to bear the costs, the general conduct and costs of the proceedings, and all other circumstances." As to costs of day in bankruptcy, see In re *James Bloyce*—Solr. J., p. 335, March 17, 1883. Costs. O. 6, R. 29.

But a master must not allow in a taxation between solicitor and client the costs of counsel on the hearing of a summons before the judge in chambers, unless the judge certifies in his order that it is a Counsel at judge's chambers.

proper case for counsel to attend: In re *Chapman*, 10 Q. B. D. 54.

Objections to allowances on taxation.

And if it is desired to impeach the amount allowed on a counsel's brief, the brief itself should be brought before the Court: *Tillett* v. *Stracey*. Any party who objects to the allowance on taxation must, before the allocatur is signed, deliver to the other party, and carry in before the taxing officer an objection in writing stating the items to which he objects, but not his reasons: *Simmons* v. *Storer*, 14 Ch. D. 154. Then the taxing officer reviews his taxation on such objection, and he may then receive further evidence; and, if required, he must state the grounds of his decision and any special facts. Then either party may apply to a judge at chambers for an order to review the taxation as to any item or part of any item which may have been thus objected to, provided it amounts to £2 in all, otherwise the taxing master's allocatur is conclusive.

Application for order to review.

Registrar in bankruptcy may go behind allocatur.

But where charges of improper conduct, as, for instance, that he was a party to an alleged fraud, are made against a solicitor who has had his bill taxed, the registrar in bankruptcy can go behind the allocatur of the taxing master and investigate the charges: Jessel, M.R., Brett and Holker, L.JJ.; see Ex parte *Harper*; In re *Pooley*, 20 Ch. D. 687. And it is presumed that the same power exists under similar circumstances and for similar purposes in any Court, although an exact expression of judicial opinion in so many words cannot be quoted by the writer.

Evidence to be used upon a review of taxation.

The evidence to be used before the judge upon a review of taxation is the same as that used before the taxing master, and no further evidence can be adduced unless the judge so directs: Costs O. 6, R. 33; and the objections taken must be the same as those taken before the taxing master in the first instance. They must, in fact, be the subjects of the objections to his certificate: In re *Snell*, a solicitor, C. A. 5 Ch. D. 835. If not, they will be too late even if otherwise valid.

Powers of the taxing master.

The taxing master can administer oaths, examine witnesses, direct production of papers and documents, and can take accounts. He can also direct what parties are to attend a taxation, and when any party neglects to bring in costs, and thereby prejudices any other party, he can allow him a nominal sum for costs. Taxing masters allow no costs which do not appear to them necessary or proper for the attainment of justice, or of defending the rights of the party, or which seem to have been the result of over caution, negligence, or mistake, or to have been incurred by the desire of one party only. But as between solicitor and client it would appear from *The Papa de Rossa*, 3 P. D. 163, that items cannot be disallowed which have been incurred even by the negligence of the solicitor, though an action by the client might lie for such negligence against the solicitor. They are to allow similar fees to those heretofore allowed, unless otherwise ordered in the Judicature Act and Rules, and the old practice as to the taxation of costs and allowance of fees which existed prior to this Act, where not inconsistent to it are to be retained. Therefore all the old rules of the Court of Chancery, except so far as they are altered by the rules under the Judicature Act are still binding, at all events in the Chancery Division. Jessel, M.R., in *Pringle* v. *Gloag*, 10 Ch. D. 678, says that it is not intended that all the rules of the Common Law Courts (as to costs) which were sometimes in conflict with the rules of the Equity Courts

Costs incurred through negligence of solicitor.

Rules for taxation.

Pringle v. *Gloag*.

are now binding upon the Chancery Division; but he does not say they are not still binding on the Common Law Division.

Costs, Order VI., r. 18.

One of the most stringent rules against unnecessary proceedings is rule 18 (of Order VI. Rules of the Supreme Court, Costs,) which not only gives the Court power in any cause or matter, whether the objection is raised or not, to disallow the costs of unnecessary proceedings, or to direct the taxing master to look into the same and to disallow the costs; but as a further safeguard gives the taxing officer power mero motu to look into and disallow the costs of the same; and also of evidence, although it may have been entered as read in any decree or order, and this power he should exercise: In re *Wormsley, Baines* v. *Wormsley*, 47 L. J. Ch. 844, 39 L. T. 85 M. R. Before this he could not do so unless especially directed: In re *Farrington*, 33 Beav. 346.

Costs of unnecessary proceedings. Power of the Court or taxing master to disallow.

Direction of Court in such cases.

The direction given by the Court is to look into the papers in the action, and to disallow such parts thereof as seem unnecessary as well as to ascertain the costs thereby caused and to deduct such costs from those payable: *Cracknall* v. *Janson*, 11 Ch. Div. 14.

Scales for taxation.

Provisions have long been made for the taxation of any items which may occur in a bill of costs upon the scale most proper for such items. Thus under the common order to tax a solicitor's bill in Chancery, the taxing masters would heretofore have referred any Common Law costs which occurred in the bill to the taxing master of the Common Law Court if they had any doubts, and a bill for Parliamentary business would be taxed upon the scale of Parliamentary allowances: In re *Ludlow* v. *Kingdom*, 11 Beav. 401. But it is to be remembered that many bills for what would be generally termed Par-

Parliamentary business.

liamentary work are not taxed on the Parliamentary scale; as for instance applications to the Board of Trade for provisional orders under the Tramways Act, 1870: In re *Morley*, L. R. 20 Eq. 17.

In re *Ditton*, Ex parte *Woods*, 13 Ch. D. 321, Cotton, L.J., said that the Registrar in Bankruptcy, was entitled to deal with the taxation of a bill under the circumstances there narrated "taking the advice of the taxing master."

Country solicitor attending proceedings.

The taxing master appears to have uncontrolled discretion as to whether a country solicitor may attend proceedings in London, either in the place of, or as well as, his London agent: In re *Foster*, Ex parte *Dickens*, 8 Ch. D. 598; *Bell* v. *Aitkin*, L. R. 3 C. P. 320.

His costs were not allowed in *Clark* v. *Malpas*, 31 Beav. 554.

Court will not interfere to review taxation upon a matter of discretion. Instances of discretionary power of taxing master.

The Court cannot interfere with the discretion of the master in the absence of anything to show that he has exercised it improperly, either as to the amount of subsistence money for witnesses detained to give evidence, or the period for which the allowance is given. Ten shillings a day for eighteen months were allowed in *Potter* v. *Rankin*, L. R. 5 C. P. 518. See also *Culvert* v. *Scinde Ry. Co.*, 18 C. B. N. S. 306.

The Court will rarely interfere to review a taxation upon a matter of discretion only, *e.g.*, additional fees to counsel on additional papers laid before them: *Wakefield* v. *Brown*, L. R. 9 C. P. 410.

Commissioner.

The Court did not interfere with the master's discretion in allowing the expenses of sending a barrister to the Canaries as commissioner to examine witnesses: *Yglesias* v. *Royal Exchange Assurance Corporation*, L. R. 5 C. P. 141.

Number of

A master can allow two counsel in a reference in-

[illegible]in a reference. volving a large sum and a long inquiry, and can increase the usual allowance to an arbitrator, though he is a barrister: *Sinclair* v. *G. E. Ry. Co.*, L. R. 5 C. P. 135.

Masters taxing as personæ designatæ. Where masters tax as personæ designatæ, and not as officers of the Court, the Court has no jurisdiction to review their taxation: *Coke's claim, Wraithby's claim*, L. R. 1 Ex. 54.

Costs of inquiry before sheriff. Nor where costs of an inquiry before the sheriff are settled by a master under s. 52 of the Lands Clauses Consolidation Act, 1845: *Owen* v. *London and North Western Ry. Co*, L. R. 3 Q. B. 54.

CHAPTER XX.

COSTS PAYABLE BY A CLIENT.

THE greater part of the chapter upon Solicitor and Client Costs was taken up in the consideration of the few instances in which costs as between solicitor and client are ordered by the Court to be paid out of a fund or by the opposite side. It is proposed here to illustrate the class of allowances that will be made by the taxing master to the solicitor when they have to be paid by his own client. The regulations contained in the rules of the Supreme Court (Costs) against unnecessary proceedings have reference almost entirely to taxation between party and party; and therefore the old rules are still in force as to a taxation between solicitor and client. The then Master of the Rolls, Lord Langdale, remarks in *Stephens v. Lord Newborough*, 11 Beav. 403, that the rules as to the costs allowed to solicitors are on a most unsatisfactory footing. That very small remuneration is allowed for obtaining instructions for a bill which often causes trouble and expenditure, not at all commensurate with the allowance made. But that on the other hand they are allowed for poing that which they never do, namely for drawing the bill. The effect of this is, that the allowance for taking the instructions, which is inadequate, and the

Old rules still in force.

System of payment in litigious business.

allowance for drawing the bill, which the solicitor does not do, and which is therefore more than adequate, together make up an amount which sufficiently pays him for his entire work. Although this was said in 1848, and strictly applies only to what was then done, the principle is not changed in 1883. The same learned judge said In re *Catlin*, 18 Beav. 508, in 1854, that the items in a bill of costs, and the principles on which they are allowed and disallowed, frequently involve matters of great nicety as to which a judge's previous experience and practice have afforded him little means of coming to a satisfactory conclusion. It is therefore necessary that in his bill a solicitor should set out exactly what he has done upon taking each step; as although for some step he may be paid inadequately, for others he may be paid more than he might at first expect.

Solicitor's diary.

A direct authority for the keeping of a diary is afforded by the words of Brett, L.J., see Ex parte *Swinbanks*, In re *Shanks*, 11 Ch. D. 536. He says, It is the interest of a solicitor to keep a diary, as it is by means of it that he makes out his charges against his clients.

Method of making out bill.

From the remarks of Baggallay, L.J., In re *Snell*, 5 Ch. D. 832, it is to be gathered that the introduction of items into a bill of costs, not from any contemporaneous notes in equal detail, but from concise notes taken in short hand at the time, and which were sufficient to guide the solicitor, in making out subsequently his detailed bill, does not afford a satisfactory explanation of items when challenged.

Jessel, M.R., on solicitor's bill of costs.

Some of the remarks of Jessel, M.R., in the same case when before him upon the form of a solicitor's bill, will not be here out of place. He says that a bill should disclose matters in sufficient detail to enable a person ordinarily acquainted with the business to tax it. There is generally too much detail in a bill, but on the other hand a solicitor must not put a whole mass of business together, and charge a lump sum so that no one can tell whether a proper allowance can be made for it or not, or whether he has overcharged or not. Particulars and details must be furnished, as without them it cannot be ascertained whether proper charges have been made. An instance of an item which illustrates this is that given at length in the Appendix to this book. The Master of the Rolls says: "The item disallows itself so to speak; it is not possible to make out what it is worth." It is true that the item was afterwards allowed by the Court of Appeal, but the strictures of his Lordship upon the form of the item are none the less entitled to the most careful consideration.

Burden of proof of each item lies on solicitor.

The burden of proof relating to each item lies upon the solicitor, and supposing the only evidence tendered were the oath of the solicitor on the one side, and that of the client on the other, the item would be disallowed.

Accounts of solicitors acting as agents.

When a solicitor is a general agent, he is bound to keep regular accounts of his money transactions, but when he is only employed for particular transactions, as to raise money on a mortgage, or to discount a bill, the client is aware of the whole nature of the transaction and should know how much he receives. Where it was the ordinary course of dealing between the parties that the costs of the particular transactions should be deducted at the time, and the balance handed over, the onus is not thrown on the solicitor to show that his costs in respect of other matters have not been paid: In re *Lee*, a solicitor,

Ex parte *Neville*, L. R. 4 Ch. 46, judgment of Lord Hatherley.

Items that will stand taxation between solicitor and client.

Supposing then that the solicitor has proper materials at hand, out of which he can make his bill, the next subject to be glanced at is what general rule can be suggested as to the items that will stand taxation between solicitor and client. It may be premised that the higher and lower scale (Rules of Court, Costs, Order V.) applies primarily to party and party taxation; and also that the question of County Court costs has been already dealt with at p. 151. But see In re *Emanuel*, 9 Q. B. D. 408, as to the rate chargeable for work not in the County Court scale. The rules, therefore, which are now proposed will be of almost universal application, in the absence of any special agreement in a taxation as between solicitor and client. And first, it may be remarked, that in the rate of charges allowed on taxation between solicitor and client, and party and party, there is no difference; it is the items which will be allowed in the one case but not in the other that the difference lies. For example, as between solicitor and client anything that the client gave special instructions for after having been properly warned by his solicitor, as for the opinion of counsel upon his chance of success during the progress of a case, or for the employment of three counsel instead of two, he would have to pay himself, although he might have got costs against his adversary; but in the taxation between party and party nothing but the ordinary and necessary steps in an action (and consequently not any opinion as to the chances of success of a party during an action, and the costs, except in an extraordinary case, of more than two counsel) would be allowed. Again, no negotiations

Rate of charges between solicitor and client and party and party are the same.

Party and party costs.

Negotiations before action brought.

which may have been going on between the parties before an action was begun, can be charged for as between party and party except one letter which must have been actually written; but the costs of such negotiations if desired by the client may properly be charged for in a bill by a solicitor to his own client. It therefore follows that even when an action is won by a client and he gets the costs of it out of his adversary, he does not get all the charges and expenses from him that he has to pay to his own solicitor; and it is with such charges whether rightly chargeable as against him or not—but certainly not chargeable against the other side—that we have now to deal.

Professional work only can be charged for.

Proof of postage can be charged for.

Unnecessary proceedings.

Affidavit not entered in the order as read.

And, first, it is only for professional work that he can charge his client. Thus, he cannot charge for addressing letters and documents and sending them to the post; but he can charge if he has to prove the posting of a document as evidence of its being sent. James, L.J., in Ex parte *Dillon*, In re *Woods*, 13 Ch. D. 320. Again, he will not be allowed to charge his client with proceedings in an action which were wholly unnecessary, unless expressly authorised by the client to take them. See p. 184 and In re *Blyth and Fanshawe*, 31 W. R. 284. Thus, the costs of an affidavit filed in support of a motion, but not entered in the order as read, will not be allowed; nor a copy of the correspondence between the parties furnished to counsel as instructions for a bill, and partially inserted therein, because the costs allowed for instructions for the bill and for drawing it should have included this. But the costs of two counsel, even in an unopposed motion made by a trustee to pay money into Court have been allowed. For the Court may consider it necessary to have an explanation of things which may not have been distinctly brought under their notice in the papers before them. Cases which seem simple in themselves may be mixed up with other matters which, perhaps, require a great deal of consideration. When briefs have been given counsel with instructions that the prayer of the petition will not be resisted, if afterwards opposition is threatened supplemental briefs with fees may be delivered: *Stephens* v. *Lord Newborough*, 11 Beav. 413. A solicitor has no right to take special journeys, or to go to foreign countries, at the expense of his client without specific instructions; otherwise the client in giving a retainer would authorise his solicitor to travel all over the world at his expense. As a general rule he has no right even to make journeys in England. Country solicitors have no right to come to town to conduct a suit there, or a solicitor to go from town to the assizes. If a client, however, sanctions a journey, and adopts the benefit of it, it is otherwise. Such was the opinion of Jessel, M.R., In re *Snell*, a solicitor, 5 Ch. D. 828, as to journeys undertaken by solicitors, and it was not disapproved of by the Court of Appeal, (although his opinion on questions of fact was overruled in this case), who did not express an opinion upon the rule thus laid down by him. This, therefore, it is submitted, upon such high authority, is a correct statement of the law upon the subject of journeys undertaken by solicitors when authorised, and when not authorised, by the client. See also In re *Barring*, 20 Beav. 146.

Journeys.

Country solicitor attending bankruptcy appeal.

It was, however, held by Bacon, C.J., In re *Foster* Ex parte *Dickens*, 8 Ch. D. 598, that a country solicitor personally attending a bankruptcy appeal in London instead of employing an agent will, on taxation, be allowed the additional charges and expenses of so doing, as he is probably better acquainted with the subject-matter than the London agent. Even where on the trial of a cause in London the country as well as the London solicitor attends the rule that the costs of the attendance of the country solicitor will not be allowed on taxation is not inflexible: *Bell* v. *Aitkin*, L. J. 3 C. P. 320.

County and town solicitors attending.

See p. 159.

When an order to change solicitors has been obtained considerable acrimony is sometimes shown in taxing the first solicitor's bill, and items are not then often consented to, as they would, perhaps, be in other taxations. Some notice is, therefore, now taken of the various items which are frequently inserted in such a bill after the order to change where the solicitor to be changed is a country one. As the order to deliver a bill requires to be served personally, no service on the London agent of this order will be allowed for.

Order for change of solicitors.

On a reference to taxation of the new solicitor's bill, where a compromise as to that of the former solicitor has been effected by the second one, the taxing master has no jurisdiction to judge of the advantage, or the opposite, to the client of such compromise unless he has himself taken proceedings to impeach it; and, therefore, a sum of £2 2s. has been allowed for perusing a bill of 190 folios to the first solicitor as well as £6 10s. for making a copy of such bill.

Taxation after compromise of solicitor's bill.

Perusing first solicitor's bill.

Copy bill.

Where a receiver is appointed who is paid so much per cent., no sum will be allowed for drawing out a scheme of the property and the holdings of the tenants whose rents he is to receive, though such a scheme may be essential for the due performance of his duties.

Where receiver paid by per centage no scheme of property allowed.

No charge for notices of adjournments of proceed-

Notice of

adjournments of proceedings before chief clerks. ings or summonses before chief clerks is allowed, because the chief clerks have themselves made arrangements by which they adjourn the proceedings or summonses, from time to time, and require all parties to take notice of such adjournments.

Fees of certificate. Only one fee of 6*s.* 8*d.* is allowed for attending for and to file a certificate of taxation, and not 6*s.* 8*d.* to bespeak the same and 6*s.* 8*d.* for attending filing the same.

Procuring execution of lease by tenant. Supposing a client to be liable to a solicitor for the costs of perusing and procuring the execution of a lease by a tenant, say two guineas, although the tenant is primarily liable, if the amount has not been paid, when the order to tax is made this charge is properly included in the client's bill.

Costs when papers delivered over. When a client requires that his papers shall be delivered over, he must pay for the affidavits and schedule of papers, though not for a list of the title deeds and of the parties named therein; as the latter is done for the use and security of the solicitor and not of the client.

Consultation with counsel when no fee for conference is charged. Where no fee is paid to counsel on a consultation, and the solicitor merely goes to counsel's chambers to confer on some small matter during the progress of a suit for which counsel does not charge a conference fee, though the time of the solicitor is taken up he cannot charge for such attendance.

Fee for instructions for brief. The fee for instructions for brief is payable to him who is the solicitor at the time of joinder of issue, not to the former solicitor. Where affidavits in another matter are necessary evidence in a cause, a list of the subjects, and a charge for perusing them may be made.

Bill cannot be altered A solicitor cannot make, nor has a taxing master any jurisdiction to permit any alteration or amendment to be made in a delivered bill, except by consent: In re *Catlin*, 18 Beav. 520. Great care should therefore be taken in drawing the bill in the first instance, as taxation cannot be avoided by amending it after delivery: In re *Heather*, L. R. 5 Ch. 694, where a bill was delivered, objected to, and returned with suggested alterations, some of which were acquiesced in. And though an amended bill was then delivered, taxation of the original bill was ordered first by the Master of the Rolls and afterwards by the Court of Appeal. But where a solicitor has delivered a second bill of costs before the first is taxed, upon the taxation of the first alone the order for delivery over of papers will not be made: Ex parte *Jarman*, 5 Ch. D. 840.

after delivery. See p. 142.

Second bill

If difficulties arise on taxation, and it seems to the taxing officer desirable to have the solicitor cross-examined on an affidavit made by him in support of his bill under the common order, he can order this to be done. And it is the duty of the examiners to take such examination: In re *Flux Argles and Rawlins*, 44 L. J. Ch. 375.

Taxing master may order solicitor to be cross-examined.

The taxing master has himself full power to decide questions as to retainer: In re *Bracey*, 8 Beav. 266; and as to the necessity for the institution of legal proceedings: Re *Atkinson*, 26 Beav. 151; and he can disallow items for work that is useless: Re *Burchall*, 21 L. J. Ch. 236.

Taxing master can decide questions of retainer. Uselessness of work done.

They also have regard to agreements as to the amount of costs to be paid by the client, as, for instance, costs out of pocket, and bills in pursuance of such agreement can be taxed: In re *Ransom*, 18 Beav. 220.

Agreements.

They can allow interest on disbursements (33 & 34 Vict. c. 28, s. 16), and also take an account of all

Interest.

moneys of the clients which have come to the hands of the solicitor, in his capacity of solicitor, and which could be applied in payment of his bill. And he may be ordered to pay interest upon any such moneys improperly retained; but the master has no power to take an account of pecuniary matters between the parties which are quite foreign to the bill of costs: *Jones* v. *James*, 1 Beav. 307.

Taxation upon application of third parties. Sec. 38.

Section 38 of the Solicitors Act, 1843, which is sometimes referred to as the third party clause, enacts that bills may be taxed upon the application of third parties who, though not the parties chargeable, are liable to pay, or who have paid the bills, refers only to costs as between solicitor and client: See In re *Cowdell*, W. N. 18, 1883. This section applies, therefore, to anyone who has guaranteed the client's costs; but not to the opposite party in an action who has to pay them through being beaten. It can, therefore, apply only to taxation as between solicitor and client: In re *Heritage*, Ex parte *Docker*, 3 Q. B. D. 729. But yet in the case of a solicitor who has acted for a trustee whose bill of costs is being taxed by one of the cestuis que trustent, the taxation under section 38 is not between solicitor and client. The solicitor should tell the trustee if anything cannot be charged against the trust estate. The principle upon which such a taxation is conducted is, whether the things charged are proper and necessary for the administration of the estate: Lord Romilly, In re *Brown*, L. R. 4 Eq. 466.

Solicitor acting for trustee.

Benefit of agreements between solicitor and client.

The benefit of any agreement made between the party chargeable and the solicitor passes to the persons who have obtained under the third party clause the usual order to tax: In re *Taylor*, 18 Beav. 169. This was a case in which persons interested in the equity of redemption taxed a solicitor's bill in respect of his employment as solicitor by his clients, the mortgagees. See also In re *Newman*, L. R. 2 Ch. 707. And in making an order for taxation under this section (s. 38), it is discretionary with the Court whether or not to order also the delivery up of papers: Ex parte *Jarman*, 4 Ch. D. 835.

Delivery up of papers.

When an order for taxation which is not obtained as of course is made under section 39 by a party interested in a property out of which the trustees or executors have paid or are intending to pay a bill, such taxation is taken between solicitor and client; nothing, notwithstanding, being able to be charged to the estate by the solicitor which was not necessary for its administration; and the party interested having the benefit of any arrangement entered into by the trustees or executors and the solicitor. For the words of Lord Langdale, In re *Taylor*, quoted above, apply as much to a taxation under section 39 as under section 38.

Order for taxation obtained under sec. 39.

The words, "party interested," mean a party interested under the trust-deed, will or intestacy, and the trustee must be really chargeable with the bill, and is only liable on his own retainer; except in the case of an executor, who stands in the place of his testator. An assignee does not come within the section.

"Party interested."

A trustee in bankruptcy is not a trustee for a bankrupt; so, although he may have obtained his discharge and become entitled to the surplus of his estate, all the creditors having been paid in full, he is not entitled under this section (s. 39) to obtain the taxation of a bill of costs paid by the trustee in bankruptcy: In re *Leadbitter*, 10 Ch. D. 388.

Not trustee in bankruptcy.

A trustee must not derive any personal advantage from the employment of a solicitor; and if he acts

Trustee acting as solicitor.

himself as a solicitor, in the absence of an express proviso to that effect enabling him in the trust-deed, he can only charge money out of pocket; he can make no profits whatever out of the employment. Still less can he obtain advantage, whether in the shape of a fixed sum or a share in the profits, from the employment of another person as such solicitor: In re *Taylor*, 18 Beav. 172. See also *Thomas* v. *Palin*, 21 Ch. D. 365.

See also Chap. xi.

Special circumstances must be shown when a bill has been taxed and settled for it to be re-taxed (s. 40).

Client out of the jurisdiction desiring taxation.

Where a client who desires the taxation of a solicitor's bill is out of the jurisdiction, he must deposit a proper sum of money as security before his application can be heard. The undertaking of his new solicitor to pay them is not sufficient: In re *Norman*, 11 Beav. 402.

CHAPTER XXI.

TAXATION AFTER TWELVE MONTHS.

PAYING a solicitor's bill under protest means nothing more than that the party paying gives notice that he will avail himself of every circumstance in the case to enable himself afterwards to upset the transaction. This he could have done just as well without any protest. Another idea, wholly without foundation, is that if when a bill is paid an intimation is given that the bill will be taxed, this is sufficient to obtain an order for taxation: In re *Harrison*, 10 Beav. 59. After payment, special circumstances must be proved by the client, as pressure and overcharges, to get taxation. If the overcharges evidence fraud, very slight circumstances will suffice. In re *Harding*, 10 Beav. 250. Overcharge alone is not sufficient to obtain taxation after payment; but in other things, as, for instance, pressure, it is. See In re *Durnford*, Sol. J., p. 277, Feb. 24, 1883.

Paying bill under protest.

To get taxation after payment of bill.

In case of fraud.

Overcharge alone is not sufficient.

The pressure and difficulty under which the client labours when the bill is paid must be such that he could not delay the payment, even though he pays it under protest at the time: In re *Stirke*, 11 Beav. 304. Where there was no pressure in the case of a woman cestui que trust, and the solicitor was entitled by agreement to charge, taxation after payment within

Pressure overcharge.

Woman cestui que trust.

twelve months was refused: In re *Wyche*, 11 Beav. 209.

Statutory provision for taxation after twelve months. Special circumstances.

The method of obtaining an order for taxation in the ordinary way having been already considered, it is proposed here to deal with the statutory provisions as to the taxation of the bill after twelve months from its delivery have elapsed. The rule is that there shall be no taxation of a solicitor's bill after twelve months have elapsed from the time of its delivery, except under special circumstances: 6 & 7 Vict. c. 73, s. 37. What special circumstances have caused the taxation of a bill, after such twelve months have elapsed, will here be considered.

Matters of objection appearing on the face of the bill

The old idea was that the bill could only be referred after such twelve months on the ground of new matter having come to the knowledge of the party chargeable. It was held, however, In re *Robinson*, L. R. 3 Ex. 4, that the special circumstances required by the section might be matters of objection appearing on the face of the bill, and that an unusual charge of a large amount, requiring explanation to justify it, was sufficient ground for referring the bill to taxation, even after the expiration of the twelve months.

Payment under undue influence. Bill re-opened after two years.

When a client pays a solicitor's bill under undue influence and without sufficient information, and much of the business charged for was unnecessary and improper, the lapse of nearly two years, although there is no actual proof of overcharge, is not fatal to an order that the matter be re-opened and the bill taxed. In this case the client was an old lady, and the bills of costs were arranged: *Watson* v. *Rodwell*, 11 Ch. D. 150. But evidence of the fact of the relation of solicitor and client existing is not alone sufficient to justify an order for taxation after the twelve months: In re *Elmslie and Co.*, Ex parte *Tower Subway Co.*, L. R. 16 Eq. 326.

Where any one ignorant of the practice as to law charges is induced to enter into an unfair bargain, the agreement, notwithstanding the lapse of the twelve months, may be reviewed.

Who has power to re-open bill of costs.

The privilege of reopening a solicitor's account is, under section 37, confined to the person who was himself liable to have an action brought against him for costs; and it does not apply to the case of a party in an action who, if defeated, must pay the costs; for in that case the costs are taxed as between party and party, and upon a different footing; and section 38 enacts that this privilege shall apply in the case of persons who are in the same position as solicitor and client, and who are to have the same rights as the client himself has. For example, anyone who has guaranteed the client's costs is entitled to be in no worse position than he is in: Cockburn, C.J., In re *Heritage*, Ex parte *Docker*, 3 Q. B. D. 729.

Where there is a series of bills.

Where there is a series of bills it will depend upon the circumstances of the case (as, for instance, where a letter corrects the earlier bills) whether they are treated as one entire bill: In re *Cartwright*, L. R. 16 Eq. 469. Where this was so, taxation of the whole was directed, although most of the bills had been delivered more than twelve months before the application. In re *Hall* v. *Barker*, 9 Ch. D. 538, the opposite was the order of the Court of Appeal. In that case solicitors had been retained to act for a trustee in bankruptcy, and also to protect the interests of a creditor, who afterwards, by arrangement, took over the estate. They delivered a bill up to a certain date, saying that there were some more items, and afterwards delivered a second bill for subsequent costs. Held that the second bill only could be taxed.

Application by official liquidator.

As on obtaining the order for taxation it is necessary to undertake to pay the amount (In re *Elmslie and Co.*, L. R. 9 Eq. 72) which shall be found due, which the official liquidator of a company in liquidation may not be able to do for some time, it does not matter in such a case that the twelve months have elapsed: In re *Marseilles Extension Railway and Land Co.*, Ex parte *Evans*, L. R. 11 Eq. 154, Malins, V.-C.

Solicitor being executor paying himself out of assets.

Upon the principle that every accounting party must vouch his items of discharge, if a solicitor, being one of the executors of a testator, pays himself out of the assets for work done for the testator, when under the decree in an administration action the accounts are brought in, the taxing master may be directed to state whether any items objected to were fair and proper to be allowed; but an order for taxation cannot be made. This was done twenty-six years after the death of the testator in *Allen* v. *Jarvis*, L. R. 4 Ch. 616.

Bill taxed on parliamentary scale.

Bills taxed on the Parliamentary scale should be taxed not later than six months after the committee's report, and not until one month after a bill of such costs is delivered to the party chargeable: *Williams* v. *Swansea Canal Navigation Co.*, L. R. 3 Ex. 158.

Taxation in bankruptcy.

In bankruptcy the power of the registrars to tax costs is independent of the Solicitors Act of 1842, and a bill of costs may, therefore, be taxed there without any special order, although twelve months have elapsed since its delivery: Ex parte *Blair*, In re *Mackie*, L. R. 5 Ch. 482.

CHAPTER XXII.

PARTY AND PARTY COSTS.

THE costs chargeable under a taxation as between party and party are all that are necessary to enable the adverse party to conduct the litigation, and no more. Any charges merely for conducting litigation more conveniently may be called luxuries, and must be paid by the party incurring them.

Thus in a suit to restrain the infringement of a patent, in which the defendant had set up several cases as anticipations, the costs of the drawing of exhibits explanatory of the exhibits to the defendant's affidavits to affix to counsel's briefs are disallowed. Example of unnecessary expenses.

Charges for attendance of the solicitor's clerk on the cross-examination of witnesses before the examiner, though he is stated to have been required on account of the great number of exhibits and the constant necessity to have some one to hand them up to counsel, is not allowed in addition to the costs of attendance of the solicitor. Five guineas is the ordinary counsel's fee per diem for the cross-examination of witnesses, but in a heavy case more may be allowed; seven guineas a day may be allowed when there are scientific witnesses. Counsel's fees for cross-examination.

All these statements are made upon the authority of *Smith* v. *Buller*, L. R. 19 Eq. 473, V.-C. Malins, which is also an authority that two counsel are ordinarily to be employed. It gives the rate also as to the allowance of refreshers after a case has lasted two days, even where the evidence is adduced by affidavit. Where a reasonable and prudent man, however, would have employed three counsel, the costs will be allowed between party and party: *Kirkwood* v. *Webster*, 9 Ch. D. 229. In this case there were eight distinct charges of fraud and misrepresentation made by the plaintiff against the defendant. No less than three contracts relating to no less than five patents were in question, and other patents entered into the history of the case. One counsel only is allowed on a reference unless the master, in his absolute discretion, allows the costs of two in a heavy case: *Sinclair* v. *Great Eastern Ry. Co.*, 5 C. P. 135. At the trial of a writ of enquiry to assess damages in an action of negligence arising out of a railway accident, two counsel may be allowed by the master. Also special jury fees to a "good" jury: *Vines* v. *London, Brighton and South Coast Ry. Co.*; *Frost* v. *The same*, L. R. 5 Ex. 201. It is a question in the discretion of the taxing master whether, on an application by the defendants that part of an affidavit might be struck out, copies of the pleadings, three for the use of the Court of Appeal and one for the use of counsel, shall be allowed or not: *Warner* v. *Mosses*, 19 Ch. D. 73. In a taxation between party and party, a shorthand writer's charges and copies of shorthand writer's notes are not allowed without a special direction from the judge at the time of the trial, before the judgment is drawn up, even though there is an agreement between the solicitors of the plaintiff and the defendant that a shorthand writer shall be employed at their

When costs of three counsel allowed.

Costs of counsel in a reference.

On trial of a writ of enquiry.

Special jury fees.

Copies of pleadings.

Shorthand writers.

joint expense: *Ashworth* v. *Outram*, 9 Ch. D. 486 (C.A.). This will be sanctioned only in extraordinary and exceptional cases: Jessel, M.R., in *Earl de la Warr* v. *Miles*, 19 Ch. D. 82; *Singer Manufacturing Co.* v. *Loog*, 31 W. R. 392.

Costs of inspection of books by an accountant.

In a reference it was ordered that a plaintiff, by an accountant to be named by the arbitrator, should inspect defendant's books. The accountant did so, and gave evidence before the arbitrator. Though the award was made in his favour, with the costs of the action, reference, and award, the plaintiff was held not entitled to the costs of the preliminary examination of the books by the accountant: *Nolan* v. *Copeman*, L. R. 8 Q. B. 84. As to the scale of payments of accountants, see *Meynott* v. *Meynott*, 33 Beav. 590.

Scale of payment of accountants.

Costs of appeal from master.

In the absence of an express order of a judge in chambers, to whom there is an appeal from a master's decision as to the costs of such appeal, the plaintiff is not entitled to them, though successful: *Mann* v. *Harbord*, L. R. 5 Ex. 17.

Interest on disbursements.

A taxing master cannot allow interest on disbursements, except in a taxation between solicitor and client; and 33 & 34 Vict. c. 28, s. 17, which gives him that power, does not even apply to a taxation of costs to be paid, as between solicitor and client, out of a fund in court belonging wholly or partly to other persons than the client: *Hartland* v. *Murrell*, L. R. 16 Eq. 285.

Model in patent case.

The expense of having a model made in a patent case will be allowed: V.-C. Bacon, in *Batley* v. *Kynock*, L. R. 20 Eq. 635, where he also states the rule that exists in the Equity Courts as to allowances by taxing masters. He says the Equity Courts require the taxing master to conform to the law of the Court, but leave to him a wide discretion as to

Rule as to discretion of taxing masters in equity.

details, reserving nevertheless the right and duty of deciding upon any question of principle.

Expenses of witnesses qualifying themselves for examination.

There can be no doubt that now the expenses of witnesses qualifying themselves for examination may be allowed, if they were necessary, under rule 8. Special allowances and general provisions, Rules of the Supreme Court—Costs. In the reference of an action for the recovery of some houses by reason of breach of covenant to repair, three surveyors were called as witnesses for the plaintiff who had been instructed by him to survey the houses and report upon their condition. It appeared that the surveys and reports were necessary for the proper conduct of his case. Judgment having been obtained, with costs, by the plaintiff, the fees paid to the surveyors were ordered to be taxed: *Mackley* v. *Chillingworth*, 2 C. P. D. 273. In *Churton* v. *Frewen*, 15 W. R. 559, the expenses of an antiquarian in deciphering and translating documents were allowed by Malins, V.-C. In an action where the parties are poor and the value of the property in dispute is small, high fees paid to surveyors and heavy charges for plans and reports should be disallowed; but, nevertheless, very considerable costs in respect of surveys and reports may sometimes be allowed if the nature of the action renders it necessary to have incurred them: Grove, J., in *Mackley* v. *Chillingworth*, 2 C. P. D. 280; Lindley, J., in the same case remarking that the rule which has been long laid down in the Equity Courts has been that the wrong-doers shall bear all the costs necessarily incurred by the person injured in getting redress. He said, further, that in his opinion, in proper cases even the cost of obtaining general knowledge and of reading up books might be allowed as between party and party. The costs of an

Costs of surveys and reports.

Rule.

antiquary making translations of ancient records were allowed in *Duke of Beaufort* v. *Earl of Ashburnham*, 32 L. J. C. P. 97. Re-searches

The reasonable expenses of witnesses qualifying themselves to give evidence is allowed in the charge—Instructions for Brief; but whether a charge may be made for correcting and revising the proofs of proceedings, as well as the printing of evidence for the Court of Appeal, was not decided in *Turnbull* v. *Janson*, 3 C. P. D. 271, Lindley and Lopes, JJ. **What instructions for brief comprises.**

The expense of bringing the defendant's witnesses to London to be cross-examined in court, though counsel in the exercise of their discretion did not think fit to cross-examine them, was allowed upon a decree in favour of the plaintiff with costs: *Clark* v. *Malpas*, 31 Beav. 554. This would not have been allowed had no notice for cross-examination been given.

A professional witness is entitled to his expenses on the scale allowed to persons of his profession, although he is not called to give professional evidence: *Parkinson* v. *Atkinson*, 31 L. J. C. P. 199. This is the case also before a special examiner. An auctioneer would be entitled to £1 1s. a day for his loss of time, and his travelling expenses, if any, first-class from his residence to the place of his examination and back again. And though sworn he may refuse to answer until paid these amounts: In re *Working Men's Mutual Society*, 21 Ch. D. 831. **Costs of professional witness.**

The costs of preparing interrogatories which were not used, owing to admissions being put in, were allowed as between party and party, as well as the costs of settling an affidavit, which was an echo of the bill by counsel: *Davies* v. *Marshall*, 1 De Gex & S. 564. **Costs of interrogatories not used.**

Interpreter.

The expense of employing an interpreter to assist the defendant (a foreigner) in preparing instructions for his answer, but not the tavern or travelling expenses of one specially brought to the country, can be allowed in the discretion of the taxing master between party and party: *Earl of Shrewsbury* v. *Trappes*, 31 L. J. Ch. 680.

In an action against lessees of a colliery two breaches of covenant were assigned: (1) Non-payment of a sleeping rent; (2) not properly working the mine. Judgment having gone by default for the plaintiffs, a writ of enquiry issued. The jury found that the plaintiffs had sustained £50 damages; but nothing in respect of not properly working the mine. The master rightly allowed the plaintiffs the full costs of witnesses summoned to prove default in properly working the mine: *Dod* v. *Evans*, 15 C. B. N. S. 621.

Subsistence-money to plaintiff.

In an action by an engineer against an Indian railway company for wrongful dismissal without notice, a verdict was taken by consent for £200, being one quarter's salary, and £150, plaintiff's passage-money to England. On taxation plaintiff was allowed subsistence-money during his stay in England waiting for the trial (one and a half years), at the rate of £300 a year, and £150 for his passage out. It appears that the company justified plaintiff's dismissal, on the ground of alleged improper conduct; and that the trial had been delayed twelve months through the company having sent a commission to examine witnesses at Lahore, the execution of which had been unnecessarily delayed, and that the plaintiff was going back to India, where he had a wife and family: *Calvert* v. *Scinde Ry. Co.*, 18 C. B. N. S. 306.

Allowance

The sum allowed for instructions on brief, which

in special cases, as, for instance, in a matter requiring the assistance of a scientific person, may be considerable, covers attendances on witnesses to take their proofs, and no special charge can be made for the execution of this duty, however onerous it may have been.

for instructions on brief, see p. 181.

At first sight this may perhaps appear to be a hard rule; but the sum allowed for such instructions is in a proper case sufficiently liberal. In order to get any costs allowed, which do not actually appear by the proceedings in the action, an affidavit of increase, as it is called, has to be made which verifies them; for the successful party being only entitled to costs as an indemnity, can only claim for such as he has actually paid. And although unnecessary costs (as of drawing briefs before notice of trial, or of witnesses whose evidence is inadmissible) are disallowed, yet a witness' expenses may be allowed, though he were not called, if there were reasonable grounds for believing that he would be wanted. In short, any recognised precaution that a reasonable man would take for his own protection his adversary is chargeable with; but unusual precautions, and, above all, unnecessary ones, he will have to pay for himself.

Affidavit of increase.

Expenses of witnesses not called.

It is a hard thing that in an ordinary action the successful party should have to pay his solicitor any charges in respect of it, and yet in the present state of things he must expect to do so, unless he makes an express agreement with him that he will not be held responsible for them. Such an express agreement, of course, overrides any ordinary rules of solicitor and client taxation. Indeed, in *Jennings* v. *Johnson*, L. R. 8 C. P. 425, it was held that an agreement made by a solicitor with his client to

Agreement by solicitor not to charge solicitor and client costs.

Jennings v. *Johnson*.

charge him nothing if he lost an action, and to take nothing for costs out of any money that might be awarded to him in such action, need not even be in writing, for that section 4 of the Solicitors Act, 1870, which says that agreements as to charges shall be in writing, has only reference to charges in excess of those which are allowed on taxation.

The wisest course for the solicitor is, before commencing an action, to tell his client about these charges, which laymen unaccustomed to litigation do not generally know of; as it often gives great dissatisfaction to a litigant, who has won his case, to have to make payments which he did not expect to have to make, and for which he does not understand the reason of his liability.

Solicitor must protect client against expenses.

Rule.

Indeed, with reference to any expenses not altogether usual that a solicitor incurs for a client, the rule is not only that the client must authorise them, but must do so after having been informed by his solicitor that they will not in any event in all probability be allowed in the taxation between party and party. Whether the solicitor has or has not informed his client of this in each case is the test which the taxing master should apply to each item in a taxation between solicitor and client; for the fact of an item having been merely authorised by the client is not sufficient to prevent its being struck out. It is, in fact, the duty of the solicitor to protect his client against unnecessary expense, as well as to point out to him in every case what charges will fall upon him, even though successful in the action. See Smith's Chancery Practice, vol. i., 7th ed., p. 1084, quoted with approval by Lindley, L.J., In re *Blyth and Fanshawe*, 31 W. R. 284. Reported also 10 Q. B. D. 207. See also the judgment of Baggallay,

L.J., in the same case. The items there objected to were the expenses of shorthand notes and experts. And see In re *Chapman*, 10 Q. B. D. 57 and 58.

Shorthand notes and experts.

As to the principles upon which parties appearing in chambers are entitled to costs, see the observations of Jessel, M.R., in *Sharp* v. *Lush*, 10 Ch. D. 473. See also *Day* v. *Batty*, 21 Ch. D. 830.

Whether a taxation is to be conducted as between party and party or between solicitor and client can hardly ever prove a subject of contention. There is, however, sometimes a difficulty in deciding whether in a taxation between party and party costs should be allowed on the higher or lower scale. Order VI., r. 1 (Rules of the Supreme Court—Costs), provides to what actions the higher scale applies. See *Rogers* v. *Jones*, 7 Ch. D. 345, and In re *Sandeman*, 7 Ch. D. 176. R. 3 gives a judge power to allow costs in whole or in part on the higher scale, but he cannot delegate this power to a master: *Corticene Floor Company* v. *Tull*, 27 W. R. 373.

Higher or lower scale.

Judge has discretion as to scale.

If a judge exercises the discretion given him under this rule, his decision is nevertheless subject to appeal. Costs on the higher scale should not be allowed in actions other than those in which they are given by Order VI., r. 1 (Costs), unless some special cause is shown, as expenditure of time and skill by the solicitor to an extent which would entitle him to higher remuneration; and it would appear that in an action which is settled they should not be allowed, nor simply because fraud is alleged: In re *Terrell*, 31 W. R. 209. Reported also, 22 Ch. D. 473. The Rules of the Supreme Court (Costs) apply both to chancery or common law actions, and there are not two separate systems as to scales of costs. There are many cases which can be brought

Appeal.

Special cause.

in the Chancery or Common Law Courts, and there was no intention on the part of the framers of the rules that the higher scale should always be given when an action is brought in the Chancery Division. A special cause must be shown in each case: Bowen, L.J., In re *Terrell.*

Bowen, L.J., In re *Terrell.*

It is a mistake to suppose that only charges can be allowed between solicitor and client which can be allowed between party and party, and that that which is necessarily reasonable in one case must be the limit of what is reasonable in the other.

What is reasonable between party and party must be reasonable between solicitor and client, but the converse is not true: In re *Blyth and Fanshawe*, 10 Q. B. D. 212.

CHAPTER XXIII.

COSTS OUT OF A FUND.

It is a great matter whether costs are ordered to be paid out of an existing fund, or whether the order is made simply against an individual who may not be able to pay.

It is therefore proposed in this chapter to consider upon what principles a particular fund can be made liable for solicitor's costs. The broad rule as to costs in an ordinary litigation is that the losing party pays them, and so in the case of appeals the successful party gets his costs: Memorandum, 1 Ch. D. 41. This is the course of justice in every Court; but the custom that the costs perhaps of various parties should be paid out of a particular fund had arisen in the Chancery Courts, where there were various parties to a suit who had been necessarily brought before the Court for the purpose of the administration of a fund which the Court had under its control. Such parties, if properly brought there, were given their costs out of the fund in Court, because no other party had done them a wrong, as a penalty for which he could be made to pay their costs; and, indeed, their presence there was owing to the existence of the fund, and it was for its administration that they were present, and there-

Costs follow the event.

Chancery practice administration.

Solicitor's lien.

fore the fund had to pay their costs. Upon such a fund the solicitor has a lien independently of the statute 23 & 24 Vict. c. 127, s. 28, generally called the Solicitors Act, 1860; and since that Act the Court has also the statutory power of declaring a solicitor entitled to a charge upon any property which can be considered as having been recovered or preserved in an action. The question of the lien which the solicitor has at common law, and which is, of course, a particular lien, is considered more fully in the chapter on Lien; and the statutory lien, which can only be enforced by an order of the Court, under the head of Charging Orders; but in this chapter the general principles under which a fund in court can be got at for payment of costs, and the kind and extent of costs allowed, is glanced at in a general way.

Statutory lien.

Solicitor paid directly out of the estate.

The rule of the Court always has been to allow the solicitor to be paid directly out of the estate, instead of making him sue his client and then allowing the client to come and ask to be indemnified and paid out of the fund. Such payment of costs out of the estate is discretionary, although it has been the custom of the Court to give trustees their costs out of an estate, when such costs have been properly incurred: 19 Ch. D. 153, Ex parte *Wainwright*, In re *Wainwright*, per Jessel, M.R. Under Order LV., which put costs in the discretion of the Court, there was a reservation, that nothing should deprive a trustee, mortgagee, or other person of any right to costs out of a particular fund to which he would be entitled according to the rules theretofore acted upon in Courts of Equity. If, however, they appeal unnecessarily or do anything they ought not, they have to bear their own costs: Ex parte *Russell*, In re *Butterworth*, 19 Ch. D. 588.

Order LV.

Unnecessary proceedings by trustees and others.

But where in the County Court a decision is in favour of a person, and in the next Court above it is not, he cannot be blamed for going to the Appeal Court: Jessel, M.R., 19 Ch. D. 152. Ex parte *Wainwright,* In re *Wainwright.* And a trustee in bankruptcy should not be deprived of his costs for purchasing the estate of the bankrupt if he explains to the creditors that he is about to buy it. It is necessary that a person asking for his costs out of an estate should have done no injury to the estate by his conduct. He must have acted properly towards those to whom the fund belongs, and from whom, in fact, he is seeking payment. Thus the solicitor to a trustee in bankruptcy must not look exclusively to the interests of his client, and forget that other people have rights and interests.

Person asking for costs out of an estate must have acted fairly towards the estate.

In Ex parte *Harper,* In re *Pooley,* Ch. D. 685, the solicitor to the trustee was refused his costs, as was also the trustee, out of the bankrupt's estate, because he had been a party to that common abuse of the bankrupt law, viz., the purchasing of debts due by the bankrupt in order to procure the appointment of a trustee favourable to the bankrupt. It cannot be too strongly urged or too clearly kept in view that the right of a solicitor to costs out of an estate is simply that of his client, and that he has no independent right. And, further, that this right will be lost if either he or his client have been guilty of misconduct.

Ex parte *Harper,* In re *Pooley.*

Misconduct is generally acting with bad faith, and where there is no bad faith it would seem that where there is a fund the feeling of the Court is that the solicitors in an action should be paid if possible. The case of Ex parte *Wainwright,* In re *Wainwright,* 19 Ch. D. 140, is a good example of this. There the Court was obliged to arrive at the con-

Ex parte *Wainwright,* In re *Wainwright.*

clusion that the trustee in bankruptcy was entitled to seize the after-acquired property of the debtor, without taking into account the hardship it felt it to be upon him; yet, although regard could not be had to that hardship in relation to the law of the case, it could as to the costs. The order was that the costs of the losing party should be paid out of the estate. The Master of the Rolls in his judgment said: "Here the trustee ruins this man, and probably deprives him and his new creditors of what they ought to have. In that position of matters he employs a solicitor to defend him. Is not that solicitor to be paid? Is it not a case in which a solicitor should be allowed to defend him, and should not go without payment for so doing? Having an estate to be administered, ought we not to make provision for the payment of the solicitor who has taken the opinion of the Courts?"

Property recovered or preserved.

Again, the Courts will give a liberal construction to the words "property recovered or preserved" in making an order under the 28th section of the Solicitors Act, 1860. In *Emden* v. *Carte*, 19 Ch. D. 311, it was held by the Court of Appeal that money paid into court by the defendant as black mail, to get rid of the trouble and expense of an action, was properly recovered or preserved. In that case an uncertificated bankrupt had brought an action to recover money for work done prior to the bankruptcy and subsequent to it, but before he was discharged; and a sum was paid into court by the defendant to get rid of the action. When the trustee heard of this he got the conduct of the proceedings. The bankrupt plaintiff tried to get the sum so paid into court out, and through the assistance of his

Emden v. *Carte.*

solicitor resisted the attempts of the trustee to get hold of the fund. The order made by the Court of Appeal was that the solicitor to the bankrupt was entitled to a charging order upon the fund up to the point where the trustee intervened. If it had not been for him the money would not have been in court, and the trustee could not have got hold of it. But the solicitor had no business to oppose the claim of the trustee to the fund when that claim was advanced, and therefore directly he did so his lien on the fund ceased.

The principle upon which this order was made was that the trustee had taken the benefit of the action by adopting it, and therefore that he ought to pay the costs of the solicitor who had instituted it and brought it to a point where it was worth adopting. Principle of *Emden v. Carte.*

Where property is recovered in an action, and a compromise made with reference to it by the parties, the solicitor is entitled to a first charge upon the money paid by way of compromise: *Twynam v. Porter*, L. R. 11 Eq. 181. But property must have been recovered and fraudulently paid over by the defendant to the plaintiff to make the defendant personally liable to the plaintiff's solicitor for costs. Compromise.

When an action was brought by a man of straw, and a verdict obtained for £25, the obtaining of which had rendered him liable to his solicitor for £100 costs, he was not prohibited from compromising with the defendant for £10, after a rule nisi for a new trial had been obtained by the defendant. Notice had been given by the plaintiff's solicitor to the defendant's solicitor of his claim, and the settlement was arrived at between the parties behind the backs of their respective solicitors: Ex parte *Morrison*, L. R. 4 Q. B. 158. Ex parte *Morrison.*

Actions between partners.

With regard to the costs in actions between partners for taking the accounts, they are like all other costs of necessary administration, and must come out of the partnership assets. If, however, an action for dissolution of partnership is caused by the misconduct of a partner; as, for instance, where a partner whose duty it is to keep accounts has neglected to do so; that partner has to pay so much of the costs as are occasioned by his misconduct. And there is no difference between the costs of the action for taking the accounts prior to the trial and the subsequent costs: *Hamer* v. *Giles, Giles* v. *Hamer*, 11 Ch. D. 945. In administration actions, where letters of administration are revoked, the administrator will not get his costs of an administration suit instituted by him with knowledge that another person claimed to administer: *Houseman* v. *Houseman*, 1 Ch. D. 535.

Misconduct of partner.

Administration action when letters of administration revoked.

Creditors' actions.

When an estate turns out to be insufficient to pay debts, the ordinary rule is that a creditor who brings an action on behalf of himself and all others the creditors of the deceased is entitled to his costs as between solicitor and client. This rule also applies to the case of a creditor who obtains the conduct of an action originally commenced by a legatee or next of kin. In re *Richardson, Richardson* v. *Richardson*, 14 Ch. D. 611. But when an estate sought to be made liable for costs was, to the knowledge of the solicitor improperly bringing or defending an action, insufficient in all probability to pay them, he may even himself be made to pay costs: *Baker* v. *Loader*, L. R. 16 Eq. 50.

Costs of incumbrancers.

With regard to the costs of incumbrancers, which afford one of the exceptions to the rule that the losers in a suit pay the costs of it, there is a well-known rule which was alluded to by the Master of the Rolls in the very late case of *Johnstone* v. *Cox*, 19 Ch. D. 19. It is that the costs of incumbrancers are allowed to be added to their securities, if any difficult questions arise as to the priority of incumbrances or such like things; and unless there has been something vexatious or something unusual in an incumbrancer's conduct, he gets them as of course if the fund is sufficient to pay them. This is all that could be desired, unless the incumbrancer has taken a security on an insufficient fund, in which case his solicitor will only have his remedy against his own client.

When they may be added to their securities.

And although an estate may be held liable for costs, and an order made that a party have his costs out of it, it may yet be that the estate is not sufficient to pay them. This is particularly to be noticed when the costs of several parties are ordered to be paid out of the estate. The question of priorities therefore is most material in such a case. As a rule, in bankruptcy the trustees' costs are entitled to priority, as was pointed out by Jessel, M.R., in Ex parte *Wainwright*, In re *Wainwright*, 19 Ch. D. p. 153, in which case the appeal was dismissed; but both parties were given their costs out of the estate all through, both in the Court of Appeal and in the Courts below; and the trustee's costs were expressly stated to have priority. And the same rule applies in the Equity Courts.

Priorities.

In the late case of *Potter* v. *Jackson*, 13 Ch. D. 846, it was pointed out by Hall, V.-C., that in an ordinary administration action costs are first paid out of an estate; but in a partnership action, if a balance is found due from the firm to one of the partners, such balance must be paid out of the assets in priority to the costs of the action.

Administration and partnership. Rule as to costs when different.

CHAPTER XXIV.

STATUTORY CHARGES.

Solicitors should rely upon their client's ability to pay costs.

BLACKBURN, J., once said in a judgment of his in 1868, reported Ex parte *Morrison*, L. R. 4 Q. B. 158, that it would be more satisfactory if solicitors relied rather upon their client's ability to pay them than upon their chances of obtaining costs from the other side as the result of litigation. That the Courts still hold this view there can be no doubt; yet side by side with it is the feeling that the solicitor should be secured fair payment for the costs properly incurred by him in preserving or recovering property or money: Brett, L.J., *Emden* v. *Carte*, 19 Ch. D. 323.

Statutory charging order, lien.

This fair payment can be secured by obtaining a charging order under the Solicitors' Act, 1860, or the solicitor can rely upon his common law lien for costs without such order, upon any fund that there may be in Court. All that he can get are costs properly incurred, and it is the duty of the judge in making an order under the Act to limit the order to the costs properly incurred, and to direct taxation of such costs properly incurred: per Jessel, M.R., 19 Ch. D. 318.

For costs properly incurred.

A charging order under 1 & 2 Vict. c. 110, ss. 14 and 18, cannot be obtained by persons held to be entitled under a decree for costs, charges, and expenses, under the Judicature Act, Order 46, for costs, charges and expenses, until they have been taxed; and a stop order is merely the consequence of the charging order: *Widgery* v. *Tepper, Hall* v. *Tepper*, judgment of James, L.J., 6 Ch. D. 369; and therefore the solicitor to such persons must not rely upon his client's being able to obtain this order as his method of securing his costs. This sort of charging order is in the nature of an execution against the property of a person ordered to pay money, and is obtained by the person to whom a judgment debt is payable, or in whose favour a decree is made, and must not be confounded with a statutory charging order, or a declaration of lien made in favour of a solicitor. This subject is treated of, among other places, in the author's Hints on Practice, ed. 1, p. 259.

Charging orders.

The lien of a solicitor in a suit upon a fund in Court for his costs of suit was, however, protected by a stop order (which, when made, is made without prejudice before taxation) under special circumstances, which prevented the suit from being effectively prosecuted in *Hobson* v. *Shearman*, 8 Beav. 486.

If he does not apply under the Solicitors' Act, 1860, s. 28, he must rely upon his particular lien, which needs an order of the Court to give active effect to it, but which is not barred by the Statute of Limitations, as an order under the Act is. The common law lien, however, does not extend to real property.

Solicitor's lien does not extend to real property.

In order, then, to set the statute in force, a declaration has to be obtained by the solicitor, which should be applied for in the Court in which the property was recovered or preserved. This expression applies to a judgment for money to be

Declaration under the Solicitors' Act.

paid, or to an order agreed to by the parties that the claim should be abandoned, and the action stayed after payment of costs. The notion is, as has been insisted on, that some benefit should have been done, through the agency of the solicitor, to the persons entitled to the fund out of which he seeks to get his costs.

Extent of lien on fund in Court.

And the solicitor's lien upon a fund in Court is not a general lien; it extends only to costs in the cause or costs immediately connected with the costs in the cause; as, for instance, the costs of successfully protecting a solicitor's right to the costs in the cause: *Lucas* v. *Peacock*, 9 Beav. 181.

Solicitor may be entitled to a lien and not to a declaration.

It will of course be noticed that it is not necessary to hold that a fund has been "recovered and preserved" for a solicitor to have his lien upon it, which is a proceeding necessary before a declaration under the Act can be obtained; and therefore it may well be that he may be entitled to the one but not to the other in a particular case. Again, in order to obtain his right under the statute the declaration must be made by the Court; and that Court must be the branch of the Court to which the suit was attached, as was held by the Court of Appeal, over-ruling the judgment of Malins, V.-C., in *Heinrick* v. *Sutton*, L. R. 6 Ch. 865. *Catlow* v. *Catlow*, 2 C. P. D. 362, illustrates this. There A., as administrator of his deceased mother, sued B. and C. for detinue in the Common Pleas at Lancaster and got judgment, but could not levy. Afterwards B. and C. sued out a plaint in the County Court for administration of the estate, and brought into Court the proceeds of the goods of the intestate. The solicitor who acted for A. in the action for detinue was held to be entitled to a charge upon the fund in the hands of the

By what Court declaration made.

Registrar, and the Common Pleas Division to be the proper Court in which to make the application.

Without doubt the particular lien exists, although no application to or declaration by the Court is made. An instance in which it was thought wise by Lindley, L.J., who was then counsel for the solicitor, to apply for a declaration of the solicitor's lien upon a fund in Court, and not for a statutory charge, was *Pritchard* v. *Roberts*, L. R. 17 Eq. 223. There the client was an infant still under age, and it was thought that *Bonser* v. *Bradshaw*, 4 Giff. 260, had decided that the word in the Solicitors' Act, 1860, s. 28, "employed," did not apply to the solicitor of an infant, because an infant could not retain a solicitor. This case is, however, further discussed at the end of this chapter (p. 201).

Lien exists independently of the declaration.

Declaration preferred to statutory charge.

Pritchard v. *Roberts*.

The chief advantage of the statutory lien is that it applies to real property as well as to personal property, which the common law lien does not; but on the other hand the Statute of Limitations applies to it, which it does not to the common law lien. The application for the order under the Act is sufficient if intituled in the action; and the order may be obtained either on summons or petition, and need not be intituled either in the matter of the Act or of the solicitor: *Hamer* v. *Giles*, *Giles* v. *Hamer*, *Austin* v. *Jackson*, 11 Ch. D. 942. There was a question whether, since the passing of the Judicature Act, 1873, s. 39, the proper course was not by summons, and the objection was taken before Fry, J., in *Brown* v. *Trotman*, 12 Ch. D. 881, but the learned judge decided that as the course of the Courts had always been to make such orders upon petition, he should not deviate from that course. He decided, however, that no other party to the

Application.

How headed

How obtained.

Brown v. *Trotman*.

Equity Courts.

Who must be served.

action than the client of the solicitor applying for the order should be served with the petition. It is stated in Mr. Cordery's Book, The Law relating to Solicitors, 1878, ed. 1, p. 233, that this application may also be made by motion, but he does not there give any authority for the assertion.

When charging order refused.

It may be well to look at a few cases in which a charging order has been refused. In *Foxon* v. *Gascoigne*, L. R. 9 Ch. 654, the defendant was alleged to have built so as to obstruct the plaintiff's ancient lights, and an interlocutory injunction was granted against the defendant's building higher, and a mandatory injunction was asked for to pull down part of what had been already built. The suit was afterwards compromised upon the terms that the building should remain at its then height. The defendant became bankrupt, and his solicitor asked to have his costs made a charge upon the defendant's property to which the suit related. The Court of Appeal, affirming the decision of the Master of the Rolls, held that no property had been recovered or preserved, although the application of the plaintiff for a mandatory injunction to pull down a part of what had been built by the defendant had been refused; upon the ground that a suit which relates only to an easement is not a suit in which it can be said that property has been recovered or preserved, even though a mandatory injunction for pulling down buildings is refused.

In suits relating to easements.

Another case, in which it was held that no property had been recovered or preserved within the meaning of the Act, and that the solicitor therefore was not entitled to any charge, was *Pinkerton* v. *Easton*, L. R. 16 Eq. 490. The facts in that case were that in a suit by a residuary legatee against the

Pinkerton v. Easton.

sole surviving trustee of a testator's estate, an administration decree had been made and a new trustee ordered to be appointed. The decree was carried into chambers, and the accounts brought in, when the plaintiff stopped all further proceedings in the suit. Upon this the plaintiff's solicitor petitioned that his costs might be charged upon the plaintiff's interest in the estate.

Statutory charge extends only to property of his own client.

Moreover, the statutory charge to which a solicitor is entitled extends to the property of his own client only, and not to that of other persons; for instance, B.'s solicitor was, in *Berrie* v. *Howitt*, L. R. 9 Eq. 1, held not to be entitled to a charge for costs on B.'s share of the settled property under the following circumstances. By a settlement real estate was assured to the use of A. for life, with remainder to his children as he should by deed or will appoint, and in default of appointment, to the use of his children as tenants in common in tail, with cross remainders in tail between them. In a suit in which B. was a defendant, an appointment by A. was set aside, so that the property was left to devolve according to the limitations of the settlement in default of appointment, and B. became thereby entitled to an estate tail in certain undivided shares of the property. B. afterwards died a batchelor, and without having executed a disentailing deed; and the shares to which he was entitled devolved under the settlement upon the plaintiff, and the defendants to the suits as tenants in common in tail. Thus, if B. (the client) had barred the entail and got the fee, the solicitor would have got the charge on the fee; but as he did not, the interest of the client was gone, and there was nothing of the client's upon which he could get the charge.

Example.

Act is to be construed liberally.

In *Scholefield* v. *Lockwood*, L. R. 7 Eq. 87, as he did also in *Berrie* v. *Howitt*, Lord Romilly, M.R., said the Act ought to be construed liberally, and that solicitors ought not to be deprived of their lien where there has been a good deal of work done. In that case the client was one of the defendants in a foreclosure suit, and upon an appeal by him the decree was varied in his favour; and he was also successful in resisting claims against the client in working out the decree. Before the certificate in the suit was made he became bankrupt, and it was then that the charge was asked for. It was held that if anything came out of the estate to him it could be charged. The solicitor took the charge for what it was worth. In *Bailey* v. *Birchall*, 2 H. & M. 371, it was decided that the solicitor was entitled to a charge, although it might turn out that the client had not any interest in the property in an administration action, as in taking the accounts he was found to be a debtor to the estate.

Meaning of the word "employed."

The word "employed" too, used in the 28th section, has received a liberal construction. V.-C. Wickens, in *Baile* v. *Baile*, L. R. 13 Eq. 497, said that it must have all reasonable weight given to it; but that to say that it did not apply to a solicitor employed in good faith by a next friend on behalf of an infant, who when he comes of age adopts the proceedings, seemed to him a narrow construction of it; and that further, if a solicitor instituted proceedings on behalf of an infant, and died during the infancy, and the proceedings were continued by a second solicitor till majority, and were then adopted by the infant, the first solicitor as well as the latter must be considered as employed within the Act. See also *Bonser* v. *Bradshaw*, 9 W. R. 229, and *Pritchard* v.

Roberts, L. R. 17 Eq. 222. Of course if the infant on coming of age repudiated the proceedings taken for him, his estate is subject to no lien in respect of such proceedings; but a voluntary conveyance before the charge is declared by the Court does not defeat it. And the personal representatives of a solicitor can apply for a charge under the statute (same case); and it would appear from *Heinrich* v. *Sutton*, In re *Fiddey*, L. R. 6 Ch. 865, that the fact of a suit having been absolutely dismissed, is no objection to an order for a charge being subsequently made in it.

Infant repudiating the proceedings upon coming of age.

One or two instances of cases in which charges have been made may perhaps be noticed with advantage here. A married woman's solicitor's costs have been charged on an annuity settled to her separate use without power of anticipation, when such costs had been incurred in defending a suit by her husband to set aside the post-nuptial settlement creating such annuity: In re *Keane*, *Lumley* v. *Desborough*, L. R. 12 Eq. 115.

Instances of charging orders.

The costs of establishing an infant's title, together with the costs of a partition suit, and of the application for the charge, are costs for which his solicitor can get a charging order under the general jurisdiction of the Court of Chancery. Mr. Lindley, Q.C., who appeared for the solicitor in *Pritchard* v. *Roberts*, L. R. 17 Eq. 223, quoted before, said that in consequence of *Bonser* v. *Bradshaw*, 4 Giff. 260, which was supposed to decide that an infant could not "employ" a solicitor so as to constitute a charge under the 28th section, a declaration of the plaintiff's lien under the general jurisdiction of the Court was asked for. Hall, V.-C., intimated that if the solicitor had sued the next friend of the infant for these costs

Pritchard v. *Roberts*.

he would have recovered them, and that the next friend might have recovered them against the infant, so that in any case the costs might have to come in a circuitous manner out of the infant's estate; and, therefore, he ordered the declaration as prayed.

Jones v. *Frost.*

If a suit is instituted by an incumbrancer whose incumbrance turns out to be entirely valueless, the solicitor is entitled to a statutory charge upon the property, upon the title to which the supposed incumbrance formed a cloud: *Jones* v. *Frost,* L. R. 7 Ch. 773. These costs are generally to be taxed as between solicitor and client: *Catlow* v. *Catlow*, 2 C. P. D. 362; but more will be found upon this head in the chapter upon solicitor and client costs; and the solicitor's bill of costs may have to be paid without taxation under certain circumstances: *De Bay* v. *Griffin*, L. R. 10 Ch. 291.

Costs how taxed.

CHAPTER XXV.

PRIORITIES OF COSTS, CHARGES, ETC.

DIFFICULT questions as to priority sometimes arise with reference to a solicitor's lien for costs, and even to charges in respect of which a declaration of the Court has been made. It must never be forgotten that the right of the solicitor is merely a claim to the protection of the Court as to his costs, when the equitable interference of the Court is asked for; as, for instance, for the purpose of setting off one judgment against another.

What solicitor's right is.

The fact that a solicitor has obtained a judgment for a client, and that costs are due to him, does not cause the relation of trustee and cestui que trust between the client and himself as to the proceeds of such judgment. The solicitor who has conducted an action to judgment for which costs are owing to him does not stand in the position of a cestui que trust having an equitable interest in the proceeds of the judgment. This lien is, in fact, only a claim or right to ask for the intervention of the Court for his protection when, after having obtained judgment for his client, he finds that there is a likelihood of his client depriving him of his costs.

Client and solicitor not truste and cestui que trust.

In an action on a judgment, a set-off of a cross-judgment could always be pleaded under the statute of set-off, and the Court could not assist the solicitor: *Mercer* v. *Graves*, L. R. 7 Q. B. 499.

When, however, an application was made to the Court to allow a cross-judgment to be set-off against another judgment (an execution being taken out), the allowance of which was discretionary with the Court, the Court would say, "You who ask for equity must do equity and pay your solicitor." Lush, L.J., same case, p. 507.

Lien and set-off.

There is sometimes, too, a question whether, when there is a set-off, the lien comes before the set-off has been deducted or not. In fact, the point is whether the lien or the set-off first takes effect. With regard to all costs arising in the same suit or action, the right of set-off is sanctioned. The principle is, that where a solicitor is employed in an action he must be considered to have adopted the proceedings from the beginning to the end and to have acted for better or worse. He has only a lien upon any balance that may appear to be in favour of his client at the end: *Roberts* v. *Buée*, 8 Ch. D. 200.

Solicitor's lien on balance appearing in favour of his client.

The set-off in a counterclaim is of course a set-off in the same action: see *The Philippine*, L. R. 1 A. & E. 309, in which case the finding on the counterclaim was for a larger sum than on the claim; yet the plaintiff's solicitor was held entitled to a statutory charge, as the result of the suit to the plaintiff was that he was entitled to a transfer of shares in the vessel for a less sum than he would have been if the suit had not been instituted.

In *The Heinrich*, L. R. 3 A. & E. 505, the solicitor's lien was allowed to have priority to necessaries and the master's wages; but the case must be referred to to be understood. This subject is more freely treated of in the chapter in which costs of a counterclaim are dealt with. With regard to costs of independent proceedings, it may be broadly taken that there is no set-off. In *Barker* v. *Hemming*, 6 Q. B. D. 809, when before the Court of Appeal, it was pointed out by James, L.J., that a set-off must be not merely between the same two persons, but between the same two parties to the same proceedings. The plaintiff in that case had got judgment against the drawer and acceptor of a bill, and had issued execution thereon upon the drawer's goods. The acceptor subsequently got the judgment set aside, with costs, by proving that his acceptance had been forged, and he claimed the goods seized. An interpleader followed, and judgment was given against the acceptor, with costs. The Court held that these costs could not be set-off by the acceptor, the proceedings in which they were incurred being separate.

No set-off of costs of independent proceedings.

If by an arbitrator's award in an action a plaintiff is ordered to pay money to the defendant, and the defendant ordered to pay plaintiff a part of his costs when taxed, the defendant can set-off the debt against the taxed costs: *Pringle* v. *Gloag*, 10 Ch. D. 676. And this is the meaning of Additional Rules of Court (Costs), 1875, r. 19. But it was pointed out by James, L.J., in Ex parte *Griffin*, In re *Adams*, 14 Ch. D. 37, that the lien of the solicitor who was the equitable owner of the costs would be prejudiced by allowing the Bankruptcy Court to permit the setting off of the costs of a proceeding in the High Court against the costs in a bankruptcy.

Set-off of debt against costs of an award.

Upon a fund in Court, the proceeds of assets in an administration suit, the solicitor's lien is a first charge on the principle qui potior est tempore potior est jure; and in partnership actions, unless some sum is found due to one of the partners, in which

Solicitor's lien is first charge on assets in administration suit.

case the solicitor's lien comes next. When a garnishee order nisi is obtained, and perhaps served before the solicitor has had his application heard in support of his lien, as the solicitor could have got a declaration of his charge either under the statute, or under the general jurisdiction of the Court, and as the garnishee order has to be made absolute, it is plain that neither party has in such a case perfected his right. Now that orders nisi will probably, under the new rules, be done away with, this may perhaps be somewhat altered; but at present the law stands thus. If the solicitor in such a case is the "meritorious cause of the recovery" of the sum attempted to be affected by the garnishee order, he has a claim upon such sum in priority to the execution creditor. If, however, the execution creditor's position were perfect, the case would be otherwise, as either party in the absence of the other is entitled to be paid the money: *Birchall* v. *Pugin*, L. R. 10 C. P. 401.

Priority of declaration of lien and execution creditor.

Garnishee order nisi creates no charge until service.

Hamer v. *Giles*.

One of the latest decisions upon this point is *Hamer* v. *Giles*, 11 Ch. D. 942, in which it was held that a garnishee order nisi does not create a charge until service of it on the garnishee. There a judgment creditor of the defendant in a partnership action obtained a garnishee order nisi to attach all monies in the hands of a receiver appointed in an action, which appeared to be due to the defendant upon the taking of the accounts which had been ordered in the action. On the following day, and before the service of the order nisi, the defendant's solicitors obtained, on a summons served on the receiver, a charging order declaring them entitled to a charge for their costs upon all monies coming to the defendant under the action. On the next day, the garnishee order nisi was served on the receiver and was subsequently made absolute. It was held that both under the Act, and independently of it, the solicitors were entitled to their costs in priority to the claim of the creditor under the garnishee order. This latter case fixes the punctum temporis at which the garnishee order nisi takes effect, namely, upon service upon the garnishee; and, therefore, if this order is served before any application for a declaration of charge is made by the solicitor, the solicitor will lose his priority owing to his own laches.

When garnishee order nisi takes effect.

However, in *Shippey* v. *Grey*, 28 W. R. 877 (which is said to have been decided by the Court of Appeal, following *Faithful* v. *Ewen*, quoted below), the solicitors to the plaintiff in an action against a railway were held entitled to a statutory charging order under these circumstances. They had signed judgment againt the railway for damages and costs; but before the costs were taxed, a judgment creditor of the plaintiff obtained ex parte a garnishee order. The solicitors then gave notice to the creditor of their lien for their costs in the action against the railway company. The Court of Appeal held that they were entitled to it. See also *The Leader*, L. R. 2 A. & E. 314, where it was held that the defendant, who, after a decree against him with costs, pays money to judgment creditors of the plaintiff under garnishee orders, should have apprised the judge of the existence of the plaintiff's solicitors' lien before such orders were made absolute, or should have given notice to the solicitors.

Shippey v. *Grey.*

If plaintiffs in a suit mortgage their interest to defendants in the suit, and the plaintiffs' solicitor approves of the draft, but nothing is said by anybody as to his lien, it will be taken that the defendants' charge is subsequent to the plaintiffs' solicitor's charge

In mortgage of plaintiffs' interest to defendants, solicitor's lien

has priority.

for costs of suit, if he afterwards applies for a charging order. The reason is, because the mortgagees, having necessarily notice of the suit in which they were themselves defendants, must be presumed to have known the rights of the solicitor of the plaintiffs, and that, therefore, his charge might not be postponed to the mortgage, unless he has been guilty of misrepresentation or concealment: *Faithful* v. *Ewen*, 7 Ch. D. 495.

Re *Mason & Taylor*.

But if solicitors prepare a mortgage deed for a client of their own, they have no priority for their lien over that of their client for the money advanced by him: In re *Mason & Taylor*, 10 Ch. D. 729.

CONCLUSION.

Perhaps at the end of a treatise like this a few words may not be out of place on the amendments in the law relating to the subjects of it which appear to be wanted at the present time.

Without dwelling upon the question whether notions like champerty and maintenance, which are practically obsolete, while wrecking petitions unfortunately are not, should still be allowed to load the legal atmosphere, when such full powers have been given to the Courts to deal with agreements between solicitor and client as they may think right (Solicitors' Act, 1870, s. 4), it may, perhaps, be fairly questioned whether sufficient freedom of contract exists between solicitors and their clients.

Surely any system of protection that is not absolutely necessary is a mistake; and can it seriously be argued that the average client, not being a woman, or infant, or very old person, is not quite capable of taking care of himself in these days?

Morgan v. *Minett.*

Morgan v. *Minett*, which has been already referred to, was a hard case; and it is difficult to see why, in the case of wills, it should be easier for a solicitor to obtain undue influence over a client, than the client's own son, daughter, or wife. In a word, the disabilities of the profession are too great.

Disabilities and responsibility.

Compare the regulations as to the appointment of solicitors as justices of the peace.

And at the same time the responsibilities of solicitors are greater than is just.

Why, for example, if a solicitor, out of pure kindness of heart, undertakes a case for a client for costs out of pocket, should he be liable for anything but for the grossest negligence?

Compromise by client.

The client, perhaps a very poor man, can get behind his back, and effect a compromise with the adversary by the payment to him of a sum of money, and then the solicitor will be unable to get even his costs out of pocket. This reminds one of the fable of the crane, who, when demanding a reward for having taken a bone out of a fox's throat, was told that he had been sufficiently rewarded by not having had his head bitten off during the transaction.

Taxation after payment.

Surely, in such a case, the client has the best of the situation; and yet it is plainly to the advantage of society that solicitors should fight the battles of those who are needy, and defend the poor in proper cases. Again, is it not a hardship that his bill of costs should be taxed after payment, except in most special cases; or that accounts stated should be reopened, except where they would as between an ordinary principal and agent? In re *Moss*, L. R. 2 Eq. 347.

Actions for negligence.

So much for the principles of the law which appear, theoretically, to be unduly severe upon the profession as regards their dealings with clients. In practice, nevertheless, an action for negligence is a rare thing. The public do not know the power they possess, and the difficulties of getting evidence in such an action are, of course, enormous.

Privilege

And yet, although the feeling as often expressed

that the barrister has facilities which the solicitor has not; as, for example, his universal right of audience, his immunity from responsibility, and his power of becoming a solicitor immediately upon passing the requisite examination; we seldom hear any complaints as to the restraints upon the solicitor in his dealings with his client; and, consequently, we may infer that because he is, in fact, so seldom attacked, he does not object to his liability to attack. *of barristers.*

If this is so, it is unnecessary to dwell upon these subjects at greater length, and we may pass on to consider the amendments to be desired in the practice as to costs. And, first, it would be well if the system of payment by length were abolished in litigious as in non-litigious business. If the discretion of the taxing officer under Costs, Order 6, r. 29, was more largely used, and the importance of the cause and the nature of the fund or person to bear the costs were really ascertained and considered in every case where costs were taxed, although, of course, there would be variations in the allowances made, there would be a reason for them, which does not at present always exist. *Payment by length.* *Discretion of taxing master.*

Now the customs of one taxing master's office are said to differ from those of another, and to depend upon unwritten laws handed down in particular offices from master to master, and not upon any principle which can be got at and understood. This subject has been glanced at in the chapter on solicitors as draftsmen, and it may be shortly stated here that what is wanted is perfect uniformity in the practice of the taxing master's offices. *Want of uniformity.* *Uniformity.*

Also, that it should be clearly defined what is the work of counsel and what that of the solicitor which will be allowed for in a party and party taxation. *Counsel's work.*

Adequate payment.

And in no case should a sum total be allowed to be made up in an illicit way; as, for instance, by the filing of unnecessary affidavits, or taking unnecessary steps, as by insisting on discovery. The habit of straining at the gnat and swallowing the camel is too frequent in taxations.

A letter or a conference is struck out, and the costs of an application for an injunction or receiver, or accounts which was quite unnecessary as between party and party, are allowed.

It is too frequently stated that large firms with well known names are allowed to do things which unknown persons would not attempt; and that the master's decision upon points which he has established as principles is not often enough appealed against; and the inuendo is that where there is smoke there is fire.

Appeals from taxing master.

Wherever a question is a question of discretion, as, for instance, whether in a particular case a particular allowance should or should not be made, the master's discretion should of course be, as it is, almost omnipotent; but when he says, "I shall not allow the costs of this writ being settled by counsel because there is a statement of claim for which the opposite party will have to pay in this action," this is an instance of a decision on principle which should be at once appealed from.

Costs of interpleader summons.

Masters frequently refuse the costs of an interpleader summons, supposing that they have no power to give costs, and relying on the statements in books of practice under the old law. But see as to this, for example, Ex parte *Streeter*, In re *Morris*, 19 Ch. D., and Jessel, M.R.'s, remarks, at p. 224.

Costs of adjournments.

Again, the costs of all adjournments in chambers ought to be looked into most carefully; and the party who was the cause of them should pay, in any case, the costs of the day. Now it is said that it is sufficient to assert that the matter in question is an agency matter to obtain almost as of course an adjournment.

These are a few crude suggestions as to the amendment of the law of costs, which are offered with great diffidence. There is, no doubt, much to be said for the existing state of things, and it is possible that some of the suggestions here made might be found, when tested, to be productive of evils which the writer knows not of.

APPENDIX.

THE SOLICITORS' REMUNERATION ACT, 1881.

[44 & 45 Vict. c. 44.]

An Act for making better provision respecting the Remuneration of Solicitors in Conveyancing and other non-contentious Business. [22nd August, 1881.]

Be it enacted by the Queen's most excellent Majesty, by and with the advice and consent of the Lords spiritual and temporal, and Commons, in this present Parliament assembled, and by the authority of the same, as follows:

Preliminary.

Short title; extent; interpretation.

1.—(1). This Act may be cited as the Solicitors' Remuneration Act, 1881.

(2). This Act does not extend to Scotland.

(3). In this Act—

"Solicitor" means a solicitor or proctor qualified according to the statutes in that behalf:

"Client" includes any person who, as a principal, or on behalf of another, or as trustee or executor, or in any other capacity, has power, express or implied, to retain or employ, a solicitor, and any person for the time being liable to pay to a solicitor, for his services, any costs, remuneration, charges, expenses, or disbursements:

"Person" includes a body of persons corporate or unincorporate:

"Incorporated Law Society" means, in England, the society referred to under that title in the Act passed in the session of the twenty-third and twenty-fourth years of Her Majesty's reign, intituled "An Act to amend the Laws relating to attorneys, solicitors, proctors, and certificated conveyancers;" and, in Ireland, the society referred to under that title in the Attorneys and Solicitors' Act, Ireland, 1866.

"Provincial law societies or associations" means all bodies of solicitors in England incorporated by Royal Charter, or under the Joint Stock Companies Act, other than the Incorporated Law Society above mentioned.

General Orders.

Power to make General Orders for remuneration in conveyancing, &c.

2. In England, the Lord Chancellor, the Lord Chief Justice of England, the Master of the Rolls, and the president for the time being of the Incorporated Law Society, and the president of one of the provincial law societies or associations, to be selected and nominated from time to time by the Lord Chancellor to serve during the tenure of office of such president, or any three of them, the Lord Chancellor being one, and, in Ireland, the Lord Chancellor, the Lord Chief Justice of Ireland, the Master of the Rolls, and the president for the time being of the Incorporated Law Society, or any three of them, the Lord Chancellor being one, may from time to time make any such General Order as to them seems fit for prescribing and regulating the remuneration of solicitors in respect of business connected with sales, purchases, leases, mortgages settlements, and other matters of conveyancing, and in

respect of other business not being business in any action, or transacted in any Court, or in the chambers of any judge or master, and not being otherwise contentious business, and may revoke or alter any such order.

3. One month at least before any such General Order shall be made, the Lord Chancellor shall cause a copy of the regulations and provisions proposed to be embodied therein to be communicated in writing to the Council of the Incorporated Law Society, who shall be at liberty to submit such observations and suggestions in writing as they may think fit to offer thereon; and the Lord Chancellor, and the other persons hereby authorised to make such order, shall take into consideration any such observations or suggestions which may be submitted to them by the said Council within one month from the day on which such communication to the said Council should have been made as aforesaid, and, after duly considering the same, may make such order, either in the form or to the effect originally communicated to the said Council, or with such alterations, additions, or amendments, as to them may seem fit.

Communication to Incorporated Law Society.

4. Any General Order under this Act may, as regards the mode of remuneration, prescribe that it shall be according to a scale of rates of commission or percentage, varying or not in different classes of business, or by a gross sum, or by a fixed sum for each document prepared or perused, without regard to length, or in any other mode, or partly in one mode and partly in another, or others, and may, as regards the amount of the remuneration, regulate the same with reference to all or any of the following among other considerations, namely:—

Principles of remuneration.

The position of the party for whom the solicitor is concerned in any business, that is, whether as vendor or as purchaser, lessor or lessee, mortgagor or mortgagee, and the like;

The place, district, and circumstances at or in which the business or part thereof is transacted;

The amount of the capital money or of the rent to which the business relates;

The skill, labour, and responsibility involved therein on the part of the solicitor;

The number and importance of the documents prepared or perused, without regard to length;

The average or ordinary remuneration obtained by solicitors in like business at the passing of this Act.

Security for costs and interest on disbursements.

5. Any General Order under this Act may authorise and regulate the taking by a solicitor from his client of security for future remuneration, in accordance with any such Order, to be ascertained by taxation or otherwise, and the allowance of interest.

Order to be laid before Houses of Parliament.

6.—(1). Any General Order under this Act shall not take effect unless and until it has been laid before each House of Parliament, and one month thereafter has elapsed.

Disallowance on address.

(2). If within that month an address is presented to the Queen by either House, seeking the disallowance of the Order, or part thereof, it shall be lawful for Her Majesty by Order in Council to disallow the Order, or that part, and the Order or part disallowed shall not take effect.

Effect of Order as to taxation.

7. As long as any General Order under this Act is in operation, the taxation of bills of costs of solicitors shall be regulated thereby.

Agreements.

Power for solicitor and client to agree on form and amount of

8.—(1). With respect to any business to which the foregoing provisions of this Act relate, whether any General Order under this Act is in operation or not, it shall be competent for a solicitor to make an agreement with his client, and for a client to make an agreement with his solicitor, before or after or in the course of the transaction of any such business, for the remuneration of the solicitor, to such amount and in such manner as the solicitor and the client think fit, either by a gross sum, or by commission or percentage, or by salary, or otherwise; and it shall be competent for the solicitor to accept from the client, and for the client to give to the solicitor, remuneration accordingly. remuneration.

(2). The agreement shall be in writing, signed by the person to be bound thereby, or by his agent in that behalf.

(3). The agreement may, if the solicitor and the client think fit, be made on the terms that the amount of the remuneration therein stipulated for either shall include or shall not include all or any disbursements made by the solicitor in respect of searches, plans, travelling, stamps, fees, or other matters.

(4). The agreement may be sued or recovered on, or impeached and set aside, in the like manner and on the like grounds as an agreement not relating to the remuneration of a solicitor; and if, under any order for taxation of goods, such agreement being relied upon by the solicitor shall be objected to by the client as unfair or unreasonable, the taxing master or officer of the Court may inquire into the facts, and certify the same to the Court; and if, upon such certificate, it shall appear to the Court or judge that just cause has been shown either for cancelling the agreement or for reducing the amount payable under the same, the Court or judge shall have power to order some cancellation or reduction, and to give all such directions necessary or proper for the purpose of carrying such Order into effect, or otherwise consequential thereon, as to the Court or judge may seem fit.

Restriction on Solicitors Act, 1870.

9. The Attorneys and Solicitors Act, 1870, shall not apply to any business to which this Act relates.

GENERAL ORDER MADE IN PURSUANCE OF THE SOLICITORS' REMUNERATION ACT, 1881,

44 & 45 VICT. c. 44.

WE, the Right Honourable Roundell Baron Selborne, Lord High Chancellor of Great Britain, the Right Honourable John Duke, Lord Coleridge, Lord Chief Justice of England, the Right Honourable Sir George Jessel, Master of the Rolls, and Enoch Harvey, Esq., President of the Incorporated Law Society of Liverpool (being four (*a*) of the persons in that behalf authorised by the statute 44 & 45 Vict. c. 44), do hereby, in pursuance and execution of the powers given to us by the said statute, and of all other powers and authorities enabling us in that behalf, order and direct in manner following:—

Sched. I. not to apply to registered titles.

1. This Order is to take effect from and after the 31st day of December, 1882, except that Schedule I. hereto shall not apply to transactions respecting real property the title to which has been registered under the Acts of 25 & 26 Vict. c. 53, 25 & 26 Vict. c. 67, and 38 & 39 Vict. c. 87.

For non-litigious business.

2. Subject to the exception aforesaid, the remuneration of a solicitor in respect of business connected with sales, purchases, leases, mortgages, settlements, and other matters of conveyancing, and in respect of other business, not being business in any action, or transacted in any

(*a*) The fifth is the President of the Incorporated Law Society, and it is to be noticed that his name is conspicuously absent.

Court, or in the chambers of any judge or master, is to be regulated as follows, namely:—

Sales, purchases, mortgages. Fees of solicitor having conduct. Sched. I., Pt. I.

(*a*.) In respect of sales, purchases and mortgages completed, the remuneration of the solicitor having the conduct of the business, whether for the vendor, purchaser, mortgagor or mortgagee, is to be that prescribed in Part I. of Schedule I. to this Order, and to be subject to the regulations therein contained.

Leases and agreements for leases. Sched. I., Pt. II.

(*b*.) In respect of leases, and agreements for leases, of the kinds mentioned in Part II. of Schedule I. to this Order, or conveyances reserving rent, or agreements for the same, when the transactions shall have been completed, the remuneration of the solicitor having the conduct of the business is to be that prescribed in Part II. of such Schedule I.

Other business and business not completed. Sched. II.

(*c*.) In respect of business not hereinbefore provided for, connected with any transaction the remuneration for which, if completed, is hereinbefore, or in Schedule I. hereto, prescribed, but which is not, in fact, completed, and in respect of settlements, mining leases or licences, or agreements therefor, re-conveyances, transfers of mortgage, or further charges, not provided for hereinbefore or in Schedule I. hereto, assignments of leases not by way of purchase or mortgage, and in respect of all other deeds or documents, and of all other business the remuneration for which is not hereinbefore, or in Schedule I. hereto, prescribed, the remuneration is to be regulated according to the present system as altered by Schedule II. hereto.

When drafts property of client.

3. Drafts and copies made in the course of business, the remuneration for which is provided for by this Order, are to be the property of the client.

Does not

4. The remuneration prescribed by Schedule I. to this

Order is not to include stamps, counsel's fees, auctioneer's or valuer's charges, travelling or hotel expenses, fees paid on searches to public officers, on registrations, or to stewards of manors, costs of extracts from any register, record, or roll, or other disbursement reasonably and properly paid, nor any extra work occasioned by changes occurring in the course of any business, such as the death or insolvency of a party to the transaction, nor is it to include any business of a contentious character, nor any proceedings in any Court, but it shall include law stationer's charges, and allowances for time of the solicitor and his clerks, and for copying and parchment, and all other similar disbursements.

include stamps, counsel's fees, and out of pocket expenses, except law stationer.

5. In respect of any business which is required to be, and is, by special exertion, carried through in an exceptionally short space of time, a solicitor may be allowed a proper additional remuneration for the special exertion, according to the circumstances.

Expedition fees.

6. In all cases to which the scales prescribed in Schedule I. hereto shall apply, a solicitor may, before undertaking any business, by writing under his hand, communicated to the client, elect that his remuneration shall be according to the present system as altered by Schedule II. hereto; but if no such election shall be made, his remuneration shall be according to the scale prescribed by this Order.

When solicitor can elect.

7. A solicitor may accept from his client, and a client may give to his solicitor, security for the amount to become due to the solicitor for business to be transacted by him, and for interest on such amount, but so that interest is not to commence till the amount due is ascertained, either by agreement or taxation. A solicitor may charge interest at four per cent. per annum on his disbursements and costs, whether by scale or otherwise, from the expiration of one month from demand from the client. And in cases where the same are payable by an infant, or out of a fund not presently available, such demand may

Security.

be made on the parent or guardian, or the trustee or other person liable.

8. In this Order, and the Schedules hereto, the following words and expressions shall have the meaning ascribed to them in the 3rd sub-section of section 1 of the Solicitors' Remuneration Act, 1881, viz.:—

Solicitor,
Client,
Person.

SCHEDULE I.

Part I.

Scale of Charges on Sales, Purchases, and Mortgages, and Rules applicable thereto.

Scale.

	(1.) For the 1st £1000.		(2.) For the 2nd and 3rd £1000.		(3.) For the 4th and each subsequent £1000 up to £10,000.		(4.) For each subsequent £1000 up to £100,000.*	
	Per £100		Per £100		Per £100		Per £100	
	s.	*d.*	*s.*	*d.*	*s.*	*d.*	*s.*	*d.*
Vendor's solicitor for negotiating a sale of property by private contract............	20	0	20	0	10	0	5	0
Do., do., for conducting a sale of property by public auction, including the conditions of sale—								
When the property is sold ...	20	0	10	0	5	0	2	6
When the property is not sold, then on the reserved price...	10	0	5	0	2	6	1	3
[N.B.—A minimum charge of £5 to be made whether a sale is effected or not.]								
Do., do., for deducing title to freehold, copyhold, or leasehold property, and perusing, and completing conveyance (including preparation of contract, or conditions of sale, if any)	30	0	20	0	10	0	5	0
Purchaser's solicitor for negotiating a purchase of property by private contract	20	0	20	0	10	0	5	0
Do., do., for investigating title to freehold, copyhold, or leasehold property, and preparing and completing conveyance (including perusal and completion of contract, if any)	30	0	20	0	10	0	5	0
Mortgagor's solicitor for deducing title to freehold, copyhold, or leasehold property, perusing mortgage, and completing	30	0	20	0	10	0	5	0
Mortgagee's solicitor for negotiating loan.............................	20	0	20	0	5	0	2	6
Do., do., for investigating title to freehold, copyhold, or leasehold property; and preparing and completing mortgage	30	0	20	0	10	0	5	0
Vendor's or mortgagor's solicitor for procuring execution and acknowledgment of deed by a married woman	£2 10*s.* extra.							

* Every transaction exceeding £100,000, to be charged for as if it were for £100,000.

Rules.

How commission chargeable.

1. The commission for deducing title and perusing and completing conveyance on a sale by auction is to be chargeable on each lot of property, except that where a property held under the same title is divided into lots for convenience of sale, and the same purchaser buys several such lots and takes one conveyance, and only one abstract is delivered, the commission is to be chargeable upon the aggregate prices of the lots.

On attempted sale.

2. The commission on an attempted sale by auction in lots is to be chargeable on the aggregate of the reserved prices. When property offered for sale by auction is bought in and terms of sale are afterwards negotiated and arranged by the solicitor, he is to be entitled to charge commission according to the above scales on the reserved price where the property is not sold, and also one-half of the commission for negotiating the sale. When property is bought in and afterwards offered by auction by the same solicitor, he is only to be entitled to the scale for the first attempted sale, and for each subsequent sale ineffectually attempted he is to charge according to the present system, as altered by Schedule II. hereto. In case of a subsequent effectual sale by auction, the full commission for an effectual sale is to be chargeable in addition, less one-half of the commission previously allowed on the first attempted sale. The provisions of this rule as to commission on sales or attempted sales by auction are to be subject to rule 2.

When property sold afterwards.

When solicitor acts for mortgagor and mortgagee.

3. Where a solicitor is concerned for both mortgagor and mortgagee, he is to be entitled to charge the mortgagee's solicitor's charges and one-half of those which would be allowed to the mortgagor's solicitor up to £5000, and on any excess above £5000, one-fourth thereof.

When draft perused for

4. If a solicitor peruses a draft on behalf of several parties having distinct interests, proper to be separately

represented, he is to be entitled to charge £2 additional for each such party after the first.

parties having different interests.

5. Where a party, other than the vendor or mortgagor, joins in a conveyance or mortgage, and is represented by a separate solicitor, the charges of such separate solicitor are to be dealt with under the old system as altered by Schedule II. hereto.

Other party's solicitor.

6. Where a conveyance and mortgage of the same property are completed at the same time, and are prepared by the same solicitor, he is to be entitled to charge only half the above fees for investigating title, and preparing the mortgage deed up to £5000, and, on any excess above £5000, one-fourth thereof, in addition to his full charges upon the purchase-money and his commissions for negotiating (if any).

Conveyance and mortgage at same time.

7. Fractions of £100, under £50, are to be reckoned as £50. Fractions of £100, above £50, are to be reckoned as £100.

How fractions reckoned.

8. Where the prescribed remuneration would, but for this provision, amount to less than £5, the prescribed remuneration shall be £5, except on transactions under £100, in which cases the remuneration of the solicitor for the vendor, purchaser, mortgagor, or mortgagee, is to be £3.

£5 minimum, except in cases under £100.

9. Where a property is sold subject to incumbrances, the amount of the incumbrances is to be deemed a part of the purchase-money, except where the mortgagee purchases, in which case the charge of his solicitor shall be calculated upon the price of the equity of redemption.

Incumbrances part of purchase-money.

10. The above scale as to mortgages is to apply to transfers of mortgages where the title is investigated, but not to transfers where the title was investigated by the same solicitor on the original mortgage or on any previous transfer; and it is not to apply to further charges where the title has been so previously investigated. As to such transfers and further charges, the remuneration is to be regulated according to the present system as altered by

When such applies to transfers.

Schedule II. hereto. But the scale for negotiating the loan shall be chargeable on such transfers and further charges where it is applicable.

Sales by auction where no commission to auctioneers.

11. The scale for conducting a sale by auction shall apply only in cases where no commission is paid by the client to an auctioneer. The scale for negotiating shall apply to cases where the solicitor of a vendor or purchaser arranges the sale or purchase and the price and terms and conditions thereof, and no commission is paid by the client to an auctioneer, or estate or other agent. As to a mortgagee's solicitor it shall only apply to cases where he arranges and obtains the loan from a person for whom he acts. In case of sales under the Lands Clauses Consolidation Act, or any other private or public Act under which the vendor's charges are paid by the purchaser, the scale shall not apply.

Where rule does not apply.

When no commission charged.

12. In cases where, under the previous portion of this Schedule, a solicitor would be entitled to charge a commission for negotiating a sale or mortgage, or for conducting a sale by auction, and he shall not charge such commission, then he shall be entitled to charge the rates allowed by the first column on all transactions up to £2000, and to charge in addition those allowed by the second column on all amounts above £2000 and not exceeding £5000, and further to charge those allowed by the third column on all amounts above £5000 and not exceeding £50,000, instead of the rates allowed up to the amounts mentioned in those columns respectively.

Part II.

Scale of Charges as to Leases, or Agreements for Leases, at Rack Rent (other than a Mining Lease, or a Lease for Building purposes, or Agreement for the same).

Lessor's solicitor for preparing, settling, and completing lease and counterpart: —

Where the rent does not exceed £100	£7 10*s.* per cent. on the rental, but not less in any case than £5.

Where the rent exceeds £100 and does not exceed £500	£7 10*s.* in respect of the first £100 of rent, and £2 10*s.* in respect of each subsequent £100 of rent.
Where the rent exceeds £500	£7 10*s.* in respect of the first £100 of rent, £2 10*s.* in respect of each £100 of rent up to £500, and £1 in respect of every subsequent £100.
Lessee's solicitor for perusing draft and completing	One-half of the amount payable to the lessor's solicitor.

Scale of Charges as to Conveyances in Fee, or for any other Freehold Estate, Reserving Rent, or Building Leases Reserving Rent, or other Long Leases not at Rack Rent (except Mining Leases) or Agreements for the same respectively.

Vendor's or lessor's solicitor for preparing, settling, and completing conveyance and duplicate, or lease and counterpart :—

Amount of Annual Rent.		Amount of Remuneration.
Where it does not exceed	£5	£5.
Where it exceeds £5 and does not exceed	£50	The same payment as on rent of £5, also 20 per cent. on the excess beyond £5.
Where it exceeds £50 but does not exceed...............	£150	The same payment as on a rent of £50, and 10 per cent. on the excess beyond £50.
Where it exceeds	£150	The same payment as on a rent of £150, and 5 per cent. on the excess beyond £150.

Where a varying rent is payable, the amount of annual rent is to mean the largest amount of annual rent.

Purchaser's or lessee's solicitor for perusing draft and completing...............	One-half of the amount payable to the vendor's or lessor's solicitor.

Rules Applicable to Part II. of Schedule I.

As to all Leases, or Conveyances at a Rent, or Agreements for the same, other than Mining Leases and Agreements therefor.

Abstract.

1. Where the vendor or lessor furnishes an abstract of title, it is to be charged for according to the present system as altered by Schedule II.

Solicitor acting for two parties.

2. Where a solicitor is concerned for both vendor and purchaser, or lessor and lessee, he is to charge the vendor's or lessor's solicitor's charges and one-half of that of the purchaser's or lessee's solicitor.

Mortgagor or mortgagee joining.

3. Where a mortgagee or mortgagor joins in a conveyance or lease the vendor's or lessor's solicitor is to charge £1 1*s.* extra.

Other party joining.

4. Where a party other than a vendor or lessor joins in a conveyance or lease, and is represented by a separate solicitor, the charges of such separate solicitor are to be dealt with under the old system as altered by Schedule II.

When partly premium, partly rent.

5. Where a conveyance or lease is partly in consideration of a money payment or premium, and partly of a rent, then, in addition to the remuneration hereby prescribed in respect of the rent, there shall be paid a further sum equal to the remuneration on a purchase at a price equal to such money payment or premium.

6. Fractions of £5 are to be reckoned as £5.

SCHEDULE II.

Instructions for and Drawing and Perusing Deeds, Wills, and other Documents.

Such fees for instructions as, having regard to the care and labour required, the number and lengths of the papers to be perused, and the other circumstances of the case, may be fair and reasonable. In ordinary cases, as to drawing, &c., the allowance shall be—

For drawing - - - - - -	2*s.* per folio.
For engrossing - - - - - -	8*d.* ,, ,,
For fair copying - - - - -	4*d.* ,, ,,
For perusing - - - - - -	1*s.* ,, ,,

Attendance.	*s.*	*d.*
In ordinary cases - - - - - -	10	0

In extraordinary cases the taxing master may increase or diminish the above charge, if for any special reasons he shall think fit.

Abstracts of Title (where not covered by the above Scales).

	s.	*d.*
Drawing each brief sheet of 8 folios - -	6	8
Fair copy - - - - - - - - -	3	4

Journeys from Home.

In ordinary cases for every day or not less than seven hours employed on business or in travelling - - - - - - -	£5	5	0
Where a less time than seven hours is so employed - - - - - per hour	0	15	0

In extraordinary cases the taxing master may increase or diminish the above allowance, if for any special reasons he shall think fit.

(Signed) Selborne, C.
Coleridge, C.J.
G. Jessel, M.R.
E. Harvey.

REMARKS ON THE SOLICITORS' REMUNERATION ACT.

Only one Order.

The first thing that strikes the careful reader of the Solicitors' Remuneration Act and the Order to it already made is, that there is a want of certainty and simplicity about it, and that as yet all has not been done that will be done eventually under it in the way of prescribing the remuneration for non-litigious work in which settlements are not included. Possibly it will soon be impossible for the solicitor to contract himself out of it, as he can now do, by making his election in writing and communicating it to the client before the business is begun; except by agreement to take a fixed sum for the work he has to do, which is specially allowed by section 8. This will, of course, be the easiest and pleasantest way of arranging his costs; but it must not be lost sight of that this agreement may be overhauled by the taxing master, just as agreements under the Solicitors Act of 1870 now can.

Act not compulsory.

Lump sum for costs.

Principle of Act.

The principle of the Act is to change the form of the remuneration of the solicitor, and instead of paying him by length, as heretofore, to pay him by commission upon the value of the property dealt with. It must not be forgotten that a scale has long been in existence, bearing the authorisation of the Law Society, which has had much the same end in view; and that this has worked very well in London, although in the country it is often complained of as being too high.

Law Society's scale.

Where

The Act is not to apply where the vendor employs

an auctioneer and pays him himself. This has caused auctioneers to complain that the solicitor is being unduly favoured at their expense. auct'oneer employed.

It may be noticed that the scale for mortgages applies only to transfers and further charges where the solicitor charging for a transfer or further charge investigated the title upon the original mortgage. Where this is not so the old method of payment remains in force. Transfer and further charges.

Interest at four per cent. upon costs, to run from one month after a demand has been properly made, as also security for such costs, may be taken by the solicitor. Interest.

An expedition fee may be charged in respect of any business, the completion of which is required in an unusually short space of time. This rule may lead to disputes, and great care should be taken in having the instructions of the client as to this exact and complete. Order CXLII., r. 4.

All drafts and copies of documents are to belong to the client. R. 3

These are the main provisions of the Act and Order; but for the details, as where a mortgage and conveyance are to be executed at the same time, or where the same solicitor is acting for the mortgagor and mortgagee, or where there are several parties to the sale, the Order itself must be referred to. Several difficulties appear likely to arise under it, and notably under r. 11 it is probable that it will often be a moot question whether or not the solicitor has or has not arranged the sale or purchase, and the price and terms and conditions thereof.

The order as to Court Fees, which came into operation on January 1 last, is given at length.

ORDER AS TO COURT FEES.

1. The following portion of the schedule to the Order as to Court Fees made on the 28th October, 1875, is hereby repealed; that is to say,

	Lower Scale. £ s. d.	Higher Scale. £ s. d.
On taking acknowledgment of a deed by a married woman - -	1 0 0	6 0 0

And instead thereof the following fees shall henceforth be chargeable in respect of the matters hereinafter mentioned (namely):

Fees under the Act 3 & 4 Will. IV. c. 74 (the Fines and Recoveries Act).

	£ s. d.
For taking the acknowledgment of a married woman by a judge of the High Court of Justice - - - - - - - -	1 0 0
To a perpetual commissioner for taking the acknowledgment of a married woman when not required to go further than a mile from his residence - - - - - - -	0 13 4
To a perpetual commissioner when required to go more than one mile, but not more than three miles, besides his reasonable travelling expenses - - - - - - - -	1 1 0

	£	s.	d.
To a perpetual commissioner where the distance exceeds three miles, besides his reasonable travelling expenses - - - - -	2	2	0
Where more than one married woman at the same time acknowledges the same deed respecting the same property, these fees are to be taken for the first acknowledgment only, and the fees to be taken for the other acknowledgment or acknowledgments, how many soever the same may be, shall be one-half of the original fees, and so also where the same married woman shall at the same time acknowledge more than one deed respecting the same property.			
To the clerk of the peace or his deputy for every search - - - - - - -	0	1	0
To the same for every copy of a list of commissioners, provided such list shall not exceed the number of 100 names - - - -	0	5	0
To the same for every further complete number of 50 names, an additional - -	0	2	6
For every official copy of a list of commissioners, provided such list shall not exceed the number of 100 names - - - - -	0	5	0
For every further complete number of 50 names, additional - - - - - -	0	2	6
For preparing every special commission -	1	0	0
For examining the certificate and affidavit, and filing and indexing the same - - -	0	5	0
Upon the return of a special commission to the central office - - - - - - -	0	5	0
For every search in the registry of certificates of acknowledgments of deeds by married women - - - - - - - - -	0	1	0
For enrolling recognisances, deeds, and other instruments, per folio of 72 words, including			

	£	s.	d.
the certificate of enrolment endorsed on the instrument, but not including maps, plans, and drawings, which are to be charged at their actual cost - - - - - - - -	0	1	0
For endorsing a certificate of enrolment on a duplicate of any enrolled instrument, for each folio of the instrument if it does not exceed 24 folios - - - - - - -	0	0	6
For the like certificate if the instrument exceeds 24 folios - - - - - - -	0	12	0
For office copies of enrolled instruments, per folio of 72 words - - - - - -	0	0	6
For examining copies of enrolled instruments and marking them as office copies, per folio of 72 words - - - - - -	0	0	2

Fees under section 48 *of the Conveyancing and Law of Property Act*, 1881.

	£	s.	d.
On depositing a power of attorney - -	0	2	0
On an application to search for a power of attorney so deposited, and inspecting the same, and the affidavit or other documents deposited therewith, for each hour or part of an hour, not exceeding on one day 10*s*. - - - -	0	2	6

If an office copy is required, and it exceeds 2*s*. 6*d*., the fee for search and inspection is to be allowed.

Copies of powers of attorney and other documents so deposited presented at the office and stamped or marked as office copies to be charged for as office copies.

2. The following fees, by the Order as to Court Fees, dated the 6th August, 1880, directed to be inserted in the

schedule to the Order as to Court Fees made on the 28th October, 1875, are hereby repealed:—

Searches and Inspections.

	Lower Scale.			Higher Scale.		
	£	*s.*	*d.*	£	*s.*	*d.*
For an official certificate of the result of a search in one name in any register or index under the custody of the Clerk of Enrolments, the Registrar of Bills of Sale, the Registrar of Certificates of Acknowledgments of Deeds by Married Women, or the Registrar of Judgments - - -	0	5	0	0	5	0
For every additional name, if included in same certificate -	0	2	0	0	2	0
For a duplicate copy of certificate, if not more than three folios	0	1	0	0	1	0
For every additional folio -	0	0	6	0	0	6
For a continuation search, if made within 14 days of date of official certificate (the result to be endorsed on such certificate) -	0	1	0	0	1	0

3. Instead of the fees so repealed, the following fees shall henceforth be chargeable in respect of the matters hereinafter mentioned, viz.:—

Searches and Inspections.

	£	*s.*	*d.*
For an official certificate of the result of a search in one name in any register or index under the custody of the Clerk of Enrolments, the Registrar of Bills of Sale, the Registrar of Certificates of Acknowledgments of Deeds by Married Women, or the Registrar of Judgments, if not more than five folios - -	0	5	0
For every additional folio - - -	0	0	6

	£	s.	d.
For every additional name, if included in the same certificate - - - - - -	0	2	0
For an office copy of the certificate of search, if not more than three folios - -	0	1	0
For every additional folio - - - -	0	0	6
For a continuation search, if made within one calendar month of date of official certificate (the result to be endorsed on such certificate)	0	1	0

4. This order shall come into operation on the 1st January, 1883.

33 & 34 Vict. c. 28.

An Act to amend the law relating to the Remuneration of Attorneys and Solicitors. [14*th July*, 1870.

Whereas it is expedient to amend the law relating to the Remuneration of Attorneys and Solicitors: Be it enacted by the Queen's most excellent Majesty, by and with the advice and consent of the Lords, spiritual and temporal, and Commons, in this present Parliament assembled, and by the authority of the same, as follows:

Preliminary.

1. This Act may be cited as "The Attorneys and Solicitors Act, 1870." Short title.

2. This Act shall not extend to Scotland. Extent of Act.

3. In the construction of this Act, unless where the context otherwise requires, the words following have the significations hereinafter respectively assigned to them; that is to say, Interpretation of terms.

The words "attorney or solicitor" mean an attorney, solicitor, or proctor, qualified according to the provisions of the Act for the time being in force, relating to the admission and qualification of attorneys, solicitors, or proctors;

"Person" includes a corporation;

"Client" includes any person who, as a principal or on behalf of another person, retains or employs, or is about to retain or employ, an attorney or solicitor, and any person who is or may be liable to pay the bill of an attorney or solicitor for any services, fees, costs, charges, or disbursements.

Part I.

Agreements between Attorneys or Solicitors and their Clients.

The remuneration of attorneys and solicitors may be fixed by agreement.

4. An attorney or solicitor may make an agreement in writing with his client respecting the amount and manner of payment for the whole or any part of any past or future services, fees, charges, or disbursements in respect of business done or to be done by such attorney or solicitor, whether as an attorney or solicitor, or as an advocate or conveyancer, either by a gross sum, or by commission or percentage, or by salary or otherwise, and either at the same or at a greater or at a less rate as or than the rate at which he would otherwise be entitled to be remunerated, subject to the provisions and conditions in this part of this Act contained: Provided always, that when any such agreement shall be made in respect of business done or to be done in any action at law or suit in equity, the amount payable under the agreement shall not be received by the attorney or solicitor until the agreement has been examined and allowed by a taxing officer of a Court having power to enforce the agreement; and if it shall appear to such taxing officer that the agreement is not fair and reasonable, he may require the opinion of a Court or a judge to be taken thereon by motion or petition, and such Court or judge shall have power either to reduce the amount payable under the agreement, or to order the agreement to be cancelled, and the costs, fees, charges, and disbursements in respect of the business done to be taxed in the same manner as if no such agreement had been made.

Amount payable under agreement not to be paid until allowed by taxing officer.

Saving of interests of

5. Such an agreement shall not affect the amount of, or any rights or remedies for the recovery of, any costs

recoverable from the client by any other person, and any such other person may require any costs payable or recoverable by him to or from the client to be taxed according to the rules for the time being in force for the taxation of such costs, unless such person has otherwise agreed: Provided always, that the client who has entered into such agreement shall not be entitled to recover from any other person under any order for the payment of any costs which are the subject of such agreement more than the amount payable by the client to his own attorney or solicitor under the same. third parties.

6. Such an agreement shall be deemed to exclude any further claim of the attorney or solicitor beyond the terms of the agreement in respect of any services, fees, charges, or disbursements in relation to the conduct and completion of the business in reference to which the agreement is made, except such services, fees, charges, or disbursements, if any, as are expressly excepted by the agreement. Agreements shall exclude further claims.

7. A provision in any such agreement that the attorney or solicitor shall not be liable for negligence, or that he shall be relieved from any responsibility to which he would otherwise be subject as such attorney or solicitor, shall be wholly void. Reservation of responsibility for negligence.

8. No action or suit shall be brought or instituted upon any such agreement, but every question respecting the validity or effect of any such agreement may be examined and determined, and the agreement may be enforced, or set aside, without suit or action on motion or petition of any person or the representative of any person, a party to such agreement, or being alleged to be liable to pay, or being or claiming to be entitled to be paid the costs, fees, charges or disbursements in respect of which the agreement is made by the Court in which the business, or any part thereof, was done, or a judge thereof, or if the business was not done in any Court, then where the amount payable under the agreement exceeds fifty pounds, by Examination and enforcement of agreements.

any Superior Court of law or equity or a judge thereof, and when such amount does not exceed fifty pounds, by the judge of a County Court which would have jurisdiction in an action upon the agreement.

Improper agreements may be set aside.

9. Upon any such motion or petition as aforesaid, if it shall appear to the Court or a judge that such agreement is in all respects fair and reasonable between the parties, the same may be enforced by such Court or judge by rule or order in such manner and subject to such conditions, if any, as to the costs of such motion or petition as such Court or judge may think fit; but if the terms of such agreement shall not be deemed by the Court or judge to be fair and reasonable, the same may be declared void, and the Court or judge shall thereupon have power to order such agreement to be given up to be cancelled, and may direct the costs, fees, charges, and disbursements incurred or chargeable in respect of the matters included therein to be taxed in the same manner and according to the same rules as if such agreement had not been made; and the Court or judge may also make such order as to the costs of and relating to such motion or petition, and the proceedings thereon, as to the said Court or judge may seem fit.

Agreements may be re-opened after payment in special cases.

10. When the amount agreed for under any such agreement has been paid by or on behalf of the client, or by any person chargeable with or entitled to pay the same, any Court or judge having jurisdiction to examine and enforce such an agreement may, upon application to the person who has paid such amount, within twelve months after payment thereof, if it appears to such Court or a judge that the special circumstances of the case require the agreement to be re-opened, re-open the same, and order the costs, fees, charges, and disbursements to be taxed, and the whole or any portion of the amount received by the attorney or solicitor to be repaid by him, on such terms and conditions as to the Court or judge may seem just.

When any such agreement is made by the client in the capacity of guardian, or of trustee under a deed or will, or of committee of any person or persons whose estate or property will be chargeable with the amount payable under such agreement, or with any part of such amount, the agreement shall before payment be laid before the taxing officer of a Court having jurisdiction to enforce the agreement, and such officer shall examine the same, and may disallow any part thereof, or may require the direction of the Court or a judge to be taken thereon by motion or petition; and if in any such case the client pay the whole or any part of the amount payable under the agreement, without the previous allowance of such officer or Court or judge as aforesaid, he shall be liable at any time to account to the person whose estate or property is charged with the amount paid, or with any part thereof for the amount so charged; and if in any such case the attorney or solicitor accept payment without such allowance, any Court which would have had jurisdiction to enforce the agreement may, if it think fit, order him to refund the amount so received by him under the agreement.

Prohibition of certain stipulations.

11. Nothing in this Act contained shall be construed to give validity to any purchase by an attorney or solicitor of the interest, or any part of the interest, of his client in any suit, action, or other contentious proceeding to be brought or maintained, or to give validity to any agreement by which an attorney or solicitor retained or employed to prosecute any suit or action, stipulates for payment only in the event of success in such suit, action, or proceeding.

Not to give validity to contracts, &c., which may be void in bankruptcy.

12. Nothing in this Act contained shall give validity to any disposition, contract, settlement, conveyance, delivery, dealing, or transfer, which may be void or invalid against a trustee or creditor in bankruptcy, arrangement, or composition, under the provisions of the laws relating to bankruptcy.

Provision in case of death or incapacity of the attorney.

13. Where an attorney or solicitor has made an agreement with his client in pursuance of the provisions of this Act, and anything has been done by such attorney or solicitor under the agreement, and before the agreement has been completely performed by him such attorney or solicitor dies or becomes incapable to act, an application may be made to any Court which would have jurisdiction to examine and enforce the agreement by any party thereto, or by the representatives of any such party, and such Court shall thereupon have the same power to enforce or set aside such agreement, so far as the same may have been acted upon, as if such death or incapacity had not happened; and such Court, if it shall deem the agreement to be in all respects fair and reasonable, may order the amount due in respect of the past performance of the agreement to be ascertained by taxation, and the taxing officer in ascertaining such amount shall have regard so far as may be to the terms of the agreement, and payment of the amount found to be due may be enforced in the same manner as if the agreement had been completely performed by the attorney or solicitor.

As to change of attorney after agreement.

14. If after any such agreement as aforesaid shall have been made, the client shall change his attorney or solicitor before the conclusion of the business to which such agreement shall relate (which he shall be at liberty to do notwithstanding such agreement), the attorney or solicitor, party to such agreement, shall be deemed to have become incapable to act under the same within the meaning of section 13 of this Act, and upon any order being made for taxation of the amount due to such attorney or solicitor in respect of the part performance of such agreement the Court shall direct the taxing master to have regard to the circumstances under which such change of attorney or solicitor has taken place; and, upon such taxation, the attorney or solicitor shall not be deemed entitled to the full amount of the remuneration agreed to be paid to him, unless it shall appear that there has been no

default, negligence, improper delay, or other conduct on his part affording reasonable ground to the client for such change of attorney or solicitor.

15. Except as in this part of this Act provided, the bill of an attorney or solicitor for the amount due under an agreement made in pursuance of the provisions of this Act shall not be subject to any taxation, nor to the provisions of the Act of the sixth and seventh Victoria, chapter seventy-three, and the Acts amending the same respecting the signing and delivery of the bill of an attorney or solicitor.

Agreements shall be exempt from taxation.

Part II.

General Provisions.

16. An attorney or solicitor may take security from his client for his future fees, charges, and disbursements, to be ascertained by taxation or otherwise.

Security may be taken for future costs.

17. Subject to any general rules or orders hereafter to be made, upon every taxation of costs, fees, charges or disbursements, the taxing officer may allow interest at such rate and from such time as he thinks just on moneys disbursed by the attorney or solicitor for his client, and on moneys of the client in the hands of the attorney or solicitor, and improperly retained by him.

Security may be taken for future costs.

18. Upon any taxation of costs, the taxing officer may, in determining the remuneration, if any, to be allowed to the attorney or solicitor for his services, have regard, subject to any general rules or orders hereafter to be made, to the skill, labour and responsibility involved.

Taxing officer to have regard to character of services.

19. Whenever any decree or order shall have been made for payment of costs in any suit, and such suit shall afterwards become abated, it shall be lawful for any person interested under such decree or order to revive such suit, and thereupon to prosecute and enforce such decree or order, and so on from time to time as often as any such abatement shall happen.

Revival of order for payment of costs.

Power to attorneys, &c., to perform acts as appertain to office of proctor.

20. From and after the passing of this Act, it shall be lawful for an attorney or solicitor to perform all such acts as appertain solely to the office of a proctor, in any Ecclesiastical Court other than the Provincial Courts of the Archbishops of Canterbury and of York, and the Diocesan Court of the Bishop of London, without incurring any forfeiture or penalty, and to make the same charges which a proctor would be entitled to make, and to recover the same, any enactments to the contrary notwithstanding.

SOLICITORS ACT, 1843.

6 & 7 VICT. C. 73, ss. 37—41.

37. And be it enacted that from and after the passing of this Act no attorney or solicitor, nor any executor, administrator, or assignee of any attorney or solicitor, shall commence or maintain any action or suit for the recovery of any fees, charges or disbursements for any business done by such attorney or solicitor, until the expiration of one month after such attorney or solicitor, or executor, administrator, or assignee of such attorney or solicitor, shall have delivered unto the party to be charged therewith, or sent by the post to or left for him at his counting-house, office of business, dwelling-house, or last known place of abode, a bill of such fees, charges, and disbursements, and which bill shall either be subscribed with the proper hand of such attorney or solicitor (or, in the case of a partnership, by any of the partners, either with his own name or with the name or style of such partnership), or of the executor, administrator, or assignee of such attorney or solicitor, or be enclosed in or accompanied by a letter subscribed in like manner, referring to such bill.

Attorneys and solicitors not to commence an action for fees till one month after delivery of bills.

And upon the application of the party chargeable by such bill within such month it shall be lawful, in case the business contained in such bill or any part thereof shall have been transacted in the High Court of Chancery, or any other Court of equity, or in any matter of bank-

Reference of bills, whether relating to business transacted in Court or

not, for taxation.

ruptcy or lunacy, or in case no part of such business shall have been transacted in any Court of law or equity, for the Lord High Chancellor or the Master of the Rolls, and in case any part of such business shall have been transacted in any other Court, for the Courts of Queen's Bench, Common Pleas, Exchequer, Court of Common Pleas at Lancaster, or Court of Pleas at Durham, or any judge of either of them, and they are hereby respectively required to refer such bill, and the demand of such attorney or solicitor, executor, administrator or assignee, thereupon to be taxed and settled by the proper officer of the Court in which such reference shall be made, without any money being brought into Court; and the Court or judge making such reference shall restrain such attorney or solicitor, or executor, administrator or assignee of such attorney or solicitor, from commencing any action or suit touching such demand pending such reference.

Taxation after one month.

And in case no such application as aforesaid shall be made within such month as aforesaid, then it shall be lawful for such reference to be made as aforesaid, either upon the application of the attorney or solicitor, or the executor, administrator, or assignee of the attorney or solicitor, whose bill may have been so as aforesaid delivered, sent or left, or upon the application of the party chargeable by such bill, with such directions and subject to such conditions as the Court or judge making such reference shall think proper; and such Court or judge may restrain such attorney or solicitor, or the executor, administrator, or assignee of such attorney or solicitor, from commencing or prosecuting any action or suit touching such demand pending such reference upon such terms as shall be thought proper.

Taxation after twelve months, under special circumstances.

Provided always, that no such reference as aforesaid shall be directed upon an application made by the party chargeable with such bill after a verdict shall have been obtained or a writ of inquiry executed in any action for the recovery of the demand of such attorney or solicitor, or executor, administrator, or assignee of such attorney or solicitor, or after the expiration of twelve months after such bill shall have been delivered, sent or left as aforesaid, except under special circumstances, to be proved to the satisfaction of the Court or judge to whom the application for such reference shall be made.

And upon every such reference, if either the attorney or solicitor, or executor, administrator or assignee of the attorney or solicitor, whose bill shall have been delivered, sent or left, or the party chargeable with such bill, having due notice, shall refuse or neglect to attend such taxation, the officer to whom such reference shall be made may proceed to tax and settle such bill and demand ex parte.

Payment of costs of taxation.

And in case any such reference as aforesaid shall be made upon the application of the party chargeable with such bill, or upon the application of such attorney or solicitor, or the executor, administrator or assignee of such attorney or solicitor, and the party chargeable with such bill shall attend upon such taxation, the costs of such reference shall, except as hereinafter provided for, be paid according to the event of such taxation; that is to say, if such bill when taxed be less by a sixth part than the bill delivered, sent or left, then such attorney or solicitor, or executor, administrator or assignee of such attorney or solicitor, shall pay such costs; and if such bill when taxed shall not be less by a sixth part than the bill delivered, sent or left, then the party chargeable with such bill, making such application or so attending, shall pay such costs; and every order to be made for such reference as aforesaid shall direct the officer to whom such reference shall be made to tax such costs of such reference to be so paid as aforesaid, and to certify what, upon such reference, shall be found to be due to or from such attorney or solicitor, or executor, administrator or assignee of such attorney or solicitor, in respect of such bill and demand, and of the costs of such reference, if payable: Provided also, that such officer shall in all cases be at liberty to certify specially any circumstances relating to such bill or taxation, and the Court or judge shall be at liberty to make thereupon any such order as such Court or judge may think right respecting the payment of the costs of such taxation: Provided also, that where such reference as aforesaid shall be made when the same is not authorised to be made except under special circumstances, as hereinbefore provided, then the said Court or judge shall be at liberty, if it shall be thought fit, to give any special directions relative to the costs of such reference.

Courts may order atttorney or solicitor to deliver his bill and to deliver up deeds, &c.

Provided also, that it shall be lawful for the said respective Courts and judges, in the same cases in which they are respectively authorised to refer a bill which has been so as aforesaid delivered, sent, or left, to make such order for the delivery by any attorney or solicitor, or the executor, administrator or assignee of any attorney or solicitor, of such bill as aforesaid, and for the delivery up of deeds, documents, or papers in his possession, custody, or power, or otherwise touching the same, in the same manner as has heretofore been done as regards such attorney or solicitor, by such Courts or judges respectively, where any such business had been transacted in the Court in which such order was made.

Evidence of delivery of bill.

Provided also, that it shall not in any case be necessary in the first instance for such attorney or solicitor, or the executor, administrator, or assignee of such attorney or solicitor, in proving a compliance with this Act, to prove the contents of the bill he may have delivered, sent, or left, but it shall be sufficient to prove that a bill of fees, charges or disbursements, subscribed in the manner aforesaid, or enclosed or accompanied by such letter as aforesaid, was delivered, sent, or left in manner aforesaid; but, nevertheless, it shall be competent for the other party to show that the bill so delivered, sent, or left was not such a bill as constituted a bonâ fide compliance with this Act.

Power to

Provided also, that it shall be lawful for any judge of

the Superior Courts of law and equity to authorise an attorney or solicitor to commence an action or suit for the recovery of his fees, charges, or disbursements against the party chargeable therewith, and also to refer his bill of fees, charges and disbursements and the demand of such attorney and solicitor thereupon to be taxed and settled by the proper officer of the Court in which such reference shall be made, although one month shall not have expired from the delivery of the bill of fees, charges, or disbursements, on proof to the satisfaction of the said judge that there is probable cause for believing that the party chargeable therewith is about to quit England, or to become a bankrupt, or a liquidating or compounding debtor, or to take any other steps, or do any other act, which in the opinion of the judge would tend to defeat or delay such attorney or solicitor in obtaining payment.

judge to authorise action or taxation before expiration of month (as amended by 38 & 39 Vict. c. 79, s. 2).

38. And be it enacted, that where any person, not the party chargeable with any such bill within the meaning of the provisions hereinbefore contained, shall be liable to pay, or shall have paid, such bill, either to the attorney or solicitor, his executor, administrator, or assignee, or to the party chargeable with such bill as aforesaid, it shall be lawful for such person, his executor, administrator, or assignee, to make such application for a reference for the taxation and settlement of such bill as the party chargeable therewith might himself make, and the same reference and order shall be made thereupon, and the same course pursued in all respects, as if such application was made by the party so chargeable with such bill as aforesaid: Provided always, that in case such application is made when, under the provisions herein contained, a reference is not authorised to be made except under special circumstances, it shall be lawful for the Court or judge to whom such application shall be made to take into consideration any additional special circumstances applicable to the person making such application, although such circumstance might not be applicable to the party so chargeable

Bills may be taxed upon the application of third parties.

with the said bill as aforesaid, if he was the party making the application.

Lord Chancellor may direct taxation of bills, chargeable on executors, &c.

39. And be it enacted, that it shall be lawful, in any case in which a trustee, executor, or administrator has become chargeable with any such bill as aforesaid, for the Lord High Chancellor or the Master of the Rolls, if in his discretion he shall think fit, upon the application of a party interested in the property out of which such trustee, executor, or administrator may have paid or be entitled to pay such bill, to refer the same, and such attorney's or solicitor's, or executor's, administrator's, or assignee's demand thereupon, to be taxed and settled by the proper officer of the High Court of Chancery, with such directions and subject to such conditions as such judge shall think fit, and to make such order as such judge shall think fit for the payment of what may be found due, and of the costs of such reference, to or by such attorney or solicitor, or the executor, administrator, or assignee of such attorney or solicitor, by or to the party making such application, having regard to the provisions herein contained relative to applications for the like purpose by the party chargeable with such bill, so far as the same shall be applicable to such cases, and in exercising such discretion as aforesaid the said judge may take into consideration the extent and nature of the interest of the party making the application: Provided always, that when any money shall be so directed to be paid by such attorney or solicitor, or the executor, administrator, or assignee of such attorney or solicitor, it shall be lawful for such judge, if he shall think fit, to order the same, or any part thereof, to be paid to such trustee, executor, or administrator, so chargeable with such bill, instead of being paid to the party making such application; and when the party making such application shall pay any money to such attorney or solicitor, or executor, administrator, or assignee of such attorney or solicitor, in respect of such bill, he shall have the same right to be paid by such trustee, exe-

cutor, or administrator so chargeable with such bill as such attorney or solicitor, or executor, administrator, or assignee of such attorney or solicitor, had.

40. And be it enacted that for the purpose of any such reference upon the application of the person not being the party chargeable within the meaning of the provisions of this Act as aforesaid, or of a party interested as aforesaid, it shall be lawful for such Court or judge to order any such attorney or solicitor, or the executor, administrator, or assignee of any such attorney or solicitor, to deliver to the party making such application a copy of such bill, upon payment of the costs of such copy:

Copy of bill to be delivered to person making application for reference for taxation.

Provided always, that no bill which shall have been previously taxed and settled shall be again referred unless, under special circumstances, the Court or judge to whom such application is made shall think fit to direct a re-taxation thereof.

No re-taxation.

41. And be it enacted, that the payment of any such bill as aforesaid shall in no case preclude the Court or judge to whom application shall be made from referring such bill for taxation, if the special circumstances of the case shall in the opinion of such Court or judge appear to require the same, upon such terms and conditions and subject to such directions as to such Court or judge shall seem right, provided the application for such reference be made within twelve calendar months after payment.

Taxation of bill after payment.

AN ITEM DISALLOWED ON TAXATION

See page 166.

In re Snell (a solicitor), L. R. 5 Ch. D. 821.

August 11th to Oct. 29th. Attending at the offices of the company on Mr. J. H. Patrick, the manager of the company, perusing the accounts of the company, and going fully into the same, and obtaining information as to the affairs of the company and the mode in which the business was carried on and numerous attendances on Mr. Patrick, Mr. Barber, and Mr. Walker, as to the amount of ore raised and sold from the mine and the debts and liabilities of the company, several attendances at the furnaces at Sandy, inspecting the books there and the mine and going through the same and comparing the workings with the plans and obtaining explanations from Mr. Collins and other persons as to the value of the mine, and afterwards attendances on Mr. Patrick, going fully with him into the charges made in the bill, which was already prepared and printed, and arranging to meet Mr. Davis, who he informed me was going to America for that purpose; and taking journey to Omaha, where the principal quantity of bullion obtained from the mine was sold, inspecting the books of the Omaha Smelting Company and taking extracts therefrom showing the quantity of bullion received and paid for since the company was formed, and attending with Mr. Patrick or Mr. Davis in New York discussing the position of matters fully with him at several interviews, and ultimately Mr. Davis said he was going to Salt Lake City and would look into matters and on his return to Paris he would be glad to see me and listen to any proposition for a settlement, but he would have nothing to do with Mr. Sergeant Sleigh, Mr. Murray, or any other member of the Committee, and attendances at Salt Lake City on Messrs. Baskin, the company's legal advisers there, conferring with them as to the action pending against the company and giving them particulars, and on its being decided to issue a commission to London to examine witnesses thereon and giving them names to whom to direct the commission - - - - - - 150 0 0

CASES ON NEGLIGENCE.

The following cases have been collected from various treatises, as being therein stated to bear upon solicitors' negligence. In searching after decisions on a particular subject, a person may, by reference to some one of them, be put on the right tack.

Acting Gratuitously.

Donaldson v. Holdane, 7 Cl. & F. 762.

Advising Litigation.

Gill v. Lougher, J C. & J. 170.
Otley v. Gilby, 14 L. J. Ch. 178; 7 Beav. 602.
Jacks v. Bell, 3 C. & P. 316.
Re Clarke, 21 L. J. Ch. 20.
Sill v. Thomas, 8 C. & P. 762.
Hill v. Finney, 4 F. & F. 625, n.

Agent, Negligence of.

Simons v. Rose, 31 Beav. 11.

Clerk, Negligence of.

Floyd v. Naugh, 3 Atk. 568.
Prestwick v. Poley, 18 C. B. N.S. 806; 34 L.J. C.P. 159.

Compensation (Courts will not interfere summarily to compel).

Dixon v. Wilkinson, 4 Drew, 614.
Re William Jones, 1 Chit. 651.
Garner v. Lawson, 1 Barnard, 101.
Rex v. Few, Say Rep. 50.

Compromise, When Solicitor may.

Fray *v.* Voules, El. & El. 839.

Prestwick *v.* Poley, 13 W. R. 757; 18 C. B. N. S. 806; 34 L. J. C. P. 189.

Straus *v.* Francis, L. R. 1 Q. B. 379; 35 L. J. Q. B. 153. Counsel's power to.

Conduct of Actions and Suits.

Williams *v.* Gibbs, 5 Ad. & E 208. Proceeding in Court which has no jurisdiction.

Jacob *v.* Bell, 3 C. & P. 317.

Harte *v.* Frame, 6 Clarke & F. 193. On wrong section of Act of Parliament.

Thwaites *v.* Mackenzie, 3 C. & P. 341. Before sufficiently investigating facts.

Gill *v.* Lougher, 1 C. & J. 170.

Montgomery *v.* Devereux, 7 Cl. & F. 188.

Long *v.* Orsi, 18 C. B. 619. Before proper preliminaries have been taken.

Hunter *v.* Caldwell, 10 Q. B. 69; 16 L. J. Q. B. 274.

Re Bolton, 9 Beav. 272. Gross mistakes in proceedings.

Ridley *v.* Tiplady, 20 Beav. 44. Not prosecuting proceedings with diligence.

Ridley *v.* Jolland, 8 Ves. 72.

Frankland *v.* Cole, 2 Cr. & J. 590.

Stokes *v.* Trumper, 2 Kay & J. 232.

Godefrey *v.* Jay, 7 Bing. 413. Allowing judgment to go by default.

Bevins *v.* Hulme, 15 M. & W. 88; 15 L. J. 226 Ex. Discharging defendant from custody without receiving satisfaction.

Godefrey *v.* Jay (*supra*). Neglecting to set aside irregular proceedings.

Flower *v.* Bolingbroke, 1 Stc. 639. Not entering up a judgment.

Shilcock *v.* Passman, 7 Car. & P. 289. Not applying for prisoner's discharge from execution under 48 Geo. III. c. 123, s. 1.

Neglecting to deliver briefs, &c. Roufigny v. Peale, 3 Taunt. 484.
Lowry v. Guilford, 5 C. & P. 234.
Hawkins v. Harwood, 4 Ex. 503.
Hoby v. Built, 3. B. & Ad. 530.

Not subpœnaing witnesses. Reece v. Rigby, 4 B. & Ald. 202.
Price v. Buller, 3 L. J. 39 K. B.

Non-attendance at trial. Nash v. Swinburne, 3 M. & G. 630.
Roufigny v. Peale, 3 Taunt. 484.
Swannell v. Ellis, 1 Bing. 347.
Atcheson v. Madock, Peaks, 163.
Dauntley v. Hyde, 6 Jur. 163.

Not instructing counsel properly. Rex v. Tew, Sayer, 50.
Doe v. Roe, 1 L. J. O. S. K. B. 154.
De Ressigny v. Peale, 3 Taunt. 484.
Dauntley v. Hyde (*supra*).

Unnecessarily suing in Superior Court. Lee v. Dixon, 3 F. & F. 744.

Omitting to make endorsement of service. Curlewis v. Broad, 31 L. J. Ex. 473; 10 W. R. 797.

Managing clerk receiving money for investment. Cornelius v. Harrison, 2 F. & F. 758.

Not issuing execution. Harrington v. Binns, 3 F. & F. 942.

Arresting on attachment, afterwards set aside. Williams v. Smith, 1 Dowl. P. C. 632.

Mistake in Order of Court. *In re* Bolton, 9 Beav. 272.
Re Spencer, 18 W. R. Ch. 240.

Neglect or ignorance of procedure. Cox v. Leech, 1 C. B. N. S. 617.
Hunter v. Caldwell, 10 Q. B. 69.
Frankland v. Cole, 2 Cr. & J. 590.
Huntley v. Bulwer, 6 Bing. N. C. 111.
Stannard v. Ullithorne, 10 Bing. 491.
Jacaud v. French, 12 East, 317.
Plant v. Pearman, 41 L. J. Q. B. 169.
Long v. Orsi, 18 C. B. 610.
Stokes v. Trumper, 2 K. & J. 232.

Williams v. Gibbs, 5 Ad. & El. 208.
Kemp v. Burt, 4 B. & Ad. 424.
Simons v. Rose, 31 Beav. 1.
Russell v. Stewart, 3 Beav. 1787.
Pitt v. Yalden, 4 Beav. 2060.
Laidler v. Elliot, 3 B. & C. 738.
Russell v. Palmer, 2 Wils. 325.
Hill v. Finney (*supra*).
Allison v. Rayner, 7 B. & C. 441. Not informing client as to costs.
Day v. Ward, 1 Stark. 409. Negligence must be the whole cause of failure.
Passmore v. Birnie, 2 Stark. 59.
Johnstone v. Alston, 1 Camp. 176.
Robinson v. Ward, 1 Ry. & M. 274. Failure of solicitor's bank.
Knight v. Lord Plymouth, 3 Atk. 480.
Rowth v. Slowell, 3 Ves. 656.
Adams v. Claxton, 6 Ves. 226.

Conduct in Matters not in Litigation.

Brooks v. Day, Dick. 572. Not examining title deeds.
Brown v. Howard, 4 B. Moore, 508.
Wilson v. Tucker, 3 Stark, 154.
Ireson v. Pearman, 3 B. & C. 799.
Wilson v. Tucker, 3 Stark. 154.
Allen v. Clarke, 1 N. R. 358.
Ireson v. Pearman, (*supra*). Drawing wrong conclusions from deeds.
Parker v. Rolls, 14 C. B. 691. Ignorance of principles of conveyancing.
Stannard v. Ullithorne, 10 Bing. 491. Allowing improper covenant.
Smith v. Pococke, 23 L. J. Ch. 545. Investment of client's money.
Craig v. Watson, 8 Beav. 427.
Hayne v. Rhodes, 8 Q. B. Rep. 342.
Whitehead v. Greatham, 2 Bing. 464.
Watts v. Porter, 3 E. & Bl. 743; 23 L. J. Q. B. 345.
Cooper v. Stephenson, 21 L. J. Q. B. 292.
King v. Waters, Pre. Ch. 19.

Dartnall *v.* Howard, 4 B. & C. 350.
Luke *v.* Bridges, Pre. Ch. 147.
Cases of mortgage. Brumbridge *v.* Massey, 28 L. J. Ex. 59.
Hayne *v.* Rhodes (*supra*).
Hopgood *v.* Parkins, L. R. 11 Eq. 74.
Watts *v.* Porter, 3 E. & B. 743.
Particulars of sale. Taylor *v.* Gorman, 4 Ir. Eq. Rep. 550.
Expenses of conveyances. Potts *v.* Dutton, 8 Beav. 493.
Deed not under seal or unattested. Elkington v. Holland, 9 M. & W. 659.
Parker *v.* Rolls (*supra*).
Money paid to him as agent of vendor. Edgill *v.* Day, 23 L. J. C. P. 7; 1 L. R. C. P. 110.
Bickford *v.* D'Arcy, 1 L. R. Ex. 354.

Counsel.

When counsel shield. Brasey *v.* Carter, 12 A. & E. 373.
Baker *v.* Chandlers, 3 Camp. 17.
Laidler *v.* Elliot, 5 D. & R. 635.
Bulmer *v.* Gilman, 4 M. & G. 108.
Kemp *v.* Burt, 1 New. & Mas. 362.
Jacobs *v.* Bell, 3 Car. & P. 316.
Donaldson *v.* Haldane, 7 Cl. & F. 702.
Hunter *v.* Caldwell, 16 L. J. N. S. 274 Q. B.
Reece *v.* Rigby, 4 B. & Ald. 202.
Jones *v.* Lewis, 9 Dowl. 143.
Hart *v.* Frame, 6 Cl. & F. 193.
Stevenson *v.* Rowland, Dowl. & Clarke, 119.
After case laid before. Andrews *v.* Handley, 26 L. J. Ex. 323.
Fray *v.* Voules (*supra*).
Manning *v.* Willkins, 12 L. T. 249.

Declaration.

Form of. Jones *v.* Lewis, 9 Dowl. 143.
Hayne *v.* Rhodes, 8 Q. B. Rep. 342.
Stannard *v.* Ullithorne, 3 Bing. N. C. 326.

Deeds and Papers lost.

Reeve *v.* Palmer, 5 Jur. N. S. 916.
N. W. Ry. Co. *v.* Sharp, 10 Ex. 451.

Reeve *v.* Palmer, 27 L. J. C. P. 324.
Wilmot *v.* Elkington, 2 L. J. K. B. 103.

Error.

Godefroy *v.* Dulton.
Laidley *v.* Elliot.

Upon points of new or rare occurrence.

Extent of Negligence.

Lamplien *v.* Phipes, 8 C. & P. 479.
Purvis *v.* Landall, 12 Cl. Q. B. 91.
Godefroy *v.* Dalton, 6 Bing. 461.
Godefroy *v.* Jay, 7 Bing. 413.
Marzetti *v.* Williams, 1 B. & Ald. 415.
Bettyes *v.* Maynard, W.N. 10 March, 1883.
Laugdon *v.* Godfrey, 4 F. & F. 445.

Must amount to lata culpa or crassa negligentia.

Amount of negligence client must show.

Liable only for particular thing for which he is retained.

Gross Negligence.

Lindler *v.* Elliot, 3 B. & C. 738.
Elkington *v.* Holland, 9 M. & W. 659.

Ignorance of Law.

Pitt *v.* Yalden, 4 Burr. 2060.
Kemp *v.* Burt, 1 New. & Man. 262.

Inattention to Facts after Notice.

Stannard *v.* Ullithorne, 10 Bing, 500.
Jacaud *v.* French, 12 East, 317.

Investing Money, Failure in.

Harman *v.* Johnson, 2 E. & Bl. 61.

Liability, whether certificated or not.

Brown *v.* Tolley, 31 L. T. N. S. 485.

Limitations, Statute of.

Howell *v.* Young, 5 B. & C. 259.

Obligation.

Fish *v.* Kelly, 17 C. B. N. S. 194.
Westaway *v.* Frost, 17 L. J. Q. B. 286.

Is with client, not with a stranger.

Hubbard *v.* Phillips, 13 M. & W. 702.
Andrews *v.* Hawley, 20 L. J. Ex. 323.

Partner, Negligence of.

Norton *v.* Cooper, 3 Sm. & Giff. 375.
Dundonald *v.* Masterman, L. R. 7 Eq. 504; 38 L. J. Ch. 350.
Bickford *v.* D'Arcy, L. R. 1 Ex. 354; 14 L. T. N. S. 629.

Patent Agents.

Lee *v.* Walker, L. R. 7 C. P. 121; 41 L. J. C. P. 91.

Privity of Contract.

Must be between the parties.

Robertson *v.* Fleming, 4 Macq. H. L. 167.
Fish *v.* Kelly, 17 C. B. 194.
Simons *v.* Rose, 31 Beav. 1.
Allen *v.* Clarke, 7 L. T. 781.

Precautions not taken.

Long *v.* Orsi, 18 C. B. 610.
Cox *v.* Leech, 1 C. B. N. S. 617.

Remedy against Solicitor.

Temple *v.* Laughlan, 2 N. R. 136.
Russell *v.* Palmer, 2 Wil. 235.
Pitt *v.* Yalden, 4 Burr. 2061.

Measure of damages.

Davis *v.* Garrett, 6 Bing. 716.
Rolin *v.* Steward, 23 L. J. C. P. 149.

Retainers.

Cannot throw up without notice.

Wadsworth *v.* Marshall, 2 Cr. & J. 665.
Hoby *v.* Built, 3 B. & Ald. 350.
Van Sandau *v.* Brown, 9 Bing. 402.

Ends when judgment is recovered.

Flower *v.* Bolingbroke, 1 Str. 639.
Brackenburg *v.* Pell, 12 East, 588.
Macbeath *v.* Ellis, 4 Bing. 578.
Hastings *v.* Hallick, 13 Cal. 203.

Pennington *v.* Yell, 6 Eng. (Ark.) 212.
Butler *v.* Knight, L. R. 2 Ex. 109; 36 L. J. Ex. 66. May be renewed, with power to compromise.

Services.

Long *v.* Orsi, 18 Com. Bench, 610; 26 L. J. C. P. 127. Where wholly useless to client.
Hill *v.* Featherstonaugh, 7 Bing. 569.
Hill *v.* Allen, 2 M. & W. 284.
Symes *v.* Nipper, 12 Ad. & E. 277, n.
Bracey *v.* Carter, *ib.* 373.
Cousins *v.* Paddon, 2 C. M. & R. 547, 556.
Randall *v.* Ikey, 4 Dowl. 682.
Huntley *v.* Bulwer, 6 Bing. N. C. 111.
Lewis *v.* Samuel, 8 Q. B. 455.
Bracey *v.* Carter, 12 A. & E. 373. At first useful, afterwards not.

Sill *v.* Thomas, 8 C. & P. 762. Benefit of compromise lost.

Shaw *v.* Aiden, 9 Bing. 257. Past useless.
Templar *v.* M'Lachlan, 2 New. R. 136. Cross action negligence, claim for remuneration.
Edward *v.* Cooper, 3 C. & P. 277.
Smith *v.* Rolt, 2 Dowl. 62.
Brazin *v.* Bryant, 2 Dowl. 600.

Undertakings by Solicitors.

Re Hilliard, 2 D. & S. 919.

INDEX.

Abandoned Motion,
costs of, 131

Account,
re-opened between solicitor and client, 69
of solicitor acting as agent, 163
action for between partners, costs, 192

Accountant,
costs of inspection by, 179
scale for payment of, 179

Action,
remitted to County Court, costs, 124
remitted to High Court, 124
and counterclaim referred to arbitrator, 126
by next of kin or legatees, 147, 148
in creditors' administration suit, costs, rule, 148

Adjournments,
for third parties to be added, 134
before chief clerk, costs, 168

Administration Action,
change of solicitors, 65
taxation of costs, 147
Chancery practice in, 182
former letters revoked, 192
brought in County Court, 151

ADMINISTRATION ACTION—*continued.*
by next of kin or legatees, 147, 148
by creditors, costs, rule, 148
and partnership, distinction, 193
priority of solicitors' costs, 205

ADMISSION,
notice of desire to be admitted, 9
clerk must be of full age, 9

ADVOCATES, SOLICITORS AS,
articled clerks, 10
preliminary enquiries, 94
proceedings before grand jury, 94
trial before magistrates, 94
in bankruptcy solicitor to parties heard, 94
in county courts, 95
solicitors' clerk, 96
articled clerk before magistrates, 96
privilege, 96

AFFIDAVIT,
of due execution of articles, 3
of due service under articles, 10
answering matter in, 15
unnecessary, 103
upon application to strike off the rolls, 116
not entered in order as read, costs, 165
of increase, 183

AGENT,
unqualified practitioner employing, 115
See *Town Agent*, 84—89

AGREEMENTS WITH SOLICITORS,
between solicitor and articled clerk, 8
to pay more than taxed costs, 74
costs out of pocket only, 74
between country solicitor and agent, 74
champerty, 75, 77, 99
not to charge anything for costs, 75
solicitor charging more than taxed costs, plea, 75

AGREEMENTS WITH SOLICITORS—*continued.*
third parties, 75
as to remuneration, 75
Solicitors' Remuneration Act, 1881,...76
agreement to be examined by taxing master, 76, 169
charges must appear reasonable, 77
opinion of Court may be taken, 77
costs before magistrates, taxation, 77
motion or petition to set aside, 77
client refusing to employ his solicitor, 78
improper agreements, 78
costs of petition for taxation, 78
re-opened within twelve months, 79
by trustees, guardians, &c., 79
not to charge solicitor and client costs, 183
undertakings by solicitors, 79—83. See *Undertakings.*
agreements to pay commission on property recovered, 99
between defendants to maintain one another, 99

ALLOWANCE,
to plaintiff for subsistence, 182

AMENDMENTS,
set up by plaintiff, costs, 135

ANNUITY,
purchase of, from client, 70

APPEALS,
costs generally, 121
time for application, 121
on questions raised on taxation, 119, 152
to Lords, costs pending, 133
security for costs, 134
vexatious, 135
new trial granted, 137
bankruptcy, costs of attendance of country solicitor, 166

APPEARANCE,
failure of solicitor to enter, 28, 32
use of defendant's name without authority, 32

APPLICATIONS,
to strike off the rolls, 13, 116
for re-admission, 14
costs of unnecessary applications, 129
to judge on taxing master's certificate, 132
for order to review taxation, 132, 156
for security for costs, 134, 136
against solicitors, costs, 137
for taxation by third parties, 170
for taxation by parties interested, 171

ARBITRATOR,
action and counterclaim referred to, 126

ARTICLED CLERKS,
duration of clerkship, 1
coupling of periods of service, 1
Solicitors Act, 1877, as to service, 1
irregular service, 2
cancellation of articles by mutual consent, 3
stamp duty on articles, 3
enrolment of articles, 3
neglect to enrol, 4
application to Court, form of order, 4
lost articles, 5
service must be continuous, 5
absence for several months, 5
service by ten years' men, 6
other engagements during articles, 6
employment under articles, 6
service, definition of, 8
agreement between master and clerk, 8
costs of clerk on application to the Court, 9
must be of full age to be admitted, 9
adoption of articles after attaining twenty-one, 9
admission, notice of, 9
affidavit of due service, 10
judge may refuse to admit, 10
as advocates, 10, 96
notaries, 10. See *Notaries*.

ARTICLES OF ASSOCIATION,
retainer of solicitor by, 24

Articles of Clerkship.
See *Articled Clerks.*

Attachment,
power of Court to issue writ of, against solicitor, 16
ability to pay must be shown, 16
when attachment issues, 17
order, notice, 17
non-compliance with order for taxation, 141
solicitor failing to give undertaking, 83

Attendance,
at taxation, 144, 150

Bankruptcy,
of solicitor, 63
of client, 63
costs of solicitor, trustee in bankruptcy, 92
solicitor to the parties may be heard in, 94
proof of solicitor's bill, 143
taxation, power of registrar, 156, 176
appeal, attendance of country solicitor, 166
solicitor cannot insist on taxation, 143
application for taxation by official liquidator, 176
trustee's priority for costs, 193

Bill of Costs,
privileged at client's desire, 40
See *Costs.*
of town agent, taxation, 138
solicitor refusing to produce, 139
time for action for costs, 140
delivery of, 141
must be signed by solicitor, 141
order for delivery of, 141
service, 142
cannot be altered after delivery, 142, 168
withdrawal of, 142
proof of in bankruptcy, 143
promissory note given for, 143
costs of taxation, 143

BILL OF COSTS—*continued.*
method of making, 162
proof of items, 163, 164
examination of solicitor in support of, 169
payment of under protest, 173
payment under undue influence, 174
solicitor, executor paying himself out of assets, 176
re-opened after two years, 174
See *Taxation.*

BRIEF,
solicitor omitting to deliver, 17
time for delivery of, 18
instructions for, costs, 181
what instructions comprise, 181

CANCELLATION
of articles of clerkship, 3

CERTIFICATE,
practising without London certificate, 85
solicitor acting without, 112
unqualified practitioners, (see) 116

CHAMBERS,
attendance of counsel at, 151

CHAMPERTY, 75, 77, 99

CHANGE OF SOLICITORS, 62—67
See *Solicitors.*

CHARGE OF SOLICITORS,
statutory, 49
on property recovered or preserved, 50
notice of to absconding client, 52
priorities, 51. See *Priorities*, 203—207
scandalous charges, 146

CHARGING ORDER.
See *Statutory Charges*, 194—202

CHARITIES,
gifts to, costs, 146

CHIEF CLERK,
costs of adjournments before, 168

CLAIM,
and counterclaim, costs, 126, 127
for fictitious amount, 128

CLERK,
solicitor acting as, 14
liability, 14
confidential clerk, privilege, 37
advocacy, 96

CLERKSHIP.
See *Articled Clerks*, 1—10

CLIENT,
retainer of solicitor. See *Retainer*, 22, 35
ratifying solicitor's actions, 24
address of privileged, 39
moneys of, solicitor's lien, 49
failure to find funds, 63
letters of, no lien on, 59
dealings with solicitors, 68
refusing to employ his solicitor, 78
no privity between client and town agent, 52, 86, 87
remedy against solicitor for negligence, 106. See *Town Agent*, 52—91
costs payable by, 161—172
taxation between solicitor and client, 161. See *Taxation between Solicitor and Client*, 145—151
old rules still in force, 161
system of payment in litigious business, 161
solicitor's diary, 162
method of making bill, 162
remarks of Jessel, M.R., on costs, 162
burden of proof of items lies on solicitor, 163
solicitor acting as agent, account, 163
items allowed between solicitor and client, 164
party and party costs, what allowed, 164
negotiations before action, 165
professional work only to be charged for, 165

CLIENT—*continued.*
unnecessary proceedings, 165
affidavits not entered in order as read, 165
journeys by solicitors, 166
costs of solicitor attending bankruptcy appeal, 166
order for a change of solicitors, 167
taxation after compromise of first solicitor's bill, 167
adjournments before chief clerk, 168
procuring execution of lease by tenant, 168
requiring papers to be delivered over, 168
conference with counsel, no fee paid, 168
fee for instructions for brief, 168
bill cannot be altered after delivery, 168
second bill before taxation of first, 169
order for examination of solicitor in support of bill, 169
taxing master can decide questions of retainer, 169
powers of taxing master, 157, 169
taxation on application of third parties, 170
solicitor acting for trustee, 170
benefits of agreements between solicitor and client, 170
discretion of Court to order delivery of papers, 171
order for taxation by party interested, 171
who are parties interested, 171
trustee employing a solicitor, 171
trustee acting as solicitor, 172
client out of jurisdiction desiring taxation, 172
solicitor must protect against expenses, 184

COMPANY,
appointment of solicitor by, 24

COMPROMISE,
power of solicitor to, 25
in defiance of instructions, 25, 105
for a "certain" sum, 106
taxation after compromise of first solicitor's bill, 167
by client, 210
after property recovered, 191

CONFIDENTIAL COMMUNICATIONS.
See *Privilege*, 36—43

CONFIDENTIAL RELATIONSHIP
between solicitor and client, 71

CONSENT,
orders by, 136

CONTRACT
or tort? 125

CORPORATIONS,
retainer of solicitor by, 24
lien on papers of by town clerk, 46

CORRESPONDENCE,
privileged, 39

COSTS GENERALLY,
of articled clerk on application to the Court, 9
agreements as to, 74, 75. See *Agreements.*
of solicitor, trustee, 92
of unqualified practitioners, 113
of useless litigation, 118
of indulgence of the Court, 119
in common law courts, 119
power to order solicitor and client costs, 119
rules as to, 120
fixing definite sum in place of, 120
jury cases, 120, 121
County Courts Act, 1867,...121
trustees and mortgagees, Order LV., r. 1,...121
on appeal, 121
time for application for costs, 121
judge can deprive successful party of costs mero motu, 122
power of Divisional Courts, 122
where there are two trials, 123
proceedings before a master, 123
appeal from master as to costs, 123
in libel and slander cases, 123
in County Courts, 123
actions remitted to County Court, 124
actions transferred to High Court, 124
where amount exceeds £500,...124
contract or tort? 125

COSTS GENERALLY—*continued.*
costs of a reference, 135
amount reduced by counterclaim, 126
action and counterclaim referred, 126
order of reference silent as to costs, 127
claim and counterclaim dismissed with costs, 127
County Court Act does not apply to counterclaims, 128
where balance is in favour of defendant, 128
claim for fictitious amount, 128
unnecessary applications in Chancery Division, 129
money paid into Court taken out, 130
costs on higher scale, 130
unnecessary expense, 131
of abandoned motion, 131
tendency to repress expense, 131
of production, 132
upon notice of withdrawal, 132
objection to allowances of taxing master, 132
appeal to judge, 132
time for taxation, 133
pending appeal to Lords, 133
set-off of costs, 133
costs of third parties, 133
adjournment for third parties to be added, 134
security, when ordered, 134
married women ordered to give security, 134
amendments set up by plaintiff, 135
insolvency of appellant, 135
vexatious appeals, 135
of application for security, 135
orders by consent as to costs, 136
interpleader, 136
appeals for, 136
new trial granted by Court of Appeal, 137
applications against solicitors, 137. See *Taxation* and *Taxing Master.*
payable by a client, 161—172. See *Client.*
party and party 177—185. See *Party and Party Costs.*
solicitor relying on result of litigation for, 194. See *Statutory Charges*, 194—202. See *Priorities of Costs, Charges, &c.*, 203—207

COSTS OUT OF A FUND,
costs following the event, 187
Chancery practice, administration, 187
lien on a fund and on property recovered, 188
solicitor paid directly out of the estate, 188
unnecessary proceedings by trustees, &c., 188
party asking costs must have acted fairly, 189
instances of costs refused, 189
right of solicitor is that of client, 189
misconduct of party claiming, 189
remarks of Jessel, M.R. as to, 190
property recovered or preserved, 190
property recovered and compromise made, 191
action for account between partners, 192
administration action, former letters revoked, 192
insufficient estate, costs of plaintiff creditor, 192
creditor obtaining conduct of action, 192
costs of incumbrancers, 192
trustee in bankruptcy has priority, 193
administration and partnership actions, distinctions, 193

COUNSEL,
conduct of during trial, 20
papers with, 63
attending judge's chambers, costs, 151, 155
fees allowed on taxation, 100, 133
no privity between client and counsel, 104
solicitors acting under opinion of, 99, 104
cannot recover fees, 104
instructing, 104
what are questions for, 104
conference when no fee charged, 168
fee for instructions for brief, 168
fees for cross-examination, 177
costs of three counsel, 178
in reference, 178

COUNTERCLAIM,
and claim referred to arbitrator, 126
and claim dismissed with costs, 127
County Court Act does not apply to, 128
when balance in favour of defendant, 128

County Courts,
solicitors as advocates, 95
Act 1867 as to costs, 121, 123
actions remitted to, costs, 124
taxation in administration actions, 151
actions under £20, costs allowed, 151

Creditor,
costs of in administration action, 148
obtaining conduct of action from legatee, 192

Cross-examination,
costs of counsel, 177

Damages,
costs not given as, 145

Day,
costs of the day, 155

Death
of donor, gift not impeached, 71

Debtors Acts,
attachment, 16

Declaration under Solicitors Act.
See *Statutory Charges*, 194—202.

Default
in payment of balance due under taxation, 15

Defence,
retainer for, 25
solicitor neglecting to defend, 32, 108
fraudulent, 33
mistake in, remedy of client, 33

Defendant,
need not enquire into authority for issuing writ, 32
solicitor using defendant's name without authority, 32

Delivery of Bill of Costs,
methods of, 141
must be proved, 141

DELIVERY OF BILL OF COSTS—*continued.*
what constitutes, 141
order for, 141
waiver of personal service of order, 142
bill cannot be altered after delivery, 142, 168

DIARY
of solicitor, 162

DISABILITIES OF SOLICITORS,
gifts and purchases from clients, 68, 73
dealings between solicitors and clients, principle, 68
independent proof, 69
purchase from client, onus of proof of payment, 69, 70
account re-opened, 69
purchase of annuity from client, 70
independent advice necessary, 71
confidential relationship, 71
gift not impeached after death of donor, 71
gifts by will, suspicion impossible, 72, 73
new solicitor called in, duty of, 72

DISBURSEMENTS,
allowance of interest on, 179

DISCHARGE
of solicitor, 62, 63, 64

DISCRETION,
costs in discretion of Court, 118
of taxing master, 153, 155, 169, 179
instances of, 159
Court will not interfere, 159
of Court as to delivery of papers, 171

DIVISIONAL COURT,
power of as to costs, 122

DOCUMENTS,
in possession of solicitor, privilege, 41
right to on change of solicitors, 62
affidavit and list of on change of solicitors, 67
affidavit of, privilege claimed, 42

DOCUMENTS—*continued.*
solicitor refusing to produce in Court, 43
order for production, lien of solicitor, 54, 60
lien no bar to order for client to produce, 54, 60
official liquidator's right to production, 54
bankruptcy trustee's right to production, 54

DRAFTING,
solicitors as draftsmen, 97—103
effect of Remuneration Act, 97
provisions of Solicitors Acts, 97
principle of, 98
agreements bad for champerty, 99
agreement to pay commission on property recovered, 99
acting under counsel's opinion, 99
drawing wrong conclusions from deeds, liability, 100
allowance of counsel's fees, 100
precedents in Acts of Parliament, 100
mistakes by solicitor, 100
endorsements of writs, costs, 101
notices, 101
special summonses, 102
pleadings, 102
interrogatories, 102
unnecessary affidavits, 103

EASEMENTS,
suits relating to, charging order refused, 198

ELECTIONEERING AGENT,
solicitor, costs of taxed, 138

EMPLOYMENT,
under articles, 6
of solicitor must be legitimate, 34
what constitutes, 200

ENDORSEMENT OF WRIT,
counsel's fees for, 101

ENQUIRY, WRIT OF,
costs of counsel, 178

Enrolment,
of articles of clerkship, 3
omission to enrol, 3

Estate,
insufficient, costs of plaintiff creditor, 192

Evidence,
when secondary evidence given, 43
before notaries, 11
solicitor neglecting to provide, 110
upon a review of taxation, 156

Examination
of solicitor in support of bill, 169

Execution,
power of solicitor to issue, 26
solicitor's lien against execution creditor, 206

Executors,
retainer of solicitor by, 27
solicitor acting as, 92
work ordinarily done by, charges, 92
taxation of costs of, 149
solicitor paying himself out of assets, 176

Fees,
town agent cannot sue client for, 87
special jury, 178
of counsel. See *Counsel*.

Firms,
retainer by, 25

Form
of retainer, 23

Fraud,
by solicitors, 13
taxation after twelve months on account of, 173

Fund,
costs out of. See *Costs out of a Fund*, 187—193
solicitor's lien upon, not a general lien, 61
lien can be actively enforced, 61

Garnishee Order Nisi,
creates no charge until service, 206
when it takes effect, 206
costs of abortive garnishee summons, 154

General Lien,
does not involve power of sale, 46

Gifts,
and purchases from clients, 68
not impeached after death of donor, 71
by will, 72
to charities, costs of proceedings, 146

Grand Jury,
solicitors in proceedings before, 94

Guardians,
agreements with solicitors, 79

Heir-at-Law,
costs of, 147

Higher Scale,
where ordered, 130, 185
discretion of judge, 185

Increase,
affidavit of, 183

Incumbrancers,
costs of, 192
costs may be added to their securities, 192
statutory charge of solicitor, 202

Indulgence
of Court, costs of obtaining, 119

Infants,
retainer of solicitor by, 29
repudiating proceedings on attaining twenty-one, 200

INJUNCTION,
costs on higher scale, 130

INQUIRY,
writ of, costs of counsel, 178

INSOLVENCY,
of country solicitor, 88
of appellant, security for costs, 135

INSPECTION,
of papers relating to prior action, 39
cannot be refused, 42
of documents by accountants, 179

INSTRUCTIONS,
for brief, what they comprise, 181
for brief, costs, 181

INTEREST,
allowance of, on disbursements, 179

INTERPLEADER,
costs of, 136

INTERPRETER,
costs of, 182

INTERROGATORIES,
answering, privilege claimed, 42
prepared and not used, costs, 181
drafting, 102

INVESTMENT
of client's money by solicitor, 112

JOURNEYS
by solicitors, costs of, 166

JUDGE,
may refuse to admit articled clerk, 10
may deprive successful party of costs mero motu, 122
costs of counsel attending at chambers, 151, 155
discretion as to scale of costs, appeal, 185

JURISDICTION,
taxation by client out of, 172

JURY,
costs of jury cases, 120, 121
solicitor in proceedings before grand jury, 94

LAW STATIONERS
acting as agents, 84

LEGATEES,
costs of, where estate insufficient, 148, 150

LETTERS
of client, no lien on, 59

LIABILITY OF SOLICITOR,
acting without retainer, 31
using plaintiff's name without authority, 31
using defendant's name without authority, 32
acting as agent, 80
drawing wrong conclusions from deeds, 100
for negligence. See *Negligence*, 104–112
for mistakes, 105
cannot be transferred, 104
employing counsel, 104, 109
exceeding his duty, 105
compromising against instructions, 105. See *Disabilities*, 68–72.

LIBEL AND SLANDER,
costs, 123

LIEN,
safeguard to client, 44
different kinds of, 44
extent of, 44, 196
on a will, 45
peculiarity of solicitor's lien, 45
what it does not extend to, 45, 195
of town clerk on corporation papers, 46
how prejudiced by order for production, 46
general lien, no power of sale, 46

LIEN—*continued.*
lien in case of change of solicitors, 46, 52. See *Solicitors, Change of*, 62—67
to what specific lien attaches, 47
to what not, 47
solicitor acting for mortgagor and mortgagee, 47
borrowing deeds from equitable mortgagee, 48
solicitor acting for two parties, 48
two bills, 48
cannot be lost except by special agreement, 49
on moneys of client, 49
not barred by Statute of Limitations, 49, 195
statutory charge of solicitors, 49
property recovered or preserved, 50, 188
charge of costs upon property recovered, 50
priorities of charges, 51, 204
charging order, how obtained, 51
next step, 51
notice when client absconds, 52
of town agent, not a general lien, 52
of town agent as against client and as against country solicitor, 53
only a right to embarrass, 53
no bar to order upon client to produce, 54, 60
no bar to right of bankruptcy trustee, 54
no bar to right of official liquidator, 54
waiver of by undertaking, 54
effect of not keeping undertaking, 54
peculiarity of solicitor's lien, 57
must be for professional services, 58
does not extend to other claims, 58
solicitor ordered to give up some of the documents, 58
no lien on client's letters and copy replies, 59
on alimony, 59
how lien may be used, 60
excuse for not producing deeds, 60
how lien may be lost, 60
solicitor acting for mortgagee and mortgagor, 60
waiver of lien, 60
lost by claiming some other right, 61
cases on lien, 61
upon a fund, 61

LIEN—*continued.*
protected by stop order, 195
exists independently of declaration, 196, 197
See *Priorities of Costs, Charges, &c.*, 203—207

LIMITATIONS, STATUTE OF,
solicitor's lien not barred by, 49, 195
in cases of solicitor's negligence, 107
statutory lien is subject to, 197

LIS PENDENS,
solicitor neglecting to register, 110

LOWER SCALE,
costs, 185

MAGISTRATES,
proceedings before, taxation, 77
solicitors as advocates, 94
articled clerks as advocates, 96

MARRIED WOMEN,
retainer of solicitor by, 29
security for costs, 134
payment of costs by, 139

MASTER,
costs of proceedings before, 123
appeals from as to costs, 133, 179

MASTER OF THE ROLLS,
power of over solicitors, 12

MISCONDUCT
of party claiming costs, 189

MISTAKES,
by solicitor, 100
in points of rare occurrence, 110
by taxing master, 153

MODELS,
costs of in patent cases, 179

MONEY,
of client, solicitor's lien on, 49
received by town agent, 86
paid into court and taken out, 130
given to solicitor for investment, 112

MORTGAGE
of plaintiff's interest to defendant's, costs, 207

MORTGAGEES,
Order LV. as to costs of, 33, 121

MORTGAGOR,
solicitor acting for mortgagor and mortgagee, 41, 47, 60, 91
borrowing deeds from equitable mortgagee, 48

MOTION,
to set aside agreement with solicitor, 77
costs of abandoned motion, 131
drawing notice of, 101
to dismiss for want of prosecution, 135

NEGLIGENCE OF SOLICITOR,
of town agent, 84, 87
no privity between client and counsel, 104
instructing counsel, 104, 107
solicitor cannot transfer his own liability, 104
what are questions for counsel, 104
liability of solicitor for mistakes, 105
exceeding his duty, 105
compromising against instructions, 105
must follow special directions, 105
acting under general retainer, 105
compromise for a "certain" sum, 106
extent of liability, 106
remedy of client, 106
Statute of Limitations runs from Act of, 107
right of client, 107
probable loss may be assessed by jury, 107
non-attendance at trial with witnesses, 107
legal proceedings occasioned by, 108
neglect to defend, 108
amount of negligence, 108

NEGLIGENCE OF SOLICITOR—*continued.*
care of client's papers, 109
notices affecting client, 109
of agent or partner, 109
acting without authority, 109. See *Retainer.*
employing counsel, 109
employing surveyor, 110
in providing evidence, 110
non-registry of lis pendens, 110
errors in points of rare occurrence, 110
failure of action through improper advice, 111
abandoning cause without notice, 111
acts which client has to answer for, 112
acting without certificate, 112
moneys given to solicitor for investment, 112
costs occasioned by, 157

NEW TRIAL
granted by Court of Appeal, costs, 137

NEXT FRIEND,
retainer by, 29
costs allowed, 150

NEXT OF KIN,
costs of when estate insufficient, 150

NOTARIES,
in London, 10
ten miles from London, 11
stamp duty, 11
duties of, 11
evidence before, 11

NOTICE,
of desire to be admitted, 9
to records and writ clerk on change of solicitors, 62
in lieu of charging order, absconding client, 52
by town agent to client not to pay money to country solicitor, 89
of motion drawing, 101
affecting client not acted upon by solicitor 109
of withdrawal, costs upon, 132

OBJECTIONS
to allowance of taxing master, 132, 156

OFFICIAL LIQUIDATOR,
application for taxation, 176

ORDER,
charging order, 51
for production, lien of solicitor on papers, 54, 60
to give up documents on change of solicitors, 62, 67
for solicitor to give undertaking, 82, 83
by consent, and for costs, 136
for delivery of solicitor's bill, attachment, 141
waiver of personal service, 142
to review taxation, 156
for change of solicitors, 167
for examination of solicitor, 169
for taxation by party interested, 171
for declaration under Solicitors Act, 197

PARLIAMENTARY SCALE,
bills taxed on, 158, 176

PARTIES,
to be served with petition for charging order, 198
taxation by interested parties, 171

PARTNERSHIP ACTION,
priority of solicitor's costs, 192, 205
differs from administration action, 193

PARTY AND PARTY COSTS,
what they consist of, 177
counsel's fees for cross-examination, 177
where costs for three counsel allowed, 178
of counsel in a reference, 178
on trial of a writ of inquiry, 178
special jury fees, 178
copies of pleadings, 178
shorthand writers' notes, 178, 185
inspection of books by accountants, 179
scale of payment of accountants, 179
costs of appeal from master, 179

Party and Party Costs—*continued.*
interest on disbursements, 179
model in patent cases, 179
discretion of taxing master in equity, 179
expenses of witnesses, 180
surveys and reports, 180
professional witnesses, 181
interrogatories prepared and not used, 181
interpreters, 182
instructions for brief, what is included, 181
subsistence money allowed to plaintiff, 182
affidavit of increase, 183
witnesses not called, 183
agreement not to charge solicitor and client costs, 183
solicitor must protect client against expenses, 184
higher and lower scale, 185
judges' discretion as to scale, appeal, 185
higher scale, when allowed, 185

Patents,
costs in suits for infringement, 151
costs of models, 179

Petition,
for charging order, 197
to set aside agreement with solicitor, 77
costs of, for taxation, 78

Plaintiff,
name used without authority, 30
allowed subsistence money, 182
creditor, insufficient estate, 192

Pleadings,
drawing, 102
costs of copies of, 178

Postage,
proof of may be charged for, 165

Precedents.
See Acts of Parliament, 100

PRIORITIES OF COSTS, CHARGES, &c.
what solicitor's right is, 203
solicitor and client after judgment, 203
lien and set-off, priority, 204
lien on balance in favour of client, 204
costs of independent proceedings, no set-off, 205
set-off of debt against costs of an award, 205
in administration suit, 205
in partnership actions, 205
solicitor's lien against execution creditor, 206
when garnishee order nisi takes effect, 206
mortgage of plaintiff's interest to defendant, lien, 207

PRIVILEGE,
foundation of, 36
privileged communications, 36
does not extend to criminal matters, 37
fraud, 37
solicitor's confidential clerk, 37
solicitor acting for two parties in a suit, 38
trustee acting for one cestui que trust against another, 38
principle in above cases, 38
residence of a ward, 39
correspondence between plaintiff and third parties, 39
inspection of papers in prior action, 39
address of client, 39
bill of costs privileged, 40
communications made to solicitors, 40
knowledge acquired by solicitor otherwise than from client, 41
documents in possession of solicitor, 41
solicitor acting for mortgagor and mortgagee, 41
must be no question of retainer, 42
inspection cannot be refused, 42
how privilege claimed, 42
secondary evidence, 43
of solicitors as advocates, 96

PRIVITY,
none between town agent and client, 86, 87
none between client and counsel, 104

PROCEEDINGS,
unnecessary, costs, 130, 158, 165

PRODUCTION,
order for, lien of solicitor, 54, 60
bankruptcy, trustee's right to, 54
how far lien is an excuse, 60
costs of, 132

PROFESSIONAL COMMUNICATIONS.
See *Privilege*, 36—43

PROMISSORY NOTE
for costs, solicitor may sue upon,

PROPERTY RECOVERED OR PRESERVED
agreement to pay commission on, 99
suits relating to easements, 198
costs, 190, 191

PROTEST.
payment of bill of costs under, 173

PURCHASES,
and gifts from clients, 68
of annuity from client, 70
independent proof necessary, 71

RE-ADMISSION
of solicitor, 14

REFERENCE,
costs generally, 125
order of, silent as to costs, 127
costs of brief copies of notes, 154
costs of counsel, 160, 178

REFRESHERS,
allowance of on taxation, 154

REFUSAL
to produce bill, 139

REGISTRAR IN BANKRUPTCY
may go behind allocatur, 156

RELATOR,
costs of in charity information

REMUNERATION,
agreement as to, 75
Act 1882,...75
effect of upon drafting, 97
recent changes, 95
remarks on Remuneration Act, 222

RETAINER OF SOLICITOR,
object of, 22
written, 22
onus of proof of, 22
form of, 23
what constitutes a retainer, 23
by companies, 24
client ratifying solicitor's actions, 24
by articles of association, 24
by corporations, 24
must come from client in person to bring action, 25
not necessarily for defence, 25
by a firm, 25
extent of, 25
power of solicitor to issue execution, 26
to compromise, 26
joint and separate, 26
by executors, 27
appearance entered without authority, 28
by third parties under general authority, 29
by infants, 29
by married women, 29
liability of solicitor acting without, 29
innocently acting under forged retainer, 29
by wrong set of directors, 30
use of plaintiff's name without authority, 30
measure of liability, 31
provisions of Judicature Acts, 31
solicitor to declare whether writ issued with his authority, 32
defendant not bound to inquire into authority, 32
undertaking to enter appearance, 32
failure to enter appearance, 32
using defendant's name without authority, 32
fraudulent defence by solicitor, 33

RETAINER OF SOLICITOR—*continued.*
mistake (bonâ fide) in defence, 33
remedy of client, 33
by trustee, costs, 33
employment must be legitimate, 34
restrained from acting for opposite party, 34
solicitor must be qualified, 34
duration of retainer, 35
work must be completed before thrown up, 35
reasonable causes for retiring, 35
taxing master can decide questions of, 169

REVIEW,
application to review taxation, 132, 156
evidence allowed, 156

ROLLS,
application to strike solicitor off, 13
punishment reduced to suspension, 14

RULES
for taxation, 157

SCALE,
costs on higher scale when ordered, 130 185
for payment of accountants, 179
for taxation, 158

SECONDARY EVIDENCE,
when admitted, 43

SECURITY,
for costs, when ordered, 134
applications for, 134, 136
married women, 135
insolvent appellant, 135
solicitors'. See *Statutory Charges*, 194—202

SERVICE,
effect of agreement to accept, 32
of order for delivery of bill of costs, 141
waiver of personal service, 142

SERVICE UNDER ARTICLES,
for five, four, or three years, 1
coupling periods of service, 1
irregular, 2
must be continuous, 5
by ten years' men, 6
definition of, 8
affidavit of due service, 10. See *Articled Clerks*, 1—10

SET-OFF,
and lien, priority, 204
of debt against costs of award, 205
of costs of independent proceedings, 132, 205

SHERIFF,
taxation of costs of inquiry, 160

SHORTHAND WRITERS,
costs of, 178, 185

SOLICITORS,
as officers of the court, 12—21
provisions of Judicature Acts, 12
frauds by, 13
striking off the rolls, 13
money misappropriated to be restored before re-admission, 14
application for re-admission, by petition, 14
application to strike off the rolls, 14
suspension, 14
clerk equally liable, 14
answering affidavits, 15
summary jurisdiction of the Court, 15
non-payment of balance due under taxation, 15
Debtors Acts, 16
attachment, 16
notice of attachment to be served, 17
order for attachment, 17
attachment under Judicature Act, 17
omitting to deliver briefs, 17
acting without authority, 18, 105
non-attendance in court at trial, 19

SOLICITORS—*continued.*
acting as advocates, 19. See *Advocates*, 94—96
writing to public press during action, 19
improper conduct during trial, 20
not ordered out of court when witness, 20
acting for two parties in a suit, 38, 48
acting for mortgagor and mortgagee, 41, 47
to trust estate under terms of a will, 35
change of solicitors, 62—67
lien in case of, 46, 52
when order to give up documents necessary, 62
notice to records and writ clerk, 62
solicitor discharging himself, right to documents, 62
first solicitor's lien, 62
when solicitor deemed to have discharged himself, 63
client failing to find funds, 63
bankruptcy of solicitor, 63
bankruptcy of client, 63
what papers will be ordered to be given up, 63
papers with counsel, 63
principle when solicitor discharges himself, 64
must not desert client during action, 64
solicitor discharged by client, 64
in administration action, 65
what is discharged by client, 66
solicitor must carry on suit to the end, 66
exceptions to above rule, 66
speculative action, 66
costs of affidavit and list of documents, 67
order for change of solicitors, 67, 167
employing unqualified practitioner, 115. See *Unqualified Practitioners*, 113—116
acting as agent, account, 163
as trustees, 90—93. See *Trustees.*
as draftsmen, 97—103. See *Drafting.*
retainer, 22—35. See *Retainer.*
privilege, 36—43. See *Privilege.*
lien of, 44—61. See *Lien.*
disabilities of, 68—73. See *Disabilities of Solicitors.*
agreements with, 74—79. See *Agreements with Solicitors.*
undertakings by, 79—83. See *Undertakings.*

SOLICITOR—*continued.*
negligence of, 104—157. See *Negligence.*
must protect client against expenses, 184
Remuneration Act, remarks on, 232

SPECIAL JURY
fees, 178

SPECIFIC LIEN,
to what it attaches, 47

STAMP DUTY,
on articles of clerkship, 3
in case of notary, 10

STATUTORY CHARGES,
solicitor relying on result of litigation for costs, 194
modes of securing payment, 194
charging order under Solicitors Act, 1860,...194
lien protected by stop order, 195
lien not barred by Statute of Limitations, 195
lien does not extend to real property, 195
declaration under Solicitors Act, 195
extent of lien on fund in court, 196
lien exists independently of declaration, 196, 197
by what Court declaration made, 196
declaration preferred to statutory charge, 197
statutory lien applies to real property, 197
are subject to Statute of Limitations, 197
application for order, 197
obtained on summons or petition, 197
parties to be served with petition, 198
cases where charging order refused, 198
suits relating to easements, 198
extend only to property of client, 199
construction of Solicitors Act, 200
employment of solicitor, what constitutes, 200
repudiating proceedings on attaining full age, 200
instances of, 201
suits by incumbrancers, 202
priority of solicitor's lien. See *Priorities.*

Steward of a Manor,
solicitor, taxation of costs, 138

Striking Off the Rolls,
applications, 13
reduced to suspension, 14

Subsistence
money allowed to plaintiff, 182

Successful Party
deprived of costs, 122

Summons,
drawing special, 102
for charging order, 197

Surveyor,
employment of by solicitor, 110

Surveys,
costs of, 180

Suspension
of solicitor, 14

Taxation,
non-payment of balance due on, 15
agreement to pay more than taxed costs, 74
costs before magistrates, 77
time for, 133
Solicitors Act, 1843,...138
electioneering agent, 138
steward of a manor, 138
bill of town agent, 139
for non-litigious business, 139
married woman employing a solicitor, 139
refusal to produce bill, 140
time for action for costs, 140
delivery of bill, 141
bill must be signed by solicitor, 141
order for delivery of bill, 141

TAXATION—*continued*.
waiver of personal service, 142
bill cannot be altered after delivery, 142
withdrawal of bill, 142
proving bill in bankruptcy, 143
jurisdiction in equity, 143
promissory note for costs, 143
costs of taxation, 143
attendance by letter, 144
between solicitor and client, 145—151, 161
party and party costs, 145
costs of trustees, &c., appeal, 145
costs not given as damages, 145
equity practice, 146
stand alone charges, 146
gifts to charities, 146
relator's costs, 147
in administration suits, 147
costs of heir-at-law, 147
costs of plaintiff legatee, 148
creditor's administration suit, 148
trustee's charges and expenses, 149
executors and administrators, 149
who may attend, 150
costs of next friend, 150
suits for infringement of patent, 151
actions in County Court under £20,...151
counsel attending judge's chambers, 151
taxation on application of third parties, 170
on application of party interested, 171
by client out of the jurisdiction, 172
after twelve months, 173—176
paying bill under protest, 173
taxation after payment of bill, 173
fraud, 173
overcharge alone insufficient, 173
pressure, 173
statutory provisions, 174
special circumstances requiring, 174
matters of objection appearing in bill, 174
payment under undue influence, 174

TAXATION—*continued.*
bill re-opened after two years, 174
who has power to re-open bill, 175
where there is a series of bills, 175
application by official liquidator, 176
solicitor, executor paying himself out of assets, 176
on parliamentary scale, 176
in bankruptcy, powers of registrar, 176

TAXING MASTER,
examining agreements between solicitor and client, 76, 169
opinion final, 152
appeals from, 152
discretionary powers of, 153, 169
gross mistakes, 153
counsel's fees, refreshers, 153, 154
brief copies of notes in a reference, 154
abortive garnishee summons, 154
when Court will interfere, 155
Order VI. as to discretion of, 155
counsel in judge's chambers, 151, 155
costs of the day, 155
objections to items allowed by, 132, 156
application for order to review, 132, 156
registrar in bankruptcy may go behind allocatur, 156
evidence on review of taxation, 156
powers of, 157, 169
costs incurred through negligence of solicitor, 157
rules for taxation, 157
costs of unnecessary proceedings, 158
power to disallow, 158
scales for taxation, 158
parliamentary business, 158
country solicitor attending proceedings, 159
Court will not interfere on matters of discretion, 159
instances of discretionary power, 159
costs of counsel in a reference, 160
taxing as persona designata, 160
costs of inquiry before a sheriff, 160

THIRD PARTIES,
retainer by, under general authority, 29
cannot benefit by agreements between solicitor and client, 75
costs of, 133
adjournment for third parties to be added, 134
taxation on application of, 170

TOWN AGENT,
lien of, not general, 52
as against client and as against country solicitor, 52
agreements between agents and country solicitor, 74
bill of, taxation, 138
solicitor acting as, accounts of, 163
country solicitor liable for negligence of, 84, 87
agency by law stationers, 84
acting ultra vires, 85
name must appear on writ, 85
acting without London certificate, 85
must not exceed instructions, 85
work must be in ordinary course of business, 86
no privity between client and London agent, 86, 87
money improperly received by, 86
money received in ordinary course of business, 86
summary jurisdiction of the Court, 86
cannot sue client for fees, 87
accountable to country solicitor for negligence, 87
insolvency of country solicitor, 88
lien on deeds, 88
employed by two solicitors, 88
extent of lien, 88, 89
notice to client not to pay money to country solicitor, 89
employed by solicitor trustee, 89
employment by unqualified practitioner, 90
charges against solicitor trustee, 91

TOWN CLERK,
lien on papers of corporation, 46

TRIAL,
two trials, costs, 123

TRUSTEES,
right to costs, 33, 121, 145
in bankruptcy, right to bankrupt's papers, 54
agreement with solicitors, 79
employing solicitor, 170, 171
in bankruptcy, priority for costs, 193
charges and expenses allowed in action, 149
solicitors as trustees, 90—93
acting as agent to fraudulent trustee, 90
paying money to one of two trustees, 90
acting for one cestui que trust against another, 90
cannot make profit out of trust estate unless authorised, 91, 172
member of a firm being a trustee, 91
town agent's charges to solicitor trustee, 91
appearing for self and co-trustee, 91
as mortgagor and also for trust estate as mortgagee, 91
provision in deed as to costs of, 92
work ordinarily done by executors, 92
trustee in bankruptcy, 92
general rule as to, 92, 93

UNDERTAKINGS BY SOLICITORS,
liability of solicitor as agent, 80
to pay costs, 80
to pay rent on part of assignees of bankrupt, 80
evidence of intention of the parties, 80
doubtful in form, 81
solicitor with only limited authority, 81
to act as officer of the Court, 82
Court where undertaking enforced, 82
must be personal, 82
construction of order to give undertaking, 82
Statute of Frauds or Limitations no bar, 83
how enforced, 83

UNDUE INFLUENCE,
accounts between solicitor and client opened, 69, 174

UNNECESSARY,
expense discouraged, 13
proceedings, costs, 158, 165
parties served, 134
proceedings by trustees, &c., 188

UNQUALIFIED PRACTITIONERS,
costs of, no remedy for, 113
Solicitors Act, 1874,...113
Stamp Act, 1870,...113
Legal Practitioners Act, 1877,...114
penalties, 114
acting in litigious business, 115
gain anticipated, 115
employing agent, 115
employed by solicitor, 115
applications to strike off the rolls, affidavits, 116
no certificate, 116

USELESS LITIGATION,
costs of, 118

VEXATIOUS APPEALS, 135

WAIVER OF LIEN.
See *Lien*, 44—61

WARD,
residence of must not be concealed, 39

WILL,
lien of solicitor upon, 45
gifts to solicitors, 72

WITHDRAWAL,
costs of notice, 132

WITNESS,
solicitor having conduct of the case, 20
expenses of, 180
professional, 181
when not called, 183

WRIT,
solicitor to declare authority to issue, 32
defendant need not inquire into authority, 32
name of agent must appear, 85
endorsements on, costs, 101

WRIT OF ENQUIRY,
costs of counsel, 178

THE END.

W. I. RICHARDSON, PRINTER, 4 AND 5, GREAT QUEEN STREET, LONDON, W.C.

A CATALOGUE OF LAW WORKS,

PUBLISHED BY

STEVENS AND SONS,

119, CHANCERY LANE, LONDON, W.C.
(*And at* 14, *Bell Yard*, *Lincoln's Inn*).

NOTE.—*All letters to be addressed to Chancery Lane*, NOT *to Bell Yard.*

A Catalogue of Modern Law Works (*including the leading American, Indian, Irish and Scotch*); *together with a complete Chronological List of all the English, Irish and Scotch Reports, Abbreviations used in reference to Law Reports and Text Books, and an Index of Subjects* (112 pp.), 8*vo, cloth lettered, may be had on application.*

Acts of Parliament.—*Public and Local Acts from an early date, may be had of the Publishers of this Catalogue, who have also on sale the largest collection of Private Acts, relating to Estates, Enclosures, Railways, Roads, &c., &c.*

ACTION AT LAW.—Foulkes' Elementary View of the Proceedings in an Action under the Rules of the Supreme Court, 1883.—(Founded on "SMITH'S ACTION AT LAW.") By W. D. I. FOULKES, Esq., Barrister-at-Law. Third Edition. (*In preparation.*)

Prentice's Proceedings in an Action in the Queen's Bench, Common Pleas, and Exchequer Divisions of the High Court of Justice. By SAMUEL PRENTICE, Esq., one of Her Majesty's Counsel. Second Edition. Royal 12mo. 1880. 12*s.*

ADMIRALTY.—Roscoe's Admiralty Practice.—A Treatise on the Jurisdiction and Practice of the Admiralty Division of the High Court of Justice, and on Appeals therefrom, with a chapter on the Admiralty Jurisdiction of the Inferior and the Vice-Admiralty Courts. With an Appendix containing Statutes, Rules as to Fees and Costs, Forms, Precedents of Pleadings and Bills of Costs. By EDWARD STANLEY ROSCOE, Esq., Barrister-at-Law. Second Edition. Revised and Enlarged. Demy 8vo. 1882. 1*l.* 4*s.*

"A clear digest of the law and practice of the Admiralty Courts."
"A comprehensive and useful manual of practice."—*Solicitors' Journal.*

ADVOCACY.—Harris' Hints on Advocacy. Conduct of Cases Civil and Criminal. Classes of Witnesses and suggestions for Cross-Examining them, &c., &c. By RICHARD HARRIS, Barrister-at-Law, of the Middle Temple and Midland Circuit. Sixth Edition. (Further Revised and Enlarged.) Royal 12mo. 1882. 7*s.* 6*d.*

"Full of good sense and just observation. A very complete Manual of the Advocate's art in Trial by Jury."—*Solicitors' Journal.*

"A book at once entertaining and really instructive. . . . Deserves to be carefully read by the young barrister whose career is yet before him."—*Law Magazine.*

AGRICULTURAL LAW.—**Beaumont's Treatise on Agricultural Holdings and the Law of Distress as regulated by the Agricultural Holdings (England) Act, 1883,** with Appendix containing Full Text of the Act, and Precedents of Notices and Awards. By JOSEPH BEAUMONT, Esq., Solicitor. Royal 12mo. 1883. 10*s.* 6*d.*

Cooke's Treatise on the Law and Practice of Agricultural Tenancies.—New edition, in great part rewritten with especial reference to Unexhausted Improvements, with Modern Forms and Precedents. By G. PRIOR GOLDNEY, of the Western Circuit, and W. RUSSELL GRIFFITHS, LL.B., of the Midland Circuit, Barristers-at-Law. Demy 8vo. 1882. 1*l.* 1*s.*

"In its present form it will prove of great value to politicians, lawyers and agriculturalists."—*Law Times.*

"A book of great practical utility to landlords and tenant farmers, as well as to the legal profession."—*Law Magazine.*

Griffith's Agricultural Holdings (England) Act, 1883, containing an Introduction; a Summary of the Act, with Notes; the complete Text of the Act, with Forms, and a specimen of an Award under the Act. By W. RUSSELL GRIFFITHS, LL.B., of the Midland Circuit. Uniform with "Cooke's Agricultural Tenancies." Demy 8vo. 1883. 5*s.*

Spencer's Agricultural Holdings (England) Act, 1883, with Explanatory Notes and Forms; together with the Ground Game Act, 1880. Forming a Supplement to "Dixon's Law of the Farm." By AUBREY J. SPENCER, B.A., Esq., Barrister-at-Law, and late Holder of Inns of Court Studentship. Demy 8vo. (*In the press.*)

ARBITRATION.—**Russell's Treatise on the Power and Duty of an Arbitrator, and the Law of Submissions and Awards;** with an Appendix of Forms, and of the Statutes relating to Arbitration. By FRANCIS RUSSELL, Esq., M.A., Barrister-at-Law. Sixth Edition. By the Author and HERBERT RUSSELL, Esq., Barrister-at-Law. Royal 8vo. 1882. 36*s.*

"The cases are carefully collected, and their effect is clearly and shortly given. . . . . This edition may be commended to the profession as comprehensive accurate and practical."—*Solicitors' Journal*, January 13, 1883.

ARTICLED CLERKS.—**Rubinstein and Ward's Articled Clerks' Handbook.**—Being a Concise and Practical Guide to all the Steps Necessary for Entering into Articles of Clerkship, passing the Preliminary, Intermediate, Final, and Honours Examinations, obtaining Admission and Certificate to Practise, with Notes of Cases, Suggestions as to Mode of Reading and Books to be read during Articles, and an Appendix. Third Edition. By J. S. RUBINSTEIN and S. WARD, Solicitors. 12mo. 1881. 4*s.*

"No articled clerk should be without it."—*Law Times.*

ARTICLES OF ASSOCIATION.—**Palmer.**—*Vide* "Conveyancing."

ASSETS, ADMINISTRATION OF.—**Eddis' Principles of the Administration of Assets in Payment of Debts.** By ARTHUR SHELLY EDDIS, one of Her Majesty's Counsel. Demy 8vo. 1880. 6*s.*

ATTORNEYS.—**Cordery.**—*Vide* "Solicitors."

Pulling's Law of Attorneys, General and Special. Third Edition. 8vo. 1862. 18*s.*

Smith.—The Lawyer and his Profession.—A Series of Letters to a Solicitor commencing Business. By J. ORTON SMITH. 12mo. 1860. 4*s.*

Whiteway.—*Vide* "Solicitors."

*** *All standard Law Works are kept in Stock, in law calf and other bindings.*

AVERAGE.—**Hopkins' Hand-Book on Average.**—Fourth Edition. 8vo. (*In preparation.*)

Lowndes' Law of General Average.—English and Foreign. Fourth Edition. By RICHARD LOWNDES, Author of "The Law of Marine Insurance," &c. (*In preparation.*)

BALLOT.—**FitzGerald's Ballot Act.**—With an INTRODUCTION. Forming a Guide to the Procedure at Parliamentary and Municipal Elections. Second Edition. By GERALD A. R. FITZGERALD, M.A., Esq., Barrister-at-Law. Fcap. 8vo. 1876. 5*s.* 6*d.*

"We should strongly advise any person connected with elections, whether acting as candidate, agent, or in any other capacity, to become possessed of this manual."

BANKING.—**Walker's Treatise on Banking Law.** Including the Crossed Checks Act, 1876, with dissertations thereon, also references to some American Cases, and full Index. By J. DOUGLAS WALKER, Esq., Barrister-at-Law. Demy 8vo. 1877. 14*s.*

BANKRUPTCY.—**Bedford's Final Examination Guide to Bankruptcy.**—Fourth Edition. (*In preparation.*)

Chitty's Index, Vol. I.—*Vide* "Digests."

Gray's Bankruptcy Manual.—The Bankruptcy Act, 1883, with short Notes, giving Cross References and References to the corresponding Provisions of the old Statutes and of the Rules and Cases incorporated, an Introduction, showing the changes effected by the Act, an Analysis of the Act, and a full Index, furnishing a Time Table and other lists of Special Provisions. By GEO. G. GRAY, LL.D., of the Middle Temple, Esq., Barrister-at-Law. Demy 8vo. 1883. 10*s.* 6*d*

Joel's Complete and Practical Manual of Bankruptcy and Bills of Sale Law, with copious Notes and Comments and the leading Cases in Bankruptcy, &c., under the 1849, 1861 and 1869 Acts, inclusive of those of 1883, and with References to the Conveyancing and Property Act, 1881; the Conveyancing Act, 1882; the Settled Land Act, 1882; the Married Women's Property Act, 1882; the Judicature Acts and the New Rules of Procedure, 1883. By J. EDMONDSON JOEL, Esq., of the Inner Temple and North-Eastern Circuit, Barrister-at-Law. Demy 8vo. (*In the press.*)

Rigg's Bankruptcy Act, 1883, and the Bills of Sale Act, 1882, with Notes, &c. By JAMES McMULLEN RIGG, Esq., Barrister-at-Law. Royal 12mo. (*In the press.*)

Salaman's Analytical Index to the Bankruptcy Act, 1883.—By JOSEPH SEYMOUR SALAMAN, Esq., Solicitor, Author of "Bankruptcy Act, 1869, with Notes," "Liquidation by Arrangement," &c. Uniform with the Act, 1883. *Net,* 3*s.*

Do., with Bankruptcy Act (official copy), in limp leather. *Net,* 9*s.*

Do., do. do. interleaved, limp leather. *Net,* 11*s.*

"That this Index is very full may be gathered from the fact that it occupies on the same sized paper as the Queen's printers' copy of the Act exactly the same number of pages as the Act. It gives references to the sections and sub-sections of the Act, and is prefaced by the Board of Trade memorandum. It will undoubtedly be found a useful addition to the Act."—*Solicitors' Journal,* September 22, 1883.

Williams' Law and Practice in Bankruptcy: Third Edition. By R. VAUGHAN WILLIAMS and W. VAUGHAN WILLIAMS, Esqrs., Barristers-at-Law. (*In preparation.*)

BILLS OF EXCHANGE.—**Chalmers' Digest of the Law of Bills of Exchange, Promissory Notes, and Cheques.** By M. D. CHALMERS, of the Inner Temple, Esq., Barrister-at-Law. Second Edition. Demy 8vo. 1881. 15*s.*

"In its present form this work contains a very complete digest of the subjects to which it relates."—*Law Times.*

*** *All standard Law Works are kept in Stock, in law calf and other bindings.*

BILLS OF LADING.—Leggett's Treatise on the Law of Bills of Lading; comprising the various legal incidents attaching to the Bill of Lading; the legal effects of each of the Clauses and Stipulations; and the Rights and Liabilities of Consignors, Consignees, Indorsees, and Vendees, under the Bill of Lading. With an Appendix, containing Forms of Bills of Lading &c. By EUGENE LEGGETT, Solicitor and Notary Public. Demy 8vo. 1880. 1*l.* 1*s.*

BILLS OF SALE.—Fithian's Bills of Sale Acts, 1878 and 1882. With an Introduction and Explanatory Notes showing the changes made in the Law with Respect to Bills of Sale. By EDWARD WILLIAM FITHIAN, of the Middle Temple, Esq., Barrister-at-Law (*Draftsman of the Bill of* 1882). Royal 12mo. 1882. 5*s.*

"Mr. Fithian's book will maintain a high place among the most practically useful editions of the Bills of Sale Acts, 1878 and 1882."—*Law Magazine.*

Joel.—*Vide* "Bankruptcy."

Rigg.—*Vide* "Bankruptcy."

CARRIERS.—Browne on Carriers.—A Treatise on the Law of Carriers of Goods and Passengers by Land and Water. With References to the most recent American Decisions. By J. H. B. BROWNE, Esq., Barrister-at-Law. 8vo. 1873. 18*s.*

CHANCERY, *and Vide* **"EQUITY."**

Chitty's Index.—*Vide* "Digests."

Daniell's Chancery Practice.—The Practice of the Chancery Division of the High Court of Justice and on appeal therefrom, being the Sixth Edition of Daniell's Chancery Practice, with alterations and additions, and references to a companion Volume of Forms. By L. FIELD, E. C. DUNN, and T. RIBTON, assisted by W. H. UPJOHN, Barristers-at-Law. In 2 vols. *Vol. I.* (*with Table of Cases and an Index*), demy 8vo. 1882. 2*l.* 2*s.*

"This new edition of the Standard Chancery Practice will be generally welcomed, and we are glad that we can speak favourably of the manner in which the editors have accomplished their difficult task of deciding what parts of the old work should be rejected, and of adapting the parts retained to the new practice. There is to be found, in every part of the book we have examined, evidence of great care; the cases are not merely jotted down, but analysed and considered, and no pains appear to have been spared to render the information given both accurate and complete. This is high praise, but we think it is fully warranted by the result of our examination of the work. . . . It is exactly what it professes to be—a concise and careful digest of the practice."—*Solicitors' Journal.*

"All the portions relating to the practice introduced by the Judicature Acts and Rules are well done."—*Law Times.*

"The learned authors have spared no pains to make this new book of practice as comprehensive in scope and as accurate in detail as that which so long enjoyed an almost unique reputation as 'Daniell's Practice.' Indeed if any fault is to be alleged it would be that the work is perhaps somewhat too exhaustive; a fault, however, which is on the right side in a book of practice, which is not intended to be read through, but to serve as a mine of information for ready reference whenever the practitioner may have occasion to seek for guidance."—*Law Magazine.*

*** *Vol. II. nearly ready.*

Daniell's Forms and Precedents of Proceedings in the Chancery Division of the High Court of Justice and on Appeal therefrom; with Dissertations and Notes. Being the Third Edition of "Daniell's Chancery Forms." By WILLIAM HENRY UPJOHN, Esq., of Gray's Inn, &c. Demy 8vo. 1879. 2*l.* 2*s.*

CHANCERY.—*Continued.*

Haynes' Chancery Practice.—The Practice of the Chancery Division of the High Court of Justice and on Appeal therefrom. By JOHN F. HAYNES, LL.D. Demy 8vo. 1879. 1*l.* 6*s.*

Morgan's Chancery Acts and Orders.—With Notes Sixth Edition. Adapted to the new Practice by the Right Hon. GEORGE OSBORNE MORGAN, one of Her Majesty's Counsel, Her Majesty's Judge Advocate General, and E. A. WURTZBURG, of Lincoln's Inn, Esq., Barrister-at-Law. (*In preparation.*)

Morgan and Wurtzburg's Chancery Costs.—*Vide* "Costs."

Peel's Chancery Actions.—A Concise Treatise on the Practice and Procedure in Chancery Actions under the Rules of the Supreme Court, 1883.—Third Edition. By SYDNEY PEEL, of the Middle Temple, Esq., Barrister-at-Law. Demy 8vo. 1883. 8*s.* 6*d.*

"Mr. Peel's little work gives a very commendable sketch of the modern practice of the Chancery Division. . . . It contains some chapters upon Proceedings at Chambers and on Further Consideration, which are likely to be valuable from the extreme paucity of all printed information upon these subjects; and it is enriched with a very full list of cases bearing upon the practice of the Chancery Division, giving references to all the Reports."—*Law Journal.*

"The book will give to the student a good general view of the effect on chancery practice of the Judicature Acts and Orders."—*Solicitors' Journal.*

CHANCERY PALATINE OF LANCASTER.—Snow and Winstanley's Chancery Practice.—The Statutes, Consolidated and General Orders and Rules of Court relating to the Practice, Pleading and Jurisdiction of the Court of Chancery, of the County Palatine of Lancaster. With Copious Notes of all practice cases to the end of the year 1879, Time Table and Tables of Costs and Forms. By THOMAS SNOW, M.A., and HERBERT WINSTANLEY, Esqrs., Barristers-at-Law. Royal 8vo. 1880. 1*l.* 10*s.*

CIVIL LAW.—Bowyer's Commentaries on the Modern Civil Law.—Royal 8vo. 1848. 18*s.*

Bowyer's Introduction to the Study and Use of the Civil Law.—Royal 8vo. 1874. 5*s.*

COLLISIONS.—Lowndes' Admiralty Law of Collisions at Sea.—8vo. 1867. 7*s.* 6*d.*

Marsden on Maritime Collision.—A Treatise on the Law of Collisions at Sea. With an Appendix containing Extracts from the Merchant Shipping Acts, the International Regulations (of 1863 and 1880) for preventing Collisions at Sea; and local Rules for the same purpose in force in the Thames, the Mersey, and elsewhere. By REGINALD G. MARSDEN, Esq., Barrister-at-Law. Demy 8vo. 1880. 12*s.*

COLONIAL LAW.—Clark's Summary of Colonial Law and Practice of Appeals from the Plantations. 8vo. 1834. 1*l.* 4*s.*

COMMENTARIES ON THE LAWS OF ENGLAND.—Broom and Hadley's Commentaries on the Laws of England. By HERBERT BROOM, LL.D., and EDWARD A. HADLEY, M.A., Barristers-at-Law. 4 vols. 8vo. 1869. (*Published at 3l. 3s.*) *Net*, 1*l.* 1*s.*

⁂ All standard Law Works are kept in Stock, in law calf and other bindings.

COMMERCIAL LAW.—Goirand's French Code of Commerce and most usual Commercial Laws. With a Theoretical and Practical Commentary, and a Compendium of the judicial organization and of the course of procedure before the Tribunals of Commerce; together with the text of the law; the most recent decisions of the Courts, and a glossary of French judicial terms. By LEOPOLD GOIRAND, Licencié en droit. In 1 vol. (850 pp.). Demy 8vo. 1880. 2*l.* 2*s.*

Levi.—*Vide* "International Law."

COMMON LAW.—Allen.—*Vide* "Pleading."

Archbold's Practice of the Queen's Bench, Common Pleas and Exchequer Divisions of the High Court of Justice in Actions, etc., in which they have a common jurisdiction—Thirteenth Edition. By SAMUEL PRENTICE, Esq., one of Her Majesty's Counsel. 2 vols. Demy 8vo. 1879. 3*l.* 3*s.*

Archibald's Country Solicitor's Practice; a Handbook of the Practice in the Queen's Bench Division of the High Court of Justice; with Statutes and Forms. By W. F. A. ARCHIBALD, Esq., Barrister-at-Law, Author of "Forms of Summonses and Orders, with Notes for use at Judges' Chambers." Royal 12mo. 1881. 1*l.* 5*s.*

"We are much mistaken if it does not become as widely used among the profession as the best known editions of the Judicature Acts. . . . In every place in which we have tested the work we find it thoroughly trustworthy. . . . Its arrangement is excellent, and altogether it is likely enough to become a popular solicitors' handybook."—*The Times.*

Ball's Short Digest of the Common Law; being the Principles of Torts and Contracts. Chiefly founded upon the works of Addison, with Illustrative Cases, for the use of Students. By W. EDMUND BALL, LL.B., late "Holt Scholar" of Gray's Inn, Barrister-at-Law and Midland Circuit. Demy 8vo. 1880. 16*s.*

"The principles of the law are very clearly and concisely stated."—*Law Journal.*

Bullen and Leake.—*Vide* "Pleading."

Chitty.—*Vide* "Forms."

Fisher's Digest of Reported Decisions in all the Courts, with a Selection from the Irish; the cases overruled and impeached and references to the Statutes, Rules and Orders of Courts from 1756 to 1883. Compiled and arranged by JOHN MEWS, assisted by CECIL MAURICE CHAPMAN, HARRY HADDEN WICKES SPARHAM and ARTHUR HORATIO TODD, Barristers-at-Law. (*In the press.*)

Foulkes.—*Vide* "Action."

Prentice.—*Vide* "Action."

Shirley.—*Vide* "Leading Cases."

Smith's Manual of Common Law.—For Practitioners and Students. Comprising the fundamental principles and the points most usually occurring in daily life and practice. By JOSIAH W. SMITH, B.C.L., Q.C. Ninth Edition. 12mo. 1880. 14*s.*

COMMONS AND INCLOSURES.—Chambers' Digest of the Law relating to Commons and Open Spaces, including Public Parks and Recreation Grounds, with various official documents; precedents of by-laws and regulations. The Statutes in full and brief notes of leading cases. By GEORGE F. CHAMBERS, Esq., Barrister-at-Law. Imperial 8vo. 1877. 6*s.* 6*d.*

COMPANY LAW.—Palmer's Private Companies, their Formation and Advantages; or, How to Convert your Business into a Private Company, and the benefit of so doing. With Notes on "Single Ship Companies." Fourth Edition. By F. B. PALMER, Esq., Barrister-at-Law. Author of "Company Precedents." 12mo. 1883. *Net,* 2*s.*

**** All standard Law Works are kept in Stock, in law calf and other bindings.*

COMPANY LAW.—*Continued.*

Palmer.—*Vide* "Conveyancing."

Palmer's Shareholders' and Directors' Legal Companion.—A Manual of every-day Law and Practice for Promoters, Shareholders, Directors, Secretaries, Creditors and Solicitors of Companies, under the Companies' Acts, 1862 to 1880. Fourth Edition. With an Appendix on the Conversion of Business Concerns into Private Companies. By F. B. PALMER, Esq., Barrister-at-Law. 12mo. 1883. *Net*, 2*s*. 6*d*

Thring.—*Vide* "Joint Stocks."

CONTINGENT REMAINDERS.—**An Epitome of Fearne on Contingent Remainders and Executory Devises.** Intended for the Use of Students. By W. M. C. Post 8vo. 1878. 6*s*. 6*d*.

"The student will find a perusal of this epitome of great value to him."—*Law Journal.*

CONTRACTS.—**Addison on Contracts.**—Being a Treatise on the Law of Contracts. Eighth Edition. By HORACE SMITH, Esq., Barrister-at-Law, Recorder of Lincoln, Author of "A Treatise on the Law of Negligence," &c. Royal 8vo. 1883. 2*l*. 10*s*.

"To the present editor must be given all praise which untiring industry and intelligent research can command. He has presented the profession with the law brought down to the present date clearly and fully stated."—*Law Times.*

"We think that this edition of Addison will maintain the reputation of the work as a satisfactory guide to the vast storehouse of decisions on contract law."—*Solicitors' Journal.*

Fry.—*Vide* "Specific Performance."

Leake on Contracts.—An Elementary Digest of the Law of Contracts (being a new edition of "The Elements of the Law of Contracts"). By STEPHEN MARTIN LEAKE, Barrister-at-Law. 1 vol. Demy 8vo. 1878. 1*l*. 18*s*.

Pollock's Principles of Contract.—Being a Treatise on the General Principles relating to the Validity of Agreements in the Law of England. **Third Edition**, revised and partly re-written. By FREDERICK POLLOCK, of Lincoln's Inn, Esq., Barrister-at-Law. Demy 8vo. 1881. 1*l*. 8*s*.

The late Lord Chief Justice of England in his judgment in ***Metropolitan Railway Company* v. *Brogden and others*, said. "The Law is well put by Mr. Frederick Pollock in his very able and learned work on Contracts."**—*The Times.*

"We have nothing but praise for this (third) edition. The material recent cases have been added and the whole work has been carefully revised."—*Solicitors' Journal.*

"A work which, in our opinion, shows great ability, a discerning intellect, a comprehensive mind, and painstaking industry."—*Law Journal.*

"For the purposes of the student there is no book equal to Mr. Pollock's."

"He has succeeded in writing a book on Contracts which the working lawyer will find as useful for reference as any of its predecessors, and which at the same time will give the student what he will seek for in vain elsewhere, a complete *rationale* of the law."—*Law Magazine and Review.*

Smith's Law of Contracts.—Seventh Edition. By V. T. THOMPSON, Esq., Barrister-at-Law. Demy 8vo. 1878. 1*l*. 1*s*.

CONVEYANCING.—**Dart.**—*Vide* "Vendors and Purchasers."

Harris and Clarkson's Conveyancing and Law of Property Act, 1881, and the Vendor and Purchaser Act, 1874; with Introduction, Notes and Copious Index. By W. MANNING HARRIS, M.A., and THOMAS CLARKSON, M.A., Barristers-at-Law. Demy 8vo. 1882. 9*s*.

"The notes in this volume are more copious and exhaustive than those in any other edition of these Acts which has at present appeared."—*The Law Journal.*

CONVEYANCING.—*Continued.*

Greenwood's Manual of Conveyancing.—A Manual of the Practice of Conveyancing, showing the present Practice relating to the daily routine of Conveyancing in Solicitors' Offices. To which are added Concise Common Forms and Precedents in Conveyancing. Seventh Edition. Including a **Supplement** written with special reference to the Acts of 1882, and an Appendix, comprising the Order under the Solicitors' Remuneration Act, 1881, with Notes thereon. Edited by HARRY GREENWOOD, M.A., Esq., Barrister-at-Law. Demy 8vo. 1882. 16*s.*

*** *The Supplement may be had separately. Price 2s.*

"We should like to see it placed by his principal in the hands of every articled clerk. One of the most useful practical works we have ever seen."—*Indermaur's Law Students' Journal.*

"The Author has carefully worked the provisions of the Act into his text, calling special attention to the effect of those sections which make absolute changes in the law, as distinguished from those which are merely optional for adoption or exclusion."—*The Law Magazine.*

Humphry's Common Precedents in Conveyancing. Adapted to the Conveyancing Acts, 1881-82, and the Settled Land Act, 1882, &c., together with the Acts, an Introduction, and Practical Notes. Second Edition. By HUGH M. HUMPHRY, M.A., Esq., Barrister-at-Law. Demy 8vo. 1882. 12*s.* 6*d.*

"The collection of Precedents is sufficiently comprehensive for ordinary use, and is supplemented by concise foot notes mainly composed of extracts from statutes necessary to be borne in mind by the draftsman."—*Law Magazine.*

"A work that we think the profession will appreciate."—*Law Times.*

Palmer's Company Precedents.—For use in relation to Companies subject to the Companies' Acts, 1862 to 1880. Arranged as follows:—Agreements, Memoranda and Articles of Association, Prospectus, Resolutions, Notices, Certificates, Debentures, Petitions, Orders, Reconstruction, Amalgamation, Arrangements, Private Acts. With Copious Notes. Second Edition. By FRANCIS BEAUFORT PALMER, of the Inner Temple, Esq., Barrister-at-Law. Royal 8vo. 1881. 1*l.* 10*s.*

"To those concerned in getting up companies, the assistance given by Mr. Palmer must be very valuable, because he does not confine himself to bare precedents, but by intelligent and learned commentary lights up, as it were, each step that he takes. . . There is an elaborate index."—*Law Times.*

"To those who are acquainted with the first edition we recommend the second edition as a great improvement."—*Law Journal.*

Prideaux's Precedents in Conveyancing.—With Dissertations on its Law and Practice. Twelfth Edition. Thoroughly revised and adapted to the Conveyancing Acts, 1881, 1882, the Settled Land Act, 1882, the Married Women's Property Act, 1882, and the Bills of Sale Act, 1882. By FREDERICK PRIDEAUX, late Professor of the Law of Real and Personal Property to the Inns of Court, and JOHN WHITCOMBE, Esqrs., Barristers-at-Law. 2 vols. Royal 8vo. 1883. 3*l.* 10*s.*

"The most useful work out on Conveyancing."—*Law Journal.*

"This work is accurate, concise, clear, and comprehensive in scope, and we know of no treatise upon conveyancing which is so generally useful to the practitioner."—*Law Times.*

"The conciseness and scientific precision of these Precedents of the Future are at once pleasing and startling. . . . . The Valuable Dissertations on the law and practice, which have always formed a feature of these volumes, have been revised thoroughly."—*Law Magazine.*

"The student who, in good time before his examination, can peruse these most valuable dissertations and refer to some of the precedents will have an immense advantage over those who have not done so."—*Law Students' Journal.*

*** *All standard Law Works are kept in Stock, in law calf and other bindings.*

CONVICTIONS.—Paley's Law and Practice of Summary Convictions under the Summary Jurisdiction Acts, 1848 and 1879; including Proceedings preliminary and subsequent to Convictions, and the responsibility of convicting Magistrates and their Officers, with Forms. Sixth Edition. By W. H. MACNAMARA, Esq., Barrister-at-Law. Demy 8vo. 1879. 1*l.* 4*s.*

Templer.—*Vide* "Summary Convictions."

Wigram.—*Vide* "Justice of the Peace."

CORONERS.—Jervis on the Office and Duties of Coroners.—With Forms and Precedents. Fourth Edition. By R. E. MELSHEIMER, Esq., Barrister-at-Law. Post 8vo. 1880. 12*s.*

COSTS.—Morgan and Wurtzburg's Treatise on the Law of Costs in the Chancery Division of the High Court of Justice.—Being the Second Edition of Morgan and Davey's Costs in Chancery. With an Appendix, containing Forms and Precedents of Bills of Costs. By the Right Hon. GEORGE OSBORNE MORGAN, one of Her Majesty's Counsel, Her Majesty's Judge Advocate General, and E. A. WURTZBURG, of Lincoln's Inn, Esq., Barrister-at-Law. Demy 8vo. 1882. 30*s.*

"Cannot fail to be of use to solicitors and their Chancery managing clerks."—*Law Times.*

Scott's Costs in the High Court of Justice and other Courts. Fourth Edition. By JOHN SCOTT, of the Inner Temple, Esq., Barrister-at-Law, Reporter of the Common Pleas Division. Demy 8vo. 1880. 1*l.* 6*s.*

"Mr. Scott's introductory notes are very useful, and the work is now a compendium on the law and practice regarding costs, as well as a book of precedents."—*Law Times.*

Scott's Costs in Bankruptcy and Liquidation under the Bankruptcy Act, 1869. Royal 12mo. 1873. *Net,* 3*s.*

Summerhays and Toogood's Precedents of Bills of Costs in the Chancery, Queen's Bench, Probate Divorce and Admiralty Divisions of the High Court of Justice; in Conveyancing; the Crown Office; Lunacy; Arbitration under the Lands Clauses Consolidation Act; the Mayor's Court, London; the County Courts; the Privy Council; and on Passing Residuary and Succession Accounts; with Scales of Allowances; Rules of Court relating to Costs; Forms of Affidavits of Increase, and of Objections to Taxation. Fourth Edition. By WM. FRANK SUMMERHAYS, and THORNTON TOOGOOD, Solicitors of the Supreme Court. Royal 8vo. 1883. (*Nearly ready.*) 1*l.* 8*s.*

Webster's Parliamentary Costs.—Private Bills, Election Petitions, Appeals, House of Lords. By EDWARD WEBSTER, Esq., of the Taxing and Examiners' Office. Fourth Edition. By C. CAVANAGH, Esq., Barrister-at-Law. Author of "The Law of Money Securities. Post 8vo. 1881. 20*s.*

"This edition of a well known work is in great part a new publication; and it contains, now printed for the first time, the Table of Fees charged at the House of Lords. . . . . We do not doubt that Parliamentary agents will find the work eminently useful."—*Law Journal.*

*** *All standard Law Works are kept in Stock, in law calf and other bindings*

COUNTY COURTS.—Pitt-Lewis' County Court Practice.—A Complete Practice of the County Courts, including Admiralty and Bankruptcy, embodying the Acts, Rules, Forms and Costs, with Additional Forms and a Full Index. Second Edition. By G. PITT-LEWIS, of the Middle Temple and Western Circuit, Esq., Barrister-at-Law, sometime Holder of the Studentship of the Four Inns of Court, assisted by H. A. DE COLYAR, Esq., Barrister-at-Law. In 2 parts. Demy 8vo. 1883. 2*l.* 10*s.*

*** *Part I., with Table of Cases, Index, &c., sold separately, price* 30*s.*

☞ *This Edition deals fully with the Employers' Liability Act, and is the only County Court Practice which contains the County Courts (Costs and Salaries) Act, 1882, the important legislation (as to Married Women's Property, Bills of Sale, Inferior Courts' Judgments, &c.) of the Session of 1882, and also the County Court Rules of March, 1883.*

"It is very clearly written, and is always practical. The Index is very elaborate, and there is an excellent tabular Index to the County Court Acts and Rules."—*Solicitors' Journal.*

"One of the best books of practice which is to be found in our legal literature."—*Law Times.*

"We have rarely met with a work displaying more honest industry on the part of the author than the one before us."—*Law Journal.*

"Mr. Pitt-Lewis has, in fact, aimed—and we are glad to say successfully—at providing for the County Courts' practitioner what 'Chitty's Archbold' and 'Daniell's Chancery Practice' have long been to practitioners in the High Court."—*Law Magazine.*

"Mr. Pitt-Lewis's work was at once admitted by the profession to the rank of a standard authority, and it must be now generally looked upon as the complete County Court Practice."—*City Press.*

CRIMINAL LAW.—Archbold's Pleading and Evidence in Criminal Cases.—With the Statutes, Precedents of Indictments, &c., and the Evidence necessary to support them. Nineteenth Edition. By WILLIAM BRUCE, Esq., Barrister-at-Law, and Stipendiary Magistrate for the Borough of Leeds. Demy 8vo. 1878. 1*l.* 11*s.* 6*d.*

Roscoe's Digest of the Law of Evidence in Criminal Cases.—Ninth Edition. By HORACE SMITH, Esq., Barrister-at-Law. Royal 12mo. 1878. 1*l.* 11*s.* 6*d.*

Russell's Treatise on Crimes and Misdemeanors.—Fifth Edition. By SAMUEL PRENTICE, Esq., one of Her Majesty's Counsel. 3 vols. Royal 8vo. 1877. 5*l.* 15*s.* 6*d.*

"What better Digest of Criminal Law could we possibly hope for than 'Russell on Crimes?'"—*Sir James Fitzjames Stephen's Speech on Codification.*

"Alterations have been made in the arrangement of the work which without interfering with the general plan are sufficient to show that great care and thought have been bestowed. . . . . We are amazed at the patience, industry and skill which are exhibited in the collection and arrangement of all this mass of learning."—*The Times.*

Shirley's Sketch of the Criminal Law.—By W. SHIRLEY SHIRLEY, M.A., Esq., Barrister-at-Law, Author of "Leading Cases made Easy," assisted by C. M. ATKINSON, M.A., B.C.L., Esq., Barrister-at-Law. Demy 8vo. 1880. 7*s.* 6*d.*

"As a primary introduction to Criminal Law, it will be found very acceptable to Students."—*Law Students' Journal*

DECREES.—Seton.—*Vide* "Equity."

*** *All standard Law Works are kept in Stock, in law calf and other bindings.*

DIARY.—Lawyer's Companion (The), Diary, and Law Directory for 1884.—For the use of the Legal Profession Public Companies, Justices, Merchants, Estate Agents, Auctioneers, &c., &c. Edited by JOHN THOMPSON, of the Inner Temple, Esq., Barrister-at-Law; and contains Tables of Costs in Conveyancing, &c.; a Digest of Useful Decisions on Costs; Monthly Diary of County, Local Government, and Parish Business; Oaths in Supreme Court; Summary of Legislation of 1883; Alphabetical Index to the Practical Statutes; a Copious Table of Stamp Duties; Legal Time, Interest, Discount, Income, Wages and other Tables; Probate, Legacy and Succession Duties; and a variety of matters of practical utility. PUBLISHED ANNUALLY. Thirty-eighth Issue. (*Now ready.*)

Contains the most complete List published of the English Bar, and London and Country Solicitors, with date of admission and appointments, and is issued in the following forms, octavo size, strongly bound in cloth:—

	s.	*d.*
1. Two days on a page, plain	5	0
2. The above, INTERLEAVED for ATTENDANCES	7	0
3. Two days on a page, ruled, with or without money columns	5	6
4. The above, INTERLEAVED for ATTENDANCES.	8	0
5. Whole page for each day, plain	7	6
6. The above, INTERLEAVED for ATTENDANCES	9	6
7. Whole page for each day, ruled, with or without money cols.	8	6
8. The above, INTERLEAVED for ATTENDANCES	10	6
9. Three days on a page, ruled blue lines, without money cols.	5	0

The Diary contains memoranda of Legal Business throughout the Year.

"An excellent work."—*The Times.*

"A publication which has long ago secured to itself the favour of the profession, and which, as heretofore, justifies by its contents the title assumed by it."—*Law Journal.*

"Contains all the information which could be looked for in such a work, and gives it in a most convenient form and very completely. We may unhesitatingly recommend the work to our readers."—*Solicitors' Journal.*

"The 'Lawyer's Companion and Diary' is a book that ought to be in the possession of every lawyer, and of every man of business."

"The 'Lawyer's Companion' is, indeed, what it is called, for it combines everything required for reference in the lawyer's office."—*Law Times.*

"It is a book without which no lawyer's library or office can be complete."—*Irish Law Times.*

DICTIONARY.—Student's (The) Pocket Law Lexicon. Explaining Technical Words, Phrases and Maxims of the English, Scotch and Roman Law, to which is added a complete List of Law Reports, with their Abbreviations. Second Edition, Revised and Enlarged. By HENRY G. RAWSON, B.A., Esq., Barrister-at-Law. (*In the press.*)

"A wonderful little legal Dictionary."—*Indermaur's Law Students' Journal.*

"A very handy, complete, and useful little work."—*Saturday Review.*

Wharton's Law Lexicon.—Forming an Epitome of the Law of England, and containing full explanations of the Technical Terms and Phrases thereof, both Ancient and Modern; including the various Legal Terms used in Commercial Business. Together with a Translation of the Latin Law Maxims and selected Titles from the Civil, Scotch and Indian Law. Seventh Edition. By J. M. LELY, Esq., Barrister-at-Law, Editor of "Chitty's Statutes," &c. Super-royal 8vo. 1883. 1*l.* 18*s.*

"On almost every point both student and practitioner can gather information from this invaluable book, which ought to be in every lawyer's office."—*Gibson's Law Notes.*

"As it now stands the Lexicon contains all it need contain, and to those who value such a work it is made more valuable still."—*Law Times*, June 2, 1883.

*** *All standard Law Works are kept in Stock, in law calf and other bindings.*

DIGESTS.—**Bedford.**—*Vide* "Examination Guides."

Chitty's Index to all the Reported Cases decided in the several Courts of Equity in England, the Privy Council, and the House of Lords, with a selection of Irish Cases, on or relating to the Principles, Pleading, and Practice of Equity and Bankruptcy; from the earliest period. The Fourth Edition, wholly revised, reclassified and brought down to the date of publication by WILLIAM FRANK JONES, B.C.L., M.A., and HENRY EDWARD HIRST, B.C.L., M.A., both of Lincoln's Inn, Esqrs., Barristers-at-Law. Volume I. Roy. 8vo. 1883. 1*l.* 11*s.* 6*d.*

*** **This Volume contains the Titles "Abandonment" to "Bankruptcy." The Title Bankruptcy is a Complete Digest of all cases, including the Decisions at Common Law.**

Volume II. is in the press, and will be issued shortly.

The Work will be completed in 5 or 6 Volumes.

Fisher's Digest of Reported Decisions in all the Courts, with a Selection from the Irish; the cases overruled and impeached and references to the Statutes, Rules and Orders of Courts from 1756 to 1883. Compiled and arranged by JOHN MEWS, assisted by CECIL MAURICE CHAPMAN, HARRY HADDEN WICKES SPARHAM, and ARTHUR HORATIO TODD, Barristers-at-Law. (*In the press.*)

Notanda Digest in Law, Equity, Bankruptcy, Admiralty, Divorce, and Probate Cases.—By H. TUDOR BODDAM, of the Inner Temple, and HARRY GREENWOOD and E. W. D. MANSON, of Lincoln's Inn, Esqrs., Barristers-at-Law.

Third Series, 1873 to 1876 inclusive, half-bound. *Net,* 1*l.* 11*s.* 6*d.*

Ditto, Fourth Series, for the years 1877, 1878, 1879, 1880, 1881, and 1882, with Index. *Each, net,* 1*l.* 1*s.*

Ditto, ditto, for 1883. By E. W. D. MANSON and PROCTER T. PULMAN, Esqrs., Barristers-at-Law. Plain Copy and Two Indexes, or Adhesive Copy for insertion in Text-Books (without Index). Annual Subscription, payable in advance. *Net,* 21*s.*

*** The numbers are issued regularly every month. Each number contains a concise analysis of every case reported in the *Law Reports, Law Journal, Weekly Reporter, Law Times,* and the *Irish Law Reports,* up to and including the cases contained in the parts for the current month, with references to Text-books, Statutes, and the Law Reports Consolidated Digest, and an ALPHABETICAL INDEX of the subjects contained IN EACH NUMBER.

DISCOVERY.—**Hare's Treatise on the Discovery of Evidence.**—Second Edition. By SHERLOCK HARE, Barrister-at-Law. Post 8vo. 1877. 12*s.*

Sichel and Chance's Discovery.—The Law relating to Interrogatories, Production, Inspection of Documents, and Discovery, as well in the Superior as in the Inferior Courts, together with an Appendix of the Acts, Forms and Orders. By WALTER S. SICHEL, M.A., and WILLIAM CHANCE, M.A., Esqrs., Barristers-at-Law. Demy 8vo. 1883. 12*s.*

"The work will, we think, be very useful in practice, and may be confidently recommended for use in judges' chambers."—*Law Times.*

"It will be of much use to practitioners to be able to find, as we do in the work before us, an intelligent account of the whole set of decisions."—*Solicitors' Journal.*

"It is evident that this work is the result of much careful and painstaking research, and we can confidently recommend it as a careful and convenient compendium, and particularly as likely to be of material assistance to those who are much engaged in judges' chambers or in the county courts."—*Law Magazine.*

DIVORCE.—Browne's Treatise on the Principles and Practice of the Court for Divorce and Matrimonial Causes:—With the Statutes, Rules, Fees and Forms relating thereto. Fourth Edition. By GEORGE BROWNE, Esq., Barrister-at-Law. Demy 8vo. 1880. 1*l.* 4*s.*

"The book is a clear, practical, and, so far as we have been able to test it, accurate exposition of divorce law and procedure."—*Solicitors' Journal.*

DOMICIL.—Dicey on the Law of Domicil as a branch of the Law of England, stated in the form of Rules.—By A. V. DICEY, B.C.L., Barrister-at-Law. Author of "Rules for the Selection of Parties to an Action." Demy 8vo. 1879. 18*s.*

EASEMENTS.—Goddard's Treatise on the Law of Easements.—By JOHN LEYBOURN GODDARD, Esq., Barrister-at-Law. Second Edition. Demy 8vo. 1877. 16*s.*

"The book is invaluable: where the cases are silent the author has taken pains to ascertain what the law would be if brought into question."—*Law Journal.*

"Nowhere has the subject been treated so exhaustively, and, we may add, so scientifically, as by Mr. Goddard. We recommend it to the most careful study of the law student, as well as to the library of the practitioner."—*Law Times.*

ECCLESIASTICAL LAW.—Dodd's Burial and other Church Fees and the Burial Act, 1880:—With Notes. By J. T. DODD, M.A., Barrister-at-Law. Royal 12mo. 1881. 4*s*

Phillimore's (Sir R.) Ecclesiastical Law.—The Ecclesiastical Law of the Church of England. With Supplement, containing the Statutes and Decisions to end of 1875. By the Right Hon. SIR ROBERT PHILLIMORE, D.C.L. 2 vols. 8vo. 1873-76. 3*l.* 7*s.* 6*d.*

*** The Supplement may be had separately, price 4*s.* 6*d.*, sewed.

ELECTIONS.—Carter's Corrupt and Illegal Practices Prevention Act, 1883, with Notes and an Index. Edited by JOHN CORRIE CARTER, Esq., Recorder of Stamford. Forming a Supplement to "Rogers on Elections." Royal 12mo. 1883. 5*s.*

"Mr. Carter's notes are explicit, and serve the useful purpose of clearly indicating all alterations in the law."—*The Law Times.*

FitzGerald.—*Vide* "Ballot."

Rogers on Elections, Registration, and Election Agency.—Thirteenth Edition, including PETITIONS and Municipal Elections and Registration. With an Appendix of Statutes and Forms. By JOHN CORRIE CARTER, of the Inner Temple, Esq., Barrister-at-Law. Royal 12mo. 1880. 1*l.* 12*s.*

"Petition has been added, setting forth the procedure and the decisions on that subject; and the statutes passed since the last edition are explained."—*The Times.*

"A book of long standing and for information on the common law of elections, of which it contains a mine of extracts from and references to the older authorities, will always be resorted to."—*Law Journal*

ELECTRIC LIGHTING.—Cunynghame's Treatise on the Law of Electric Lighting, with the Acts of Parliament, and Rules and Orders of the Board of Trade, a Model Provisional Order, and a set of Forms, to which is added a Description of the Principal Apparatus used in Electric Lighting, with Illustrations. By HENRY CUNYNGHAME, Barrister-at-Law. Royal 8vo. 1883. 12*s.* 6*d.*

"As an original work it demands special praise, and we congratulate Mr. Cunynghame on his production."—*Law Times.*

"Among the many works upon electric lighting which have come before us, we think that Mr. Cunynghame's cannot fail to gain and keep a high place."—*Solicitors' Journal.*

EMPLOYERS' LIABILITY ACT.—Macdonell.—*Vide* "Master and Servant."

Smith.—*Vide* "Negligence."

*** *All standard Law Works are kept in Stock, in law calf and other bindings.*

EQUITY, *and Vide* CHANCERY.

Chitty's Index.—*Vide* "Digests."

Seton's Forms of Decrees, Judgments, and Orders in the High Court of Justice and Courts of Appeal, having especial reference to the Chancery Division, with Practical Notes. Fourth Edition. By R. H. LEACH, Esq., Senior Registrar of the Chancery Division; F. G. A. WILLIAMS, of the Inner Temple, Esq.; and the late H. W. MAY, Esq.; succeeded by JAMES EASTWICK, of Lincoln's Inn, Esq., Barristers-at-Law. 2 vols. in 3 parts. Royal 8vo. 1877—79. 4*l.* 10*s.*

*** Vol. II., Parts 1 and 2, separately, price each 1*l.* 10*s.*

"The Editors of this new edition of Seton deserve much praise for what is almost, if not absolutely, an innovation in law books. In treating of any division of their subject they have put prominently forward the result of the latest decisions, settling the law so far as it is ascertained, thus avoiding much useless reference to older cases. . . There can be no doubt that in a book of practice like Seton, it is much more important to be able to see at once what the law is than to know how it has become what it is; and the Editors have evidently taken great pains to carry out this principle in presenting the law on each division of their labours to their readers."—*The Times.*

"Of all the editions of 'Seton' this is the best. . . . We can hardly speak too highly of the industry and intelligence which have been bestowed on the preparation of the notes."—*Solicitors' Journal.*

"Now the book is before us complete; and we advisedly say *complete*, because it has scarcely ever been our fortune to see a more *complete* law book than this. Extensive in sphere, and exhaustive in treatise, comprehensive in matter, yet apposite in details, it presents all the features of an excellent work . . . The index, extending over 278 pages, is a model of comprehensiveness and accuracy."—*Law Journal.*

Smith's Manual of Equity Jurisprudence.—A Manual of Equity Jurisprudence for Practitioners and Students, founded on the Works of Story, Spence, and other writers, and on more than a thousand subsequent cases, comprising the Fundamental Principles and the points of Equity usually occurring in General Practice. By JOSIAH W. SMITH, B.C.L., Q.C. Thirteenth Edition. 12mo. 1880. 12*s.* 6*d.*

"There is no disguising the truth; the proper mode to use this book is to learn its pages by heart."—*Law Magazine and Review.*

"It will be found as useful to the practitioner as to the student."—*Solicitors' Journal.*

Smith's Practical Exposition of the Principles of Equity, illustrated by the Leading Decisions thereon. For the use of Students and Practitioners. By H. ARTHUR SMITH, M.A., LL.B., of the Middle Temple, Esq., Barrister-at-Law. Demy 8vo. 1882. 20*s.*

"The book seems to us to be one of great value to students."—*Solicitors' Journal.*

"In a moderately-sized volume, such as no lawyer who has his own advantage in view could object to 'read, mark, learn, and inwardly digest,' Mr. Smith sets forth succinctly and in due order all the fundamental principles administered by Courts of Equity, showing how they have by recent enactment been engrafted on the Common and carefully abstaining from overlaying his subject-matter with multifarious details of practice which might tend to confuse and mystify. . . . We must again state our opinion that this is a most remarkable book, containing in a reasonable space more information, and that better arranged and conveyed, than almost any other law book of recent times which has come under our notice."—*Saturday Review.*

EXAMINATION GUIDES.—Bedford's Guide to the Preliminary Examination for Solicitors.—Fourth Edition. 12mo. 1874. *Net,* 3*s.*

Bedford's Digest of the Preliminary Examination Questions in Latin Grammar, Arithmetic, French Grammar, History and Geography, with the Answers. Second Edition. Demy 8vo. 1882. 18*s.*

Bedford's Preliminary Guide to Latin Grammar.—12mo. 1872. *Net,* 3*s.*

Bedford's Student's Guide to Smith on Contracts. Demy 8vo. 1879. 3*s.* 6*d.*

EXAMINATION GUIDES.—*Continued.*

Bedford's Final Examination Guide to Bankruptcy.—Fourth Edition. (*In preparation.*)

Bedford's Student's Guide to the Ninth Edition of Stephen's New Commentaries on the Laws of England.—Third Edition. Demy 8vo. 1883. 7*s.* 6*d.*

Bedford's Final Examination Digest: containing a Digest of the Final Examination Questions in matters of Law and Procedure determined by the Chancery, Queen's Bench, Common Pleas, and Exchequer Divisions of the High Court of Justice, and on the Law of Real and Personal Property and the Practice of Conveyancing, with the Answers. 8vo. 1879. 16*s.*

"Will furnish students with a large armoury of weapons with which to meet the attacks of the examiners of the Incorporated Law Society."—*Law Times.*

Haynes and Nelham's Honours Examination Digest, comprising all the Questions in Conveyancing, Equity, Common Law, Bankruptcy, Probate, Divorce, Admiralty, and Ecclesiastical Law and Practice asked at the Solicitors' Honours Examinations since their establishment to the present time, with Answers thereto. By JOHN F. HAYNES, LL.D., Author of "Chancery Practice," "The Students' Leading Cases," &c., and THOMAS A. NELHAM, Solicitor (Honours). Demy 8vo. 1883. 15*s.*

"Students going in for honours will find this one to their advantage."—*Law Times*, September 22, 1883.

"Answers are appended which, judging from an examination of several of them, appears to be careful and accurate."—*Solicitors' Journal*, October 13, 1883.

Shearwood's Law Student's Annual.—Containing the Questions with Answers to the Solicitor's and Bar Examinations (Michaelmas Term, 1881, to Trinity Term, 1882, inclusive), with Remarks and Comments. A list of Books suggested for Students, &c., &c. Edited by JOSEPH A. SHEARWOOD, Esq., Barrister-at-Law, Author of "A Concise Abridgment of Real Property," and of "Personal Property," etc. Demy 8vo. 1882. 5*s.*

"This is a book of a thorough character. . . . Much care and labour have evidently been expended on the book, which will be found of great advantage to students."—*Law Journal.*

"We know of no other manual which contains the same quantity of information in such a concise form."—*Solicitors' Journal.*

"The remarks on the examinations are very interesting, and there are some valuable hints as to what books the candidate for honours and a pass respectively should use."—*Gibson's Law Notes.*

Shearwood's Student's Guide to the Bar, the Solicitor's Intermediate and Final and the Universities Law Examinations.—With Suggestions as to the books usually read, and the passages therein to which attention should be paid. By JOSEPH A. SHEARWOOD, B.A., Esq., Barrister-at-law. 8vo. 1879. 5*s.* 6*d.*

"Any student of average intelligence who conscientiously follows the path and obeys the instructions given him by the author, need not fear to present himself as a candidate for any of the examinations to which this book is intended as a guide."—*Law Journal.*

EXECUTORS.—**Macaskie's Treatise on the Law of Executors and Administrators**, and of the Administration of the Estates of Deceased Persons. With an Appendix of Statutes and Forms. By STUART CUNNINGHAM MACASKIE, of Gray's Inn, Esq., Barrister-at-Law. 8vo. 1881. 10*s.* 6*d.*

"An able summary of the law of administration, now forming one of the subjects set for the general examination for call to the bar."

"Students may read the book with advantage as an introduction to 'Williams,' and by practitioners not possessing the larger work it will undoubtedly be found useful."—*Law Journal.*

**** All standard Law Works are kept in Stock, in law calf and other bindings.*

EXECUTORS.—*Continued.*

Williams' Law of Executors and Administrators.—By the Rt. Hon. Sir EDWARD VAUGHAN WILLIAMS, late one of the Judges of Her Majesty's Court of Common Pleas. Eighth Edition. By WALTER VAUGHAN WILLIAMS and ROLAND VAUGHAN WILLIAMS, Esqrs., Barristers-at-Law. 2 vols. Royal 8vo. 1879. 3*l.* 16*s.*

"A treatise which occupies an unique position and which is recognised by the Bench and the profession as having paramount authority in the domain of law with which it deals."—*Law Journal.*

EXTRADITION.—Kirchner's L'Extradition.—Recueil Renfermant in Extenso tous les Traités conclus jusqu'au 1er Janvier, 1883, entre les Nations civilisées, et donnant la solution précise des difficultés qui peuvent surgir dans leur application. Avec une Préface de McGEORGES LACHAUD, Avocat à la Cour d'Appel de Paris. Publié sous les auspices de M. C. E. HOWARD VINCENT, Directeur des Affaires Criminelles de la Police Métropolitaine de Londres; Membre de la Faculté de Droit et de la Société Générale des Prisons de Paris. Par F. J. KIRCHNER, Attaché à la Direction des Affaires Criminelles. In 1 vol. (1150 pp.) Royal 8vo. 2*l.* 2*s.*

FACTORY ACTS.—Notcutt's Law relating to Factories and Workshops. Second Edition. 12mo. 1879. 9*s.*

FARM, LAW OF.—Cooke.—*Vide* "Agricultural Law."

Dixon's Law of the Farm.—A Digest of Cases connected with the Law of the Farm, and including the Agricultural Customs of England and Wales. Fourth Edition. By HENRY PERKINS, Esq., Barrister-at-Law and Midland Circuit. Demy 8vo. 1879. 1*l.* 6*s.*

"It is impossible not to be struck with the extraordinary research that must have been used in the compilation of such a book as this."—*Law Journal.*

*** Supplement to above, containing the Agricultural Holdings (England) Act, 1883, with explanatory Notes and Forms; together with the Ground Game Act, 1880. By AUBREY J. SPENCER, Esq., Barrister-at-Law. Demy 8vo. 1883. (*In the press.*)

FOREIGN JUDGMENTS.—Piggott's Foreign Judgments their effect in the English Courts. Part I. The English Doctrine, Defences, Judgments in Rem. Status.—By F. T. PIGGOTT, M.A., LL.M., of the Middle Temple, Esq., Barrister-at-Law. Royal 8vo. 1879. 15*s.*

Part II.—The Effect of an English Judgment Abroad. Service on Absent Defendants. Royal 8vo. 1881. 15*s.*

FORMS.—Allen.—*Vide* "Pleading."

Bullen and Leake.—*Vide* "*Pleading.*"

Chitty's Forms of Practical Proceedings in the Queen's Bench, Common Pleas and Exchequer Divisions of the High Court of Justice: with Notes containing the Statutes, Rules and Practice relating thereto. Eleventh Edition. By THOS. WILLES CHITTY, Esq., Barrister-at-Law. Demy 8vo. 1879. 1*l.* 18*s.*

Daniell's Forms and Precedents of Proceedings in the Chancery Division of the High Court of Justice and on Appeal therefrom; with Dissertations and Notes, forming a complete guide to the Practice of the Chancery Division of the High Court and of the Courts of Appeal. Being the Third Edition of "Daniell's Chancery Forms." By WILLIAM HENRY UPJOHN, Esq., of Gray's Inn, &c., &c. Demy 8vo. 1879. 2*l.* 2*s.*

FRENCH COMMERCIAL LAW.—Goirand.—*Vide* "Commercial Law."

HIGHWAYS—Baker's Law of Highways in England and Wales, including Bridges and Locomotives. Comprising a succinct code of the several provisions under each head, the statutes at length in an Appendix; with Notes of Cases, Forms, and copious Index. By THOMAS BAKER, of the Inner Temple, Esq., Barrister-at-Law. Royal 12mo. 1880. 15*s.*

"This is distinctly a well-planned book, and cannot fail to be useful, not only to lawyers, but to those who may be locally engaged in the management of highways."—*Law Journal.*

"The general plan of Mr. Baker's book is good. He groups together condensed statements of the effect of the provisions of the different Highway Acts relating to the same matter, giving in all cases references to the sections, which are printed in full in the appendix. To each condensed section, or group of sections, he appends a note, stating concisely the effect of the decisions."—*Solicitors' Journal.*

Chambers' Law relating to Highways and Bridges, being the Statutes in full and brief Notes of 700 Leading Cases; together with the Lighting Act, 1833. By GEO. F. CHAMBERS, Esq., Barrister-at-Law. 1878. 12*s.*

INJUNCTIONS.—Seton.—*Vide* "Equity."

INLAND REVENUE CASES.—Highmore's Summary Proceedings in Inland Revenue Cases in England and Wales. By NATHANIEL JOSEPH HIGHMORE, of the Middle Temple, Esq., Barrister-at-Law, and of the Inland Revenue Department. Royal 12mo. 1882. 6*s.*

"A complete treatise on procedure applied to cases under the Revenue Act, and as a book of practice it is the best we have seen."—*The Justice of the Peace*, Jan. 28, 1882.

INSURANCE.—Arnould on the Law of Marine Insurance.—Fifth Edition. By DAVID MACLACHLAN, Esq., Barrister-at-Law. 2 vols. Royal 8vo. 1877. 3*l.*

"As a text book, 'Arnould' is now all the practitioner can want, and we congratulate the editor upon the skill with which he has incorporated the new decisions."—*Law Times.*

Lowndes on the Law of Marine Insurance.—A Practical Treatise. By RICHARD LOWNDES. Author of "The Law of General Average," &c. Second Edition. (*In preparation.*)

"It is rarely, indeed, that we have been able to express such unqualified approval of a new legal work."—*Solicitors' Journal.*

INTERNATIONAL LAW.—Amos' Lectures on International Law.—By SHELDON AMOS, M.A., Professor of Jurisprudence (including International Law) to the Inns of Court, &c. Royal 8vo. 1874. 10*s.* 6*d.*

Dicey.—*Vide* "Domicil."

Kent's International Law.—Kent's Commentary on International Law. Edited by J. T. ABDY, LL.D., Judge of County Courts. Second Edition. Revised and brought down to the present time. Crown 8vo. 1878. 10*s.* 6*d.*

"Altogether Dr. Abdy has performed his task in a manner worthy of his reputation. His book will be useful not only to Lawyers and Law Students, for whom it was primarily intended, but also for laymen."—*Solicitors' Journal.*

Levi's International Commercial Law.—Being the Principles of Mercantile Law of the following and other Countries—viz.: England, Ireland, Scotland, British India, British Colonies, Austria, Belgium, Brazil, Buenos Ayres, Denmark, France, Germany, Greece, Hans Towns, Italy, Netherlands, Norway, Portugal, Prussia, Russia, Spain, Sweden, Switzerland, United States, and Wurtemberg. By LEONE LEVI, Esq., F.S.A., F.S.S., Barrister-at-Law, &c. Second Edition. 2 vols. Royal 8vo. 1863. 1*l.* 15*s.*

⁂ All standard Law Works are kept in Stock, in law calf and other bindings.

INTERNATIONAL LAW.—*Continued.*

Vattel's Law of Nations.—By JOSEPH CHITTY, Esq. Royal 8vo. 1834. 1*l.* 1*s.*

Wheaton's Elements of International Law; Second English Edition. Edited with Notes and Appendix of Statutes and Treaties, bringing the work down to the present time. By A. C. BOYD, Esq., LL.B., J.P., Barrister-at-Law. Author of "The Merchant Shipping Laws." Demy 8vo. 1880. 1*l.* 10*s.*

"Mr. Boyd, the latest editor, has added many useful notes; he has inserted in the Appendix public documents of permanent value, and there is the prospect that, as edited by Mr. Boyd, Mr. Wheaton's volume will enter on a new lease of life."—*The Times.*

"Both the plan and execution of the work before us deserves commendation. . . . The text of Wheaton is presented without alteration, and Mr. Dana's numbering of the sections is preserved. . . . The Index, which could not have been compiled without much thought and labour, makes the book handy for reference."—*Law Journal.*

"Students who require a knowledge of Wheaton's text will find Mr. Boyd's volume very convenient."—*Law Magazine.*

INTERROGATORIES.—**Sichel and Chance.**—*Vide* "Discovery."

JOINT OWNERSHIP.—**Foster.**—*Vide* "Real Estate."

JOINT STOCKS.—**Palmer.**—*Vide* "Conveyancing" and "Company Law."

Thring's (Sir H.) Joint Stock Companies' Law.—The Law and Practice of Joint Stock and other Companies, including the Companies Acts, 1862 to 1880, with Notes, Orders, and Rules in Chancery, a Collection of Precedents of Memoranda and Articles of Association, and all the other Forms required in Making, Administering, and Winding-up a Company; also the Partnership Law Amendment Act, The Life Assurance Companies Acts, and other Acts relating to Companies. By SIR HENRY THRING, K.C.B., The Parliamentary Counsel. Fourth Edition. By G. A. R. FITZ-GERALD, Esq., M.A., Barrister-at-Law. Demy 8vo. 1880. 1*l.* 5*s.*

"This, as the work of the original draughtsman of the Companies' Act of 1862, and well-known Parliamentary counsel, Sir Henry Thring, is naturally the highest authority on the subject."—*The Times.*

"One of its most valuable features is its collection of precedents of Memoranda and Articles of Association, which has, in this Edition, been largely increased and improved."—*Law Journal.*

Jordan's Joint Stock Companies.—A Handy Book of Practical Instructions for the Formation and Management of Joint Stock Companies. Seventh Edition. 12mo. 1881. *Net,* 2*s.* 6*d.*

JUDGMENTS.—**Piggott.**—*Vide* "Foreign Judgments."

Walker's Practice on Signing Judgment in the High Court of Justice. With Forms. By H. H. WALKER, Esq., of the Judgment Department, Exchequer Division. Crown 8vo. 1879. 4*s.* 6*d.*

"The book undoubtedly meets a want, and furnishes information available for almost every branch of practice."

"We think that solicitors and their clerks will find it extremely useful."—*Law Journal.*

JUDICATURE ACTS.—**Whiteway's Hints on Practice;** or Practical Notes on the Judicature Acts, Orders, Rules and Regulations of the Supreme Court. Illustrated by the Latest Cases. **Together with the Rules of the Supreme Court, 1883.** With an Introduction, References, Notes, and Index. By A. R. WHITEWAY, M.A., of the Equity Bar and Midland Circuit, Author of "Hints to Solicitors." Second Edition. Royal 12mo. 1883. 14*s.*

Sold separately "Hints on Practice," with Cases and Index, 7*s.* 6*d.*

The Rules, edited with Notes, Cross References, and Index, *limp leather,* 7*s.* 6*d.*

"An excellently printed edition of the new Rules, with notes containing cross references and stating the sources of the Rules."—*Solicitors' Journal,* October 13, 1883.

JUDICATURE ACTS.—*Continued.*

Wilson's Supreme Court of Judicature Acts, Rules of the Supreme Court, 1883, and Forms. With other Acts, Orders, Rules and Regulations relating to the Supreme Court. With Practical Notes. Fourth Edition. By M. D. CHALMERS, of the Inner Temple, and M. MUIR MACKENZIE, of Lincoln's Inn, Barristers-at-Law. Royal 12mo. 1883. 25*s.*

*** A LARGE PAPER EDITION FOR MARGINAL NOTES. ROYAL 8VO. 1883. 30*s.*

Extract from Preface to the Fourth Edition.—The present edition contains the Rules of the Supreme Court, 1883, with notes and comments. Where a repealed rule is reproduced without alteration a reference to its former Order and number is given in the margin. Where a repealed rule is reproduced with modifications the marginal reference to it is preceded by the prefix *cf.* Where a rule is new it is stated to be so in the note, and reference is made to any statute, consolidated order, or common law or Admiralty rule upon which it appears to be founded.

This edition further includes the provisions of the Bankruptcy Act, 1883, in so far as they relate to or affect the Supreme Court, and the Statute Law Revision and Civil Procedure Act, 1883, &c.

The Editors have also entirely re-constructed the Index.

"Wilson's 'Judicature Acts' remains what it always was, one of the most handy as well as one of the best appreciated editions of the Acts."—*Law Magazine.*

"Wilson's 'Judicature Acts' is now the latest, and we think it is the most convenient of the works of the same class. . . . The practitioner will find that it supplies all his wants."—*Law Times.*

Woodfall.—*Vide* "Rules of the Supreme Court."

JUSTINIAN, INSTITUTES OF.—**Mears.**—*Vide* "Roman Law."

Ruegg's Student's "Auxilium" to the Institutes of Justinian.—Being a complete synopsis thereof in the form of Question and Answer. By ALFRED HENRY RUEGG, of the Middle Temple, Barrister-at-Law. Post 8vo. 1879. 5*s.*

"The student will be greatly assisted in clearing and arranging his knowledge by a work of this kind."—*Law Journal.*

JUSTICE OF THE PEACE.—**Burn's Justice of the Peace and Parish Officer.**—Edited under the Superintendence of JOHN BLOSSETT MAULE, Esq., Q.C. The Thirtieth Edition. Five large vols. 8vo. 1869. 7*l.* 7*s.*

Stone's Practice for Justices of the Peace, Justices Clerks and Solicitors at Petty and Special Sessions, in Summary matters, and Indictable Offences, with a list of Summary Convictions, and matters not Criminal. With Forms. Ninth Edition. By WALTER HENRY MACNAMARA, Esq., Barrister-at-Law. Demy 8vo. 1882. 25*s.*

"A very creditable effort has been made to condense and abridge, which has been successful, whilst the completeness of the work has not been impaired."—*Law Times.*

Wigram's Justices' Note Book.—Containing a short account of the Jurisdiction and Duties of Justices, and an Epitome of Criminal Law. By W. KNOX WIGRAM, Esq., Barrister-at-Law, J.P. Middlesex and Westminster. Third Edition. Corrected and revised to December, 1882. With a copious Index. Royal 12mo. 1883. 12*s.* 6*d.*

"We have found in it all the information which a Justice can require as to recent legislation."—*The Times.*

"This is altogether a capital book. Mr. Wigram is a good lawyer and a good justices' lawyer."—*Law Journal.*

"We can thoroughly recommend the volume to magistrates."—*Law Times.*

*** *All standard Law Works are kept in Stock, in law calf and other bindings.*

LAND ACT.—*See* "Settled Estates."—**Middleton.**

LAND TAX.—Bourdin's Land Tax.—An Exposition of the Land Tax; its Assessment and Collection, with a statement of the rights conferred by the Redemption Acts. By MARK A. BOURDIN (late Registrar of Land Tax). Second Edition. 1870. 4*s.*

LANDLORD AND TENANT.—Woodfall's Law of Landlord and Tenant.—With a full Collection of Precedents and Forms of Procedure. Containing also an Abstract of Leading Propositions, and Tables of certain Customs of the Country. Twelfth Edition. In which the Precedents of Leases have been revised and enlarged, with the assistance of L. G. G. Robbins, Esq. By J. M. LELY, Esq., Barrister-at-Law. Royal 8vo. 1881. 1*l.* 18*s.*

"The editor has expended elaborate industry and systematic ability in making the work as perfect as possible."—*Solicitors' Journal.*

LANDS CLAUSES ACTS.—Jepson's Lands Clauses Consolidation Acts; with Decisions, Forms, & Table of Costs. By ARTHUR JEPSON, Esq., Barrister-at-Law. Demy 8vo. 1880. 18*s.*

"The work concludes with a number of forms and a remarkably good index."—*Law Times.*

"As far as we have been able to discover, all the decisions have been stated, and the effect of them correctly given."—*Law Journal.*

LAW LIST.—Law List (The).—Comprising the Judges and Officers of the different Courts of Justice, Counsel, Special Pleaders, Draftsmen, Conveyancers, Solicitors, Notaries, &c., in England and Wales; the Circuits, Judges, Treasurers, Registrars, and High Bailiffs of the County Courts; Metropolitan and Stipendiary Magistrates, Law and Public Officers in England and the Colonies, Foreign Lawyers with their English Agents, Sheriffs, Under-Sheriffs, and their Deputies, Clerks of the Peace, Town Clerks, Coroners, &c., &c., and Commissioners for taking Oaths, Conveyancers Practising in England under Certificates obtained in Scotland. So far as relates to Special Pleaders, Draftsmen, Conveyancers, Solicitors, Proctors and Notaries. Compiled by WILLIAM HENRY COUSINS, of the Inland Revenue Office, Somerset House, Registrar of Stamped Certificates, and of Joint Stock Companies, and Published by the Authority of the Commissioners of Inland Revenue. 1883. (*Net Cash,* 9*s.*) 10*s.* 6*d.*

LAW REPORTS.—A very large Stock of second-hand and new Reports. Prices on application.

LAW STUDENT'S ANNUAL.—*Vide* "Examination Guides."

LAW SUIT.—The Humourous Story of Farmer Bumpkin's Law Suit. By RICHARD HARRIS. Barrister-at-Law, of the Middle Temple and Midland Circuit, Author of "Hints on Advocacy." Second Edition. Royal 12mo. 1883. 6*s.*

"Most of the standing grievances of suitors find a place in this book."—*Law Times.*

"He was obviously quite as eager for a good battle in court as ever was Dandy Dinmont."—*Saturday Review,* September 15, 1883.

LAWYER'S COMPANION.—*Vide* "Diary."

LEADING CASES.—Haynes' Student's Leading Cases. Being some of the Principal Decisions of the Courts in Constitutional Law, Common Law, Conveyancing and Equity, Probate, Divorce, Bankruptcy, and Criminal Law. With Notes for the use of Students. By JOHN F. HAYNES, LL.D. Demy 8vo. 1878. 16*s.*

"Will prove of great utility, not only to Students, but Practitioners. The Notes are clear, pointed and concise."—*Law Times.*

"We think that this book will supply a want . . . . . the book is singularly well arranged for reference."—*Law Journal.*

*** *All standard Law Works are kept in Stock, in law calf and other bindings.*

LEADING CASES.—*Continued.*

Shirley's Leading Cases.—A Selection of Leading Cases in the Common Law, with Notes, and a Sketch of some of the principal changes introduced by the Rules of Supreme Court, 1883. By W. SHIRLEY SHIRLEY, M.A., B.C.L., Esq., Barrister-at-Law. Second Edition. Demy 8vo. 1883. 15*s.*

"The book is deserving of high praise, and we commend it in all confidence."—*Gibson's Law Notes*, April. 1883.

"The selection is very large, though all are distinctly 'leading cases,' and the notes are by no means the least meritorious part of the work."—*Law Journal.*

"Mr. Shirley writes well and clearly, and evidently understands what he is writing about."—*Law Times.*

LEGACY DUTIES.—*Vide* "Taxes on Succession."

LEXICON.—*Vide* "Dictionary."

LIBEL AND SLANDER.—**Odgers on Libel and Slander.**—A Digest of the Law of Libel and Slander, with the Evidence, Procedure and Practice, both in Civil and Criminal Cases, with Precedents of Pleadings. With Appendix of Statutes including the Newspaper Libel and Registration Act, 1881. By W. BLAKE ODGERS, M.A., LL.D., Barrister-at-Law. Demy 8vo. 1881. 24*s.*

"We have rarely examined a work which shows so much industry. . . So good is the book, which in its topical arrangement is vastly superior to the general run of law books, that criticism of it is a compliment rather than the reverse."—*Law Journal.*

"The excuse, if one be needed, for another book on Libel and Slander, and that an English one, may be found in the excellence of the author's work. A clear head and a skilled hand are to be seen throughout."—*Extract from Preface to American reprint.*

LIBRARIES AND MUSEUMS.—**Chambers' Digest of the Law relating to Public Libraries and Museums and Literary and Scientific Institutions generally.** Second Edition. By G. F. CHAMBERS, Barrister-at-Law. Imperial 8vo. 1879. 8*s.* 6*d.*

LICENSING.—**Hindle's Treatise on the Legal Status of Licensed Victuallers and other License-Holders, as affected by recent Legislation and Decisions**; containing a full Report of the Proceedings and Judgment in the recent Darwen Licensing Appeals, with Notes. Third Edition. By FREDK. G. HINDLE, Esq., Solicitor. Demy 8vo. 1883. *Net*, 2*s.* 6*d.*

Lely and Foulkes' Licensing Acts, 1828, 1869, 1872, and 1874; containing the Law of the Sale of Liquors by Retail and the Management of Licensed Houses; with Notes to the Acts, a Summary of the Law, and an Appendix of Forms. Second Edition. By J. M. LELY and W. D. I. FOULKES, Esqrs., Barristers-at-Law. Royal 12mo. 1874. 8*s*

LIQUIDATION BY ARRANGEMENT.—**Salaman's Practical Treatise on Liquidation by Arrangement and Composition with Creditors, under the Bankruptcy Act, 1869**: comprising the Practice of the Office for Registration of Arrangement Proceedings; the Practice as to Receivers, Injunctions, Meetings of Creditors, &c.; all the Authorised and Original Forms, Bills of Costs under Liquidation and Composition; Notes of Cases; the Sections of the Bankruptcy and Debtors' Acts; and the Rules applicable to Liquidation and Composition; the Rules of 1871. With Index. By JOSEPH SEYMOUR SALAMAN, Solicitor. Crown 8vo. Re-issue. 10*s.*

LUNACY.—**Elmer's Practice in Lunacy.**—Seventh Edition. By JOSEPH ELMER, of the Office of the Masters in Lunacy.

(*In preparation.*)

**** All standard Law Works are kept in Stock, in law calf and other bindings.*

MAGISTERIAL LAW.—Shirley's Elementary Treatise on Magisterial Law, and on the Practice of Magistrates' Courts.—By W. SHIRLEY SHIRLEY, M.A., B.C.L., Esq., Barrister-at-Law. Royal 12mo. 1881. *6s. 6d.*

Wigram.—*Vide* "Justice of the Peace."

MAYOR'S COURT PRACTICE.—Candy's Mayor's Court Practice.—The Jurisdiction, Process, Practice, and Mode of Pleading in Ordinary Actions in the Mayor's Court, London (commonly called the "Lord Mayor's Court"). **Founded on Brandon.** By GEORGE CANDY, Esq., Barrister-at-Law. Demy 8vo. 1879. *14s.*

MARRIED WOMEN'S PROPERTY. — Smith's Married Women's Property Act, 1882, with an Introduction and Critical and Explanatory Notes, together with the Married Women's Property Acts, 1870 and 1874, &c. By H. ARTHUR SMITH, Esq., Barrister-at-Law. Royal 12mo. 1882. *5s.*

"There are some excellent critical and explanatory notes, together with a good index, and reference to something like two hundred decided cases."—*Law Times.*

MASTER AND SERVANT.—Macdonell's Law of Master and Servant. Part I, Common Law. Part II, Statute Law. By JOHN MACDONELL, M.A., Esq., Barrister-at-Law. Demy 8vo. 1883. *1l. 5s.*

"Mr. Macdonell has done his work thoroughly and well. He has evidently bestowed great care and labour on his task, and has, therefore, produced a work which will be of real value to the practitioner. The information, too, is presented in a most accessible form."—*Law Times*, January 27, 1883.

MERCANTILE LAW.—Russell's Treatise on Mercantile Agency. Second Edition. 8vo. 1873. *14s.*

Smith's Compendium of Mercantile Law.—Ninth Edition. By G. M. DOWDESWELL, of the Inner Temple, Esq., one of Her Majesty's Counsel. Royal 8vo. 1877. *1l. 18s.*

Tudor's Selection of Leading Cases on Mercantile and Maritime Law.—With Notes. By O. D. TUDOR, Esq., Barrister-at-Law. Third Edition. (*In the press.*)

Wilson's Mercantile Handbook of the Liabilities of Merchant, Shipowner, and Underwriter on Shipments by General Vessels. By ALEXANDER WILSON, Solicitor and Notary. Royal 12mo. 1883. *6s.*

METROPOLIS BUILDING ACTS.—Woolrych's Metropolitan Building Acts, together with such clauses of the Metropolis Management Acts as more particularly relate to the Building Acts, with Notes and Forms. Third Edition. By W. H. MACNAMARA, Esq., Barrister-at-Law. 12mo. 1882. *10s.*

"We may safely recommend this new edition to those who have to find their way among these statutes."—*The Builder*, March 31, 1883.

MINES.—Rogers' Law relating to Mines, Minerals, and Quarries in Great Britain and Ireland; with a Summary of the Laws of Foreign States, &c. Second Edition Enlarged. By ARUNDEL ROGERS, Esq., Judge of County Courts. 8vo. 1876. *1l. 11s. 6d.*

"The volume will prove invaluable as a work of legal reference."—*The Mining Journal.*

MONEY SECURITIES.—Cavanagh's Law of Money Securities.—In Three Books. I. Personal Securities. II. Securities on Property. III. Miscellaneous; with an Appendix of Statutes. By C. CAVANAGH, B.A., LL.B. (Lond.), of the Middle Temple, Esq., Barrister-at-Law. In 1 vol. Demy 8vo. 1879. *21s.*

"An admirable synopsis of the whole law and practice with regard to securities of every sort."—*Saturday Review.*

*** *All standard Law Works are kept in Stock, in law calf and other bindings.*

MORTGAGE.—Coote's Treatise on the Law of Mortgage.—Fourth Edition. Thoroughly revised. By WILLIAM WYLLYS MACKESON, Esq., one of Her Majesty's Counsel. In 1 Vol. (1436 pp.) Royal 8vo. 1880. 2*l.* 2*s.*

"A complete, terse, and practical treatise for the modern lawyer."—*Solicitors' Journal.*
"Will be found a valuable addition to the library of every practising lawyer."—*Law Journal.*

MUNICIPAL CORPORATIONS. Lely's Law of Municipal Corporations.—Containing the Municipal Corporation Act, 1882, and the Enactments incorporated therewith, with a Selection of Supplementary Enactments, including therein the Electric Lighting Act, 1882, with Notes thereon. By J. M. LELY, of the Inner Temple, Esq., Barrister-at-Law. Editor of "Chitty's Statutes," &c. Demy 8vo. 1882. 15*s.*

"An admirable edition of one of the most important consolidating statutes of the year. . . . The summary is tersely written, and the notes appear to be to the point. Nothing required for the due understanding and working of the Act seems to be absent."—*Law Journal.*

NAVY.—Thring's Criminal Law of the Navy, with an Introductory Chapter on the Early State and Discipline of the Navy, the Rules of Evidence, and an Appendix comprising the Naval Discipline Act and Practical Forms. Second Edition. By THEODORE THRING, Barrister-at-Law, and C. E. GIFFORD, Assistant-Paymaster, Royal Navy. 12mo. 1877. 12*s.* 6*d.*

NEGLIGENCE.—Smith's Treatise on the Law of Negligence, with a Supplement containing "The Employers' Liability Act, 1880," with an Introduction and Notes. By HORACE SMITH, B.A., Esq., Barrister-at-Law, Recorder of Lincoln. Demy 8vo. 1880. 10*s.* 6*d.*

NISI PRIUS.—Roscoe's Digest of the Law of Evidence on the Trial of Actions at Nisi Prius.—Fifteenth Edition. By MAURICE POWELL, Esq., Barrister-at-Law. (*In the Press.*)

NOTANDA.—*Vide* "Digests."

NOTARY.—Brooke's Treatise on the Office and Practice of a Notary of England.—With a full collection of Precedents. Fourth Edition. By LEONE LEVI, Esq., F.S.A., of Lincoln's Inn, Barrister-at-Law. 8vo. 1876. 1*l.* 4*s.*

OATHS.—Braithwaite's Oaths in the Supreme Courts of Judicature.—A Manual for the use of Commissioners to Administer Oaths in the Supreme Courts of Judicature in England and Ireland, &c. Fourth Edition. By T. W. BRAITHWAITE, of the Central Office. Fcap. 8vo. 1881. 4*s.* 6*d.*

"The recognised guide of commissioners to administer oaths."—*Solicitors' Journal.*

PARISH LAW.—Steer's Parish Law; being a Digest of the Law relating to the Civil and Ecclesiastical Government of Parishes and the Relief of the Poor. Fourth Edition. By W. H. MACNAMARA, Esq., Barrister-at-Law. Demy 8vo. 1881. 16*s.*

"An exceedingly useful compendium of Parish Law."—*Law Times.*

PARTNERSHIP.—Pollock's Digest of the Law of Partnership.—Second Edition, with Appendix, containing an annotated reprint of the Partnership Bill, 1880, as amended in Committee. By FREDERICK POLLOCK, Esq., Barrister-at-Law. Author of "Principles of Contract at Law and in Equity." Demy 8vo. 1880. 8*s.* 6*d.*

"Of the execution of the work, we can speak in terms of the highest praise. The language is simple, concise, and clear."—*Law Magazine.*
"Mr. Pollock's work appears eminently satisfactory . . . the book is praiseworthy in design, scholarly and complete in execution."—*Saturday Review.*

*** *All standard Law Works are kept in Stock, in law calf and other bindings.*

PATENTS.—**Hindmarch on the Law of Patents for Inventions.** Second Edition, brought down to the present time. By E. MACRORY, and J. C. GRAHAM, Esqrs., Barristers-at-Law. *(In preparation.)*

PAWN.—**Turner's Contract of Pawn,** as it exists at Common Law, and as modified by the Factors' Acts, the Pawnbrokers' Acts, and other Statutes. By FRANCIS TURNER, Esq., Barrister-at-Law. Second Edition. 8vo. 1883. 12*s.*

Turner's Pawnbrokers' Act, 1872.—With Explanatory Notes. By FRANCIS TURNER, Esq., Barrister-at-Law. Third Edition. 1883. *Net,* 2*s.* 6*d.*

PERPETUITIES.—**Marsden's Rule against Perpetuities.**—A Treatise on Remoteness in Limitation; with a chapter on Accumulation and the Thelluson Act. By REGINALD G. MARSDEN, Esq., Barrister-at-Law. Demy 8vo. 1883. 16*s.*

"Mr. Marsden's work is entitled to be called a new one both in treatment and in design. He has handled a difficult subject with intelligence and clearness."—*Law Times.*

PERSONAL PROPERTY.—**Shearwood's Concise Abridgment of the Law of Personal Property;** showing analytically its Branches and the Titles by which it is held. By J. A. SHEARWOOD, Esq., Barrister-at-Law. 1882. 5*s.* 6*d.*

"Will be acceptable to many students, as giving them, in fact, a ready-made note book."—*Indermaur's Law Students' Journal.*

Smith.—*Vide* "Real Property."

PLEADING.—**Allen's Forms of Indorsements of Writs of Summons, Pleadings, and other Proceedings in the Queen's Bench Division prior to Trial, pursuant to the Rules of the Supreme Court, 1883;** with Introduction, showing the principal changes introduced by these Rules, and a Supplement of Rules and Forms of Pleadings applicable to the other Divisions. By GEORGE BAUGH ALLEN, Esq., Special Pleader, and WILFRED B. ALLEN, Esq., Barrister-at-Law. Royal 12mo. 1883. 18*s.*

Bullen and Leake's Precedents of Pleadings, with Notes and Rules relating to Pleading. Fourth Edition. By THOMAS J. BULLEN, Esq., of the Inner Temple, and CYRIL DODD, Esq., Barrister-at-Law. Part I. (containing (1) Introductory Notes on Pleading; (2) Forms of Statements of Claim in Actions on Contracts and Torts, with Notes relating thereto). Royal 12mo. 1882. *(Part II. in the press.)* 1*l.* 4*s.*

"Mr. Thomas Bullen and Mr. Cyril Dodd have done their work of adaptation admirably."—*Law Journal.*

POISONING.—**Reports of Trials for Murder by Poisoning; by Prussic Acid, Strychnia, Antimony, Arsenic and Aconitine;** including the trials of Tawell, W. Palmer, Dove, Madeline Smith, Dr. Pritchard, Smethurst, and Dr. Lamson. With Chemical Introductions and Notes on the Poisons used. By G. LATHAM BROWNE, of the Midland Circuit, Barrister-at-Law, Author of "Narratives of State Trials in the Nineteenth Century," and C. G. STEWART, Senior Assistant in the Laboratory of St. Thomas's Hospital, &c. Demy 8vo. 1883. 12*s.* 6*d*

"The work will be found alike useful to the lawyer as to the medical man."—*Law Times.*

"As a guide to barristers anxious to post themselves up in points to ask, and to scientific witnesses to see the possible pitfalls to avoid, it will be invaluable."—*The Analyst,* August, 1883.

**** All standard Law Works are kept in Stock, in law calf and other bindings.*

POWERS.—Farwell on Powers.—A Concise Treatise on Powers. By GEORGE FARWELL, B.A., of Lincoln's Inn, Esq., Barrister-at-Law. 8vo. 1874. 1*l.* 1*s.*

"We recommend Mr. Farwell's book as containing within a small compass what would otherwise have to be sought out in the pages of hundreds of confusing reports."—*The Law.*

PROBATE.—Browne's Probate Practice: a Treatise on the Principles and Practice of the Court of Probate, in Contentious and Non-Contentious Business. Revised, enlarged, and adapted to the Practice of the High Court of Justice in Probate business. By L. D. POWLES, Barrister-at-Law. Including Practical Directions to Solicitors for Proceedings in the Registry. By T. W. H. OAKLEY, of the Principal Registry, Somerset House. 8vo. 1881. 1*l.* 10*s.*

"This edition will thus supply the practitioners in both branches of the profession with all the information that they may require in connection with the probate of wills."—*The Times.*

"In its present form this is undoubtedly the most complete work on the Practice of the Court of Probate. . . . . This is strictly a practical book. No principle of law, statute or form which could be of service to the practitioner in the Probate Division appears to have been omitted."—*The Law Times.*

PUBLIC HEALTH.—Chambers' Digest of the Law relating to Public Health and Local Government.—With Notes of 1260 leading Cases. The Statutes in full. A Table of Offences and Punishments, and a Copious Index. Eighth Edition (with Supplement corrected to February 8, 1883). Imperial 8vo. 1881. 1*l.* 14*s.*

Or, the above with the Law relating to Highways and Bridges. 2*l.*

PUBLIC MEETINGS.—Chambers' Handbook for Public Meetings, including Hints as to the Summoning and Management of them. By GEORGE F. CHAMBERS, Esq., Barrister-at-Law. 12mo. 1878. *Net*, 2*s.* 6*d.*

QUARTER SESSIONS.—Leeming & Cross's General and Quarter Sessions of the Peace.—Their Jurisdiction and Practice in other than Criminal matters. Second Edition. By HORATIO LLOYD, Esq., Judge of County Courts, and H. F. THURLOW, Esq., Barrister-at-Law. 8vo. 1876. 1*l.* 1*s.*

Pritchard's Quarter Sessions.—The Jurisdiction, Practice and Procedure of the Quarter Sessions in Criminal, Civil, and Appellate Matters. By THOS. SIRRELL PRITCHARD, of the Inner Temple, Esq., Barrister-at-Law, Recorder of Wenlock. 8vo. 1875. 2*l.* 2*s.*

RAILWAYS.—Browne and Theobald's Law of Railway Companies.—Being a Collection of the Acts and Orders relating to Railway Companies, with Notes of all the Cases decided thereon, and Appendix of Bye-Laws and Standing Orders of the House of Commons. By J. H. BALFOUR BROWNE, Esq., Registrar to the Railway Commissioners, and H. S. THEOBALD, Esq., Barristers-at-Law. Demy 8vo. 1881. 1*l.* 12*s.*

"Contains in a very concise form the whole law of railways."—*The Times.*

"A marvel of wide design and accurate and complete fulfilment. . . . A complete and valuable repository of all the learning as to railway matters."—*Saturday Review.*

"As far as we have examined the volume the learned authors seem to have presented the profession and the public with the most ample information to be found whether they want to know how to start a railway, how to frame its bye-laws, how to work it, how to attack it for injury to person or property, or how to wind it up."—*Law Times.*

RATES AND RATING.—Castle's Practical Treatise on the Law of Rating. By EDWARD JAMES CASTLE, of the Inner Temple, Esq., Barrister-at-Law. Demy 8vo. 1879. 1*l.* 1*s.*

"Mr. Castle's book is a correct, exhaustive, clear and concise view of the law."—*Law Times.*

*** *All standard Law Works are kept in Stock, in law calf and other bindings.*

RATES AND RATING.—*Continued.*

Chambers' Law relating to Rates and Rating; with especial reference to the Powers and Duties of Rate-levying Local Authorities, and their Officers. Being the Statutes in full and brief Notes of 550 Cases. By G. F. CHAMBERS, Esq., Barrister-at-Law. Imp. 8vo. 1878. *Reduced to* 10s.

REAL ESTATE.—Foster's Law of Joint Ownership and Partition of Real Estate. By EDWARD JOHN FOSTER, M.A., late of Lincoln's Inn, Barrister-at-Law. 8vo. 1878. 10*s.* 6*d.*

REAL PROPERTY.—Greenwood's Real Property Statutes. Second Edition. By HARRY GREENWOOD, M.A., Esq., Barrister-at-Law. (*In the press.*)

Leake's Elementary Digest of the Law of Property in Land.—Containing: Introduction. Part I. The Sources of the Law.—Part II. Estates in Land. By STEPHEN MARTIN LEAKE, Barrister-at-Law. 8vo. 1874. 1*l.* 2*s.*

*** The above forms a complete Introduction to the Study of the Law of Real Property.

Shearwood's Real Property.—A Concise Abridgment of the Law of Real Property and an Introduction to Conveyancing. Designed to facilitate the subject for Students preparing for Examination (incorporating the changes effected by the Conveyancing Act). By JOSEPH A. SHEARWOOD, of Lincoln's Inn, Esq., Barrister-at-Law. Second Edition. Demy 8vo. 1882. 7*s.* 6*d.*

"We heartily recommend the work to students for any examination on real property and conveyancing, advising them to read it after a perusal of other works and shortly before going in for the examination."—*Law Student's Journal*, April 1, 1882.

"A very useful little work, particularly to students just before their examination." —*Gibson's Law Notes*, May, 1882.

"Excellently adapted to its purpose, and is in the present edition brought well down to date."—*Law Magazine*, May, 1882.

"A very excellent specimen of a student's manual."—*Law Journal*, May 20, 1882.

"Will be found useful as a stepping-stone to the study of more comprehensive works."—*Law Times*, June 17, 1882.

Shelford's Real Property Statutes.—Ninth Edition. By T. H. CARSON, Esq., Barrister-at-Law. (*In the press.*)

Smith's Real and Personal Property.—A Compendium of the Law of Real and Personal Property, primarily connected with Conveyancing. Designed as a second book for Students, and as a digest of the most useful learning for Practitioners. By JOSIAH W. SMITH, B.C.L., Q.C. Sixth Edition. (Enlarged, and embodying the alterations made by the recent Statutes.) By the AUTHOR and J. TRUSTRAM, LL.M., of Lincoln's Inn, Barrister-at-Law. 2 vols. Demy 8vo. (*In the press.*)

"He has given to the student a book which he may read over and over again with profit and pleasure."—*Law Times.*

"The work before us will, we think, be found of very great service to the practitioner." —*Solicitors' Journal.*

REGISTRATION.—Browne's (G. Lathom) Parliamentary and Municipal Registration Act, 1878 (41 & 42 Vict. cap. 26); with an Introduction, Notes, and Additional Forms. By G. LATHOM BROWNE, of the Middle Temple, Esq., Barrister-at-Law. 12mo. 1878. 5*s.* 6*d.*

Rogers.—*Vide* "Elections."

REGISTRATION CASES.—Hopwood and Coltman's Registration Cases.—Vol. I. (1868-1872). *Net*, 2*l.* 18*s.* Calf. Vol. II. (1873-1878). *Net*, 2*l.* 10*s.* Calf.

Coltman's Registration Cases.—Vol. I. Part I. (1879—80. *Net*, 10*s.* Part II. (1880). *Net*, 3*s.* 6*d.* Part III. (1881). *Net*, 9*s.* Part IV. (1882). *Net*, 4*s.*

*** *All standard Law Works are kept in Stock, in law calf and other bindings.*

ROMAN LAW.—Greene's Outlines of Roman Law. Consisting chiefly of an Analysis and Summary of the Institutes. For the use of Students. By T. WHITCOMBE GREENE, B.C.L., of Lincoln's Inn, Barrister-at-Law. Third Edition. Foolscap 8vo. 1875. 7*s*. 6*d*.

Mears' Student's Gaius and Justinian.—The Text of the Institutes of Gaius and Justinian, The Twelve Tables, and the CXVIII. and CXXVII. Novels, with Introduction and Translation by T. LAMBERT MEARS, M.A., LL.D., of the Inner Temple, Barrister-at-Law. Post 8vo. 1882. 18*s*.

"The translation seems to be carefully done, and displays more neatness and elegance than is usually found in renderings of Roman legal texts."—*The Times*.

Mears' Student's Ortolan.—An Analysis of M. Ortolan's Institutes of Justinian, including the History and Generalization of ROMAN LAW. By T. LAMBERT MEARS, M.A., LL.D. Lond., of the Inner Temple, Barrister-at-Law. *Published by permission of the late M. Ortolan.* Post 8vo. 1876. 12*s*. 6*d*.

Ruegg.—*Vide* "Justinian."

RULES OF THE SUPREME COURT: The Rules of the Supreme Court, 1883 (official copy). Sewed. *Net*, 2*s*. 2*d*.

Do. interleaved. do. *Net*, 4*s*. 6*d*.
Do. bound in limp leather. *Net*, 6*s*. 6*d*.
Do. do. do. interleaved. *Net*, 8*s*. 6*d*.

Do., with an Index. By M. D. CHALMERS and M. MUIR MACKENZIE, Esqrs., Barristers-at-Law, Editors of "Wilson's Judicature Acts." Sewed. *Net*, 4*s*. 6*d*.

Do. bound in limp leather. *Net*, 9*s*.
Do. do. do. interleaved. *Net*, 10*s*. 6*d*.

The Rules of the Supreme Court, 1883.—With Introduction, References, Notes, and Index, by A. R. WHITEWAY, M.A., of the Equity Bar and Midland Circuit. Author of "Hints to Solicitors" and "Hints on Practice." Royal 12mo. 1883. 7*s*. 6*d*.

"An excellently printed edition of the new Rules, with notes containing cross references and stating the sources of the Rules."—*Solicitors' Journal*, October 13, 1883.

Woodfall's Guide to the New Rules and Practice.—Being a Synopsis of the Rules of the Supreme Court, 1883, with Notes and References to Cases overruled and illustrative. By ROBERT WOODFALL, of the Inner Temple and South Wales Circuit, Barrister-at-Law. Royal 12mo. 1883. 5*s*.

SETTLED ESTATES STATUTES.—Middleton's Settled Estates Statutes, including the Settled Estates Act, 1877, Settled Land Act, 1882, Improvement of Land Act, 1864, and the Settled Estates Act Orders, 1878, with Introduction, Notes and Forms. Third Edition. With Appendix of Rules and Forms under the Settled Land Act, 1882. By JAMES W. MIDDLETON, B.A., Barrister-at-Law. Royal 12mo. 1882. 7*s*. 6*d*.

"In form the book is very simple and practical, and having a good index it is sure to afford material assistance to every practitioner who seeks its aid."—*Law Journal*.

"The book is intended for the legal adviser and equity draftsman, and to these it will give considerable assistance."—*Law Times*.

"The best manual on the subject of settled estates which has yet appeared."

SHERIFF LAW.—Churchill's Law of the Office and Duties of the Sheriff, with the Writs and Forms relating to the Office. Second Edition. By CAMERON CHURCHILL, B.A., of the Inner Temple, Barrister-at-Law. Demy 8vo. 1882. 1*l*. 4*s*.

"A very complete treatise."—*Solicitors' Journal*.

"Under-sheriffs, and lawyers generally, will find this a useful book."—*Law Mag.*

*** *All standard Law Works are kept in Stock, in law calf and other bindings.*

SHIPPING.—**Boyd's Merchant Shipping Laws**; being a Consolidation of all the Merchant Shipping and Passenger Acts from 1854 to 1876, inclusive; with Notes of all the leading English and American Cases, and an Appendix. By A. C. BOYD, LL.B., Esq., Barrister-at-Law. 8vo. 1876. 1*l.* 5*s.*

"We can recommend the work as a very useful compendium of shipping law."—*Law Times.*

Foard's Treatise on the Law of Merchant Shipping and Freight.—By JAMES T. FOARD, Barrister-at-Law. Royal 8vo. 1880. *Half calf,* 1*l.* 1*s.*

SLANDER.—**Odgers.**—*Vide* "Libel and Slander."

SOLICITORS.—**Cordery's Law relating to Solicitors of the Supreme Court of Judicature.**—With an Appendix of Statutes and Rules. By A. CORDERY, of the Inner Temple, Esq., Barrister-at-Law. Demy 8vo. 1878. 14*s.*

"Mr. Cordery writes tersley and clearly, and displays in general great industry and care in the collection of cases."—*Solicitors' Journal.*

Turner.—*Vide* "Vendors and Purchasers"

Whiteway's Hints to Solicitors.—Being a Treatise on the Law relating to their Duties as Officers of the High Court of Justice; with Notes on the Recent Changes affecting the Profession; and a *vade mecum* to the Law of Costs. By A. R. WHITEWAY, M.A., of the Equity Bar and Midland Circuit. Author of "Hints on Practice." Royal 12mo. 1883. 6*s.*

"A concise treatise of useful information."—*Law Times.*

"He writes tersely and practically, and the cases he gives, if not exhaustive of the subject, are numerous and pithily explained. The book will altogether be found of great practical value."—*Law Journal,* May 19, 1883.

SPECIFIC PERFORMANCE.—**Fry's Treatise on the Specific Performance of Contracts.**—By the Hon. Sir EDWARD FRY, one of the Judges of the High Court of Justice (now a Lord Justice of Appeal). Second Edition. By the Author and W. DONALDSON RAWLINS, of Lincoln's Inn, Esq., Barrister-at-Law, M.A. Royal 8vo. 1881. 1*l.* 16*s.*

STAMP LAWS.—**Tilsley's Treatise on the Stamp Laws.**—8vo. 1871. 18*s.*

STATUTE LAW.—**Wilberforce on Statute Law.**—The Principles which govern the Construction and Operation of Statutes. By E. WILBERFORCE, Esq., Barrister-at-Law. 1881. 18*s*

STATUTES. and *vide* "Acts of Parliament."

Chitty's Collection of Statutes from Magna Charta to 1880.—**A Collection of Statutes of Practical Utility;** arranged in Alphabetical and Chronological order, with Notes thereon. The Fourth Edition, containing the Statutes and Cases down to the end of the Second Session of the year 1880. By J. M. LELY, Esq., Barrister-at-Law. In 6 very thick vols. Royal 8vo. (8,346 pp.) 1880. 12*l.* 12*s.*

Supplements to above, 44 & 45 *Vict.* (1881). 8*s.* 45 & 46 *Vict.* (1882). 16*s.*

*** **This Edition is printed in larger type than former Editions, and with increased facilities for Reference.**

"It is needless to enlarge on the value of "Chitty's Statutes" to both the Bar and to solicitors, for it is attested by the experience of many years. It only remains to point out that Mr. Lely's work in bringing up the collection to the present time is distinguished by care and judgment. The difficulties of the editor were chiefly those of selection and arrangement. A very slight laxness of rule in including or excluding certain classes of Acts would materially affect the size and compendiousness of the work. Still more important, however, is the way in which the mechanical difficulties of arrangement are met. The Statutes are compiled under sufficiently comprehensive

STATUTES.—*Continued.*

titles, in alphabetical order. Mr. Lely, moreover, supplies us with three indices—the first, at the head of each title, to the enactments comprised in it; secondly, an index of Statutes in chronological order; and, lastly, a general index. By these cross references research into every branch of law governed by the Statutes is made easy both for lawyer and layman."—*The Times.*

"A very satisfactory edition of a time-honoured and most valuable work, the trusty guide of present, as of former judges, jurists, and of all others connected with the administration or practice of the law."—*Justice of the Peace.*

"The practitioner has only to take down one of the compact volumes of Chitty, and he has at once before him all the legislation on the subject in hand."—*Solicitors' Journal.*

"'Chitty' is pre-eminently a friend in need. Those who do not possess a complete set of the statutes turn to its chronological index when they wish to consult a particular Act of Parliament. Those who wish to know what Acts are in force with reference to a particular subject turn to that head in 'Chitty,' and at once find all the material of which they are in quest. Moreover, they are, at the same time, referred to the most important cases which throw light on the subject."—*Law Journal.*

*Public General Statutes, royal 8vo, issued in parts and in complete volumes, and supplied immediately on publication.

* Printed by Her Majesty's Printers, and Sold by STEVENS & SONS.

SUMMARY CONVICTIONS.—Highmore.—*Vide* "Inland Revenue Cases."

Paley's Law and Practice of Summary Convictions under the Summary Jurisdiction Acts, 1848 and 1879; including Proceedings preliminary and subsequent to Convictions, and the responsibility of convicting Magistrates and their Officers, with Forms. Sixth Edition. By W. H. MACNAMARA, Esq., Barrister-at-Law. Demy 8vo. 1879. 1*l.* 4*s.*

"We gladly welcome this good edition of a good book."—*Solicitors' Journal.*

Templer's Summary Jurisdiction Act, 1879.—Rules and Schedules of Forms. With Notes. By F. G. TEMPLER, Esq., Barrister-at-Law. Demy 8vo. 1880. 5*s.*

"We think this edition everything that could be desired."—*Sheffield Post.*

Wigram.—*Vide* "Justice of the Peace."

TAXES ON SUCCESSION.—Trevor's Taxes on Succession.—A Digest of the Statutes and Cases (including those in Scotland and Ireland) relating to the Probate, Legacy and Succession Duties, with Practical Observations and Official Forms. Completely rearranged and thoroughly revised. By EVELYN FREETH and ROBERT J. WALLACE, of the Legacy and Succession Duty Office. Fourth Edition, containing full information as to the Alterations made in the above Taxes by the 44 Vict. c. 12, and the Stamp Duty thereby imposed on "Accounts." Royal 12mo. 1881. 12*s.* 6*d.*

"Contains a great deal of practical information, which is likely to make it very useful to solicitors."—*Law Journal.*

"The mode of treatment of the subject adopted by the authors is eminently practical."—*Solicitors' Journal.*

TORTS.—Addison on Wrongs and their Remedies.—Being a Treatise on the Law of Torts. By C. G. ADDISON, Esq., Author of "The Law of Contracts." Fifth Edition. Re-written. By L. W. CAVE, Esq., M.A., one of Her Majesty's Counsel (now a Justice of the High Court). Royal 8vo. 1879. 1*l.* 18*s.*

"As now presented, this valuable treatise must prove highly acceptable to judges and the profession."—*Law Times.*

"Cave's 'Addison on Torts' will be recognized as an indispensable addition to every lawyer's library."—*Law Magazine.*

Ball.—*Vide* "Common Law."

*** *All Standard Law Works are kept in Stock, in law calf and other bindings.*

TRADE MARKS.—**Hardingham's Trade Marks**: Notes on the British, Foreign, and Colonial Laws relating thereto. Compiled for the use of Manufacturers, Merchants, and others interested in Commerce. By GEO. GATTON MELHUISH HARDINGHAM, Assoc. Mem. Inst. C.E., Mem. Inst. M.E., Consulting Engineer and Patent Agent. Royal 12mo. 1881. *Net, 2s. 6d.*

Sebastian on the Law of Trade Marks.—The Law of Trade Marks and their Registration, and matters connected therewith, including a chapter on Goodwill. Together with Appendices containing Precedents of Injunctions, &c.; The Trade Marks Registration Acts, 1875—7, the Rules and Instructions thereunder; The Merchandise Marks Act, 1862, and other Statutory enactments; The United States Statute, 1870 and 1875, the Treaty with the United States, 1877; and the Rules and Instructions issued in February, 1878. With a copious Index. By LEWIS BOYD SEBASTIAN, B.C.L., M.A., Esq., Barrister-at-Law. 8vo. 1878. 14s.

"The Master of the Rolls in his judgment in *Re* Palmer's Trade Marks, said 'He was glad to see that the well-known writer on trade marks, Mr. Sebastian, had taken the same view of the Act.'"—*The Times.*

"Mr. Sebastian has written the fullest and most methodical book on trade marks which has appeared in England since the passing of the Trade Marks Registration Acts."—*Trade Marks.*

Sebastian's Digest of Cases of Trade Mark, Trade Name, Trade Secret, Goodwill, &c., decided in the Courts of the United Kingdom, India, the Colonies, and the United States of America. By LEWIS BOYD SEBASTIAN, B.C.L., M.A., Esq., Barrister-at-Law. 8vo. 1879. 1*l.* 1s.

"A digest which will be of very great value to all practitioners who have to advise on matters connected with trade marks."—*Solicitors' Journal.*

Trade Marks Journal.—4to. Sewed. (*Issued fortnightly.*)
Nos. 1 to 294 are now ready. *Net, each* 1s.
Index to Vols. I. to VI. *Net, each* 3s.
Do. Vol. VII. *Net*, 4s. 6d.

TRAMWAYS.—**Sutton's Tramway Acts of the United Kingdom**; with Notes on the Law and Practice, an Introduction, including the Proceedings before the Committees, Decisions of the Referees with respect to Locus Standi, and a Summary of the Principles of Tramway Rating, and an Appendix containing the Standing Orders of Parliament, Rules of the Board of Trade relating to Tramways, &c. Second Edition. By HENRY SUTTON, B.A., assisted by ROBERT A. BENNETT, B.A., Barristers-at-Law. Demy 8vo. 1883. 15s.

"The book is exceedingly well done, and cannot fail not only to be the standard work on its own subject, but to take a high place among legal text-books."—*Law Journal*, April 21, 1883.

TRIALS FOR MURDER BY POISONING.—**Browne and Stewart.**—*Vide* "Poisons."

TRUSTS AND TRUSTEES.—**Godefroi's Digest of the Principles of the Law of Trusts and Trustees.**—By HENRY GODEFROI, of Lincoln's Inn, Esq., Barrister-at-Law. Joint Author of "Godefroi and Shortt's Law of Railway Companies." Demy 8vo. 1879. 1*l.* 1s.

"As a digest of the law, Mr. Godefroi's work merits commendation, for the author's statements are brief and clear, and for his statements he refers to a goodly array of authorities. In the table of cases the references to the several contemporaneous reports are given, and there is a very copious index to subjects."—*Law Journal.*

USES.—**Jones (W. Hanbury) on Uses.**—8vo. 1862. 7s.

VENDORS AND PURCHASERS.—Dart's Vendors and Purchasers.—A Treatise on the Law and Practice relating to Vendors and Purchasers of Real Estate. By J. HENRY DART, Esq., one of the Six Conveyancing Counsel of the High Court of Justice, Chancery Division. Fifth Edition. By the AUTHOR and WILLIAM BARBER, Esq., Barrister-at-Law. 2 vols. Royal 8vo. 1876. *3l. 13s. 6d.*

"A standard work like Mr. Dart's is beyond all praise."—*The Law Journal.*

Turner's Duties of Solicitor to Client as to Sales, Purchases, and Mortgages of Land. By EDWARD F. TURNER, Solicitor, Lecturer on Real Property and Conveyancing, and one of the Assistant Examiners for Honours to the Incorporated Law Society for 1882-3. (*Published by permission of the Incorporated Law Society*). Demy 8vo. 1883. *10s. 6d.*

"A careful perusal of these lectures cannot fail to be of great advantage to students, and more particularly, we think, to young practising solicitors."—*Law Times*, September 22, 1883.

VOLUNTEER LAW.—A Manual of the Law regulating the Volunteer Forces.—By W. A. BURN and W. T. RAYMOND, Esqrs., Barristers-at-Law, and Captains in H.M. Volunteer Forces. Royal 12mo. 1882. *Net, 2s.*

WILLS.—Rawlinson's Guide to Solicitors on taking Instructions for Wills.—8vo. 1874. *4s.*

Theobald's Concise Treatise on the Law of Wills.—With Statutes, Table of Cases and Full Index. By H. S. THEOBALD, Esq., Barrister-at-Law. **Second Edition.** Demy 8vo. 1881. *1l. 4s.*

"Mr. Theobald has certainly given evidence of extensive investigation, conscientious labour, and clear exposition."—*Law Magazine.*

"A book of great ability and value. It bears on every page traces of care and sound judgment. It is certain to prove of great practical usefulness."—*Solicitors' Journal.*

"His arrangement being good, and his statement of the effect of the decisions being clear, his work cannot fail to be of practical utility."—*Law Times.*

Weaver's Precedents of Wills.—A collection of concise Precedents of Wills, with Introduction, Notes, and an Appendix of Statutes. By *Charles Weaver*, B.A. Post 8vo. 1882. *5s.*

WRONGS.—Addison.—*Vide* "Torts."

REPORTS.—*A large stock new and second-hand. Prices on application.*

BINDING.—*Executed in the best manner at moderate prices and with dispatch.*

The Law Reports, Law Journal, and all other Reports, bound to Office Patterns, at Office Prices.

PRIVATE ACTS.—*The Publishers of this Catalogue possess the largest known collection of Private Acts of Parliament (including Public and Local), and can supply single copies commencing from a very early period.*

VALUATIONS.—*For Probate, Partnership, or other purposes.*

LIBRARIES PURCHASED.

www.ingramcontent.com/pod-product-compliance
Lightning Source LLC
Chambersburg PA
CBHW021110270326
41929CB00009B/808